A child poverty rate of 10 per cent could mean that every tenth child is always poor, or that all children are in poverty for one month in every ten. Knowing where reality lies between these extremes is vital to understanding the problem facing many countries of poverty among the young. This unique study goes beyond the standard analysis of child poverty based on poverty rates at one point in time and documents how much movement into and out of poverty by children there actually is, covering a range of industrialised countries – the USA, the UK, Germany, Ireland, Spain, Hungary and Russia. Five main topics are addressed: conceptual and measurement issues associated with a dynamic view of child poverty; cross-national comparisons of child poverty rates and trends; cross-national comparisons of children's movements into and out of poverty; country-specific studies of child poverty dynamics; and the policy implications of taking a dynamic perspective.

Bruce Bradbury is Senior Research Fellow at the Social Policy Research Centre at the University of New South Wales. During 1998 he was a consultant at the UNICEF Innocenti Research Centre, Florence. His research interests include inequality and poverty, income support and labour-market policies, household equivalance scales and intra-household allocation.

Stephen P. Jenkins is Professor of Applied Economics at the Institute for Social and Economic Research, University of Essex, and Research Professor at the German Institute for Economic Research, Berlin. His current research focuses on poverty, income and labour-market dynamics. He was co-editor of *The Distribution of Welfare and Household Production* (1998).

John Micklewright is Head of Research at the UNICEF Innocenti Research Centre, Florence, and Research Fellow of the Centre for Economic Policy Research, London. His current work focuses on various aspects of child well-being in industrialised and transition countries. He was the co-author of *Economic Transformation in Eastern Europe and the Distribution of Income* (1992) and *The Welfare of Europe's Children* (2000).

The Dynamics of Child Poverty in Industrialised Countries

edited by

Bruce Bradbury, Stephen P. Jenkins
and John Micklewright

CAMBRIDGE
UNIVERSITY PRESS

PUBLISHED BY THE PRESS SYNDICATE OF THE UNIVERSITY OF CAMBRIDGE
The Pitt Building, Trumpington Street, Cambridge, United Kingdom

CAMBRIDGE UNIVERSITY PRESS
The Edinburgh Building, Cambridge CB2 2RU, UK
40 West 20th Street, New York, NY 10011-4211, USA
10 Stamford Road, Oakleigh, VIC 3166, Australia
Ruiz de Alarcón 13, 28014 Madrid, Spain
Dock House, The Waterfront, Cape Town 8001, South Africa

http://www.cambridge.org

First published 2001

Printed in the United Kingdom at the University Press, Cambridge

Typeface Times New Roman 10/12 pt   *System* QuarkXPress™ [SE]

A catalogue record for this book is available from the British Library

ISBN 0 521 80310 1 hardback
ISBN 0 521 00492 6 paperback

To Charlotte, Harriet, Rosanna and Simone,
and in memory of Nikos

Contents

Summary and policy conclusions

Figures

Tables

Notes on the contributors

J. Lawrence Aber is director of the National Center for Children in Poverty, School of Public Health, Columbia University. His research focuses on the relationships between child development and poverty, and on policies for children and families at risk.

Bruce Bradbury is a Senior Research Fellow at the Social Policy Research Centre at the University of New South Wales. During 1998 he was a consultant at the UNICEF Innocenti Research Centre. His research interests include inequality and poverty, income support and labour-market policies, household equivalence scales, and intra-household allocation.

Olga Cantó is Lecturer in Public Economics at the Departamento de Economía Aplicada, Universidad de Vigo. She defended her Ph.D. thesis, on poverty dynamics in Spain, at the European University Institute in 1998. Her current research focuses on poverty, income dynamics and wage inequality in Southern European countries.

Sheldon Danziger is Henry J. Meyer Collegiate Professor of Social Work and Public Policy and director of the Center on Poverty, Risk and Mental Health at the University of Michigan. His research focuses on the causes and consequences of trends in American poverty and income inequality and the evaluation of welfare reform. He is the co-author of *America Unequal* (1995) and *Detroit Divided* (2000).

David T. Ellwood is Lucius N. Littauer Professor of Political Economy at Harvard University's John F. Kennedy School of Government. His current research focuses on poverty, public assistance, income inequality and family structure change. Previously he served as Assistant Secretary for the Department of Health and Human Services under President Clinton.

Péter Galasi is Professor of Labour Economics at the Department of Human Resources, Budapest University of Economic Sciences and Public

Administration. He has written on income inequalities and earnings differences in Hungary.

Peter Gottschalk is Professor of Economics at Boston College and a Research Affiliate of the Institute for Research on Poverty, University of Wisconsin Madison. His current research focuses on wage and employer dynamics of less-educated workers and the measurement of mobility. His published work has focused on poverty and low-wage labour markets.

Martha S. Hill is Senior Research Scientist at the Institute for Social Research, University of Michigan. Her research interests focus on the economics of the family with special attention to intergenerational and life course issues. Current research topics include children's well-being, poverty and sufficiency, transitions to adulthood, interrelationships between generations and time allocation.

Markus Jäntti is Professor of Economics at the University of Tampere, and was formerly Senior Research Fellow with the Academy of Finland. His research focuses on social mobility, income inequality and poverty. He recently co-authored a survey of poverty in advanced countries for the *Handbook of Income Distribution* (2000).

Stephen P. Jenkins is Professor of Applied Economics at the Institute for Social and Economic Research, University of Essex, and Research Professor at the German Institute for Economic Research (DIW), Berlin. His current research focuses on poverty, income and labour-market dynamics. He was co-editor of *The Distribution of Welfare and Household Production* (1998).

Jeni Klugman is a senior economist in the Poverty Reduction and Economic Management group of the World Bank, Washington DC. Her current work focuses on national poverty-reduction strategies in low-income countries in Africa and East Asia, with research interests in poverty, safety nets and labour markets. She is the editor of *Poverty in Russia: Public Policy and Private Responses* (1997).

Alexandre Kolev is an economist at the World Bank, and was formerly at the UNICEF Innocenti Research Centre, Florence. His research focuses on poverty, income and labour markets in transition economies.

Bertrand Maître is a statistical analyst at the Economic and Social Research Institute, Dublin. He carries out analysis of the Living in Ireland Survey and the European Community Household Panel on a range of topics. His current research focuses on poverty and income distribution.

Magda Mercader-Prats is Lecturer in Public Economics at the Departament d'Economia Aplicada, Universitat Autònoma de Barcelona. Her current research focuses on economic poverty and inequality and redistributive policies in Europe and Spain.

John Micklewright is Head of Research at the UNICEF Innocenti Research Centre, Florence, and Research Fellow of the Centre for Economic Policy Research, London. His current work focuses on various aspects of child well-being in industrialised and transition countries. He was the co-author of *Economic Transformation in Eastern Europe and the Distribution of Income* (1992) and *The Welfare of Europe's Children* (2000).

Gyula Nagy is Professor of Labour Economics in the Department of Human Resources, Budapest University of Economic Sciences and Public Administration. His current research topics include unemployment, labour-market dynamics and labour-market policies.

Brian Nolan is Research Professor at the Economic and Social Research Institute, Dublin. His current research focuses on poverty, income inequality and low pay. He was co-author of *Resources, Deprivation and Poverty* (1996) and *Poverty in the 1990s* (1996).

Christian Schluter is Lecturer in the Economics Department of the University of Bristol and a Research Associate of the Centre for the Analysis of Social Exclusion at the London School of Economics. His research interests include the analysis of inequality, poverty and income dynamics.

Dorothy Watson is a research officer at the Economic and Social Research Institute, Dublin. Her research interests include the study of social inequality, values and belief systems, crime and survey methodology.

Acknowledgements

This book results from a project on 'Children In and Out of Poverty' at the UNICEF Innocenti Research Centre, Florence, and has therefore benefited from the core funding of the Italian government to the Centre. Stephen Jenkins' work was partly supported by the Institute for Social and Economic Research's core funding from the University of Essex and the UK Economic and Social Research Council, and by the European Union TMR Network 'Living Standards, Inequality and Taxation' (contract no. ERBFMRXCT 980248). Bruce Bradbury's work was partly supported by an Australian Research Council Small Grant. We are grateful to Tony Atkinson, Jonathan Bradshaw, Greg Duncan, Tim Smeeding, Robert Walker and the chapter authors for their encouragement and suggestions, and to Chris Harrison and his colleagues at Cambridge University Press for their work on the book's production. The Press's anonymous referees made useful comments on draft chapters. Finally, we thank Cinzia Iusco Bruschi of the UNICEF Innocenti Research Centre for great secretarial and administrative support throughout the course of the project, and Janice Webb of the Institute for Social and Economic Research, University of Essex, for her very efficient assistance in the preparation of the final manuscript.

Bruce Bradbury
Stephen P. Jenkins
John Micklewright

1 Beyond the snapshot: a dynamic view of child poverty

BRUCE BRADBURY, STEPHEN P. JENKINS AND
JOHN MICKLEWRIGHT

1.1 Why study child poverty dynamics?

If one in ten children is currently poor (a child poverty rate of 10 per cent), it could mean that every tenth child is in poverty all the time or, at the other extreme, it could mean that all children are poor for one month in every ten. This book sheds light on where the reality lies between these extremes. For a range of industrialised countries it documents how much movement into and out of poverty by children there actually is. It is therefore a book about poverty among children and about the dynamic aspects of that poverty – how individual children move into and out of being poor.

The focus on the poverty of children as opposed to any other group in the population needs little justification. Children represent a country's future, an obvious reason for societal concern with child well-being. There are innate feelings of protection towards the young and assumptions of their blamelessness for the situation in which they find themselves. Children are unable to take full responsibility for their circumstances and are dependent on others to look after and raise them. Their vulnerability provides a powerful moral imperative in favour of collective action in general to help them, and a welfare state in particular (see, for example, Goodin 1988). To implement this requires prior knowledge about the nature of child poverty and its consequences, plus knowledge of what the causes are.

But why should one wish to know about children's movements into and out of poverty in addition to their poverty at a point in time (the conventional perspective)? First, for the individual child, the adverse impact on his or her living standards of being poor this year depends on past poverty. Poor children who have already been poor a long time are likely to be worse off than those who are newly poor, as families' capacities to get by are used up over time. It is not only the length of the current poverty spell which may matter but also the pattern of poverty throughout childhood: whether, for

1

example, it consists of a series of intermittent spells of poverty, a single long spell of moderate poverty, or a short spell of extreme poverty.

Second, the accumulation over time of each child's poverty history tells us whether poverty is concentrated among a small group of children or is an experience that is widely shared. Assuming that society has at least some aversion to 'unequal shares', then the greater the concentration of poverty experience, the greater the concern.

Third, child poverty has impacts which last beyond childhood into adulthood, and the effects depend on the nature of the poverty experienced. There is evidence that the impact of childhood poverty on a variety of outcomes in future life depends on the length of time spent poor. A long period (or repeated shorter periods) of low living standards can be expected to have a greater impact on a child's development and future life chances than an isolated short period.

Fourth, a focus on movements into and out of poverty is useful for explaining who is currently poor and why. A rising child poverty rate may come about either because the number of children entering poverty is rising or because the number of poor children who leave poverty is falling. Thus to understand the incidence of child poverty at a point in time, and its trends, one needs to know about child poverty inflow and outflow rates. At a more fundamental level, analysis of why poverty flows differ provides a more natural way to understand the causes of poverty than does analysis of why poverty rates *per se* differ, particularly since the factors which determine entry (or re-entry) to the ranks of the poor may well differ from the factors determining escape from poverty.

Fifth, and finally, the design of policy to reduce the number of poor children depends on the nature of movements to and from poverty.[1] If turnover in child poverty is low, then policy can concentrate on the relatively unchanging group of poor families that experience long periods of low living standards. If turnover is high, then the target group is continually changing and the challenge for policy is a different one. The whole approach to anti-poverty policy may be influenced by taking a dynamic perspective, emphasising the prevention of entry into poverty and the promotion of exits (as recent US and British experience illustrates), rather than only paying benefits to the currently poor:

[D]ynamic analysis gets us closer to treating causes, where static analysis often leads us towards treating symptoms . . . If, for example, we ask who are the poor today, we are led to questions about the socioeconomic identity of the existing poverty population. Looking to policy, we then typically emphasise income supplementation

[1] The relevance of dynamic perspectives for policy design has also been stressed by Walker (1994) and Leisering and Walker (1998).

strategies. The obvious static solution to poverty is to give the poor more money. If instead, we ask what leads people into poverty, we are drawn to events and structures, and our focus shifts to looking for ways to ensure people escape poverty (Ellwood 1998: 49).

The analogy with the study of unemployment and policies to deal with it is instructive. Both academic research and public policy have long recognised that the unemployed are not an unchanging pool. Unemployment is widely seen as an essentially dynamic process – people move *into* unemployment and in general move *out* again. Some people move out much more slowly than others – these are the long-term unemployed and their number is both routinely reported by statistical offices throughout the industrialised world and is a closely monitored statistic, on grounds that are analogous to those for interest in the dynamics of child poverty.[2]

The state of discussion of child poverty is nowhere near this situation: for example, the number of persistently poor children is a rarely presented national poverty statistic. Quite simply, the body of knowledge on the dynamics of child poverty does not match the need for information on the subject, and this provides the motivation for the current volume. There are important recent books on childhood poverty and deprivation that, like this one, provide a cross-national perspective (for example, Cornia and Danziger 1997, Vleminckx and Smeeding 2001) but none to our knowledge that focuses on the dynamic aspects of the subject.

It is true that in some countries there *is* quite a lot that is already known about the dynamics of child poverty. In these countries the two requirements have been fulfilled: there has been the collection of the necessary data – through repeated interviews over time of the same persons ('panel surveys') – and the appropriate research has taken place that uses this information. In particular, a great deal has been discovered about the dynamics of child poverty in the USA, which definitely leads the field in this respect. Appropriate longitudinal data have been collected for a long time, including the widely used Panel Study of Income Dynamics (PSID). There has been considerable investigation of the issues following the pioneering research during the 1980s by Bane and Ellwood (1986) which built on earlier use of the PSID (see, for example, Duncan *et al.* 1984, Hill 1981). Ten years later, Ashworth *et al.* were able to comment that the distribution of the number of years during childhood spent poor was 'quite familiar territory' in the USA (1994: 663). The authors show that if poverty had been evenly distributed among American children, each child born in 1969–73

---

[2] Long-term unemployment is unpleasant at the time for the individuals concerned and may have a negative impact on their futures as well. Also long-term unemployment may lead to persistent under-performance of the national economy (the so-called hysteresis effect).

would have spent two years in poverty (defined on the basis of annual family incomes) in the first fifteen years of their lives, whereas in reality 62 per cent were never poor; on the other hand 7 per cent of children were poor in at least eleven years (Ashworth *et al.* 1994: table 2). National government statistics include information on the duration of childhood poverty (for example, Federal Interagency Forum on Child and Family Statistics 1998).

In countries other than the USA, there has been recent progress as new data have become available and the necessary research has been carried out. For example, Robert Walker noted in his 1994 book, *Poverty Dynamics*, that 'little is known about the duration of poverty in Britain', and his empirical investigation relied largely on data recording movements in and out of receipt of income-tested cash benefits.[3] Since then the British Household Panel Survey (BHPS), which started in 1991, has begun to reveal much about poverty dynamics, although most of the research using this source has not focused on childhood *per se* (for example, Jarvis and Jenkins 1997, Department of Social Security 1998). Evidence on the persistence of childhood deprivation in Britain has started to feature in analyses of poverty by government departments as well as by academic researchers (HM Treasury 1999). The new annual government report on poverty and social exclusion that was announced in 1999 will include some information on the persistence of childhood poverty. Nonetheless data spanning the whole of childhood are still not yet available for the UK as they are in the USA.

Several other European countries have longer-running socio-economic panel surveys than Britain. Germany, the Netherlands and Sweden have panels that began in the mid-1980s. Some analyses of movements into and out of poverty have certainly been made with these (for example, van Leeuwen and Pannekoek 1999, Krause 1998), although the focus has not been on children. An important paper by Duncan *et al.* (1993) pulled together evidence from panel surveys for eight different countries to document movements into and out of poverty by families with children.

But in many industrialised countries the picture describing the dynamics of child poverty remains to be painted. As far as the availability of data is concerned, the creation of the European Community Household Panel (ECHP) in the mid-1990s is a major step forward, providing longitudinal data on a comparable basis for most of the European Union member states (Eurostat 1999). This survey will become an increasingly important source as the period covered lengthens (assuming that funding for the data collection will continue). However, the mere collection of the data is no guarantee

[3] The work of Hancock (1985) was an early investigation into the dynamics of poverty among families with children in Britain, but was restricted to use of a single follow-up survey after twelve months of a sample of low-income families.

that the necessary analysis to shed light on the dynamics of child poverty will be undertaken. For example, there has been no early move by Eurostat (the European Union's statistical office) to use the data to measure the well-being of children in this way.

The main aim of this book is to make a start in filling the gap in current knowledge about child poverty dynamics, showing what can be revealed about the movements by children into and out of poverty, with a particular focus on seven industrialised countries: the USA, Britain, Germany, Ireland, Spain, Hungary and Russia. A part of the book provides results on a basis that is as comparable as possible for these countries. The cross-national perspective provides a yardstick against which the results for individual countries that we present (and also the results of other researchers) may be compared. Additional goals are to demonstrate the possibilities for analysis of child well-being with longitudinal data and to stimulate research on child poverty dynamics in European Union and other industrialised countries. We hope to highlight the issues that can be addressed, while at the same time marking out some of the pitfalls in this area of measurement and analysis. The book covers policy issues at various points (and this is the particular focus of the final chapter), as described below. It is not principally a book about policy to reduce child poverty, however. Rather it aims to provide analysis that is relevant to policy.

In the remainder of this chapter we provide an introduction to the rest of the book and summarise and highlight its principal findings. After introducing the countries that we analyse and explaining our selection of them (section 1.2), we outline the main topics to be addressed and the organisation of the volume as a whole (section 1.3). Then the findings of each chapter are reviewed in turn (section 1.4). Although the book addresses some complex issues, we have attempted to make the results accessible to as wide an audience as possible without compromising rigour.

1.2 The countries covered

The industrialised countries covered in the book differ in various dimensions. These include the level of economic development, the availability of longitudinal data, the place of the family in society, and the type and strength of welfare state. These features are discussed in more detail in chapter 3 which provides a comprehensive analysis of child poverty based on cross-section surveys. Twenty-five countries are included: see table 1.1 which provides a full list. Clearly the sample is extensive and covers a diverse set of nations. The majority (fifteen) are in Western Europe, but the

Table 1.1. *Countries covered in the book*

Western Europe	North America
Austria	Canada
Belgium	**United States**
Denmark	
Finland	*Transition economies*
France	Czech Republic
Germany	**Hungary**
Ireland	Poland
Italy	**Russia**
Luxembourg	Slovakia
Netherlands	
Norway	*Other economies*
Spain	Australia
Sweden	Israel
Switzerland	Taiwan
United Kingdom	

Note: All the countries listed are included in the analysis in chapter 3. Those with names shown in boldface are analysed in chapter 4 and part II.

coverage also extends to North America (two countries), five are so-called 'transition economies' from Central and Eastern Europe, and there are three countries from other regions. The selection of countries represents the largest number available for analysis using the Luxembourg Income Study (LIS) database of household surveys (more about this in chapter 3).

Our analysis of the dynamics of child poverty – the main focus of the book – covers a sub-set of seven countries (the names in boldface in table 1.1). What are the grounds for our selection of these?

The USA picks itself. This is the country with the longest history of research on the dynamics of child poverty. The available data allow issues to be addressed for this country that cannot be tackled elsewhere, and the prevalence of childhood poverty in the USA has long been a concern. The proportion of children below the official US poverty line rose notably in the last quarter of the twentieth century, from 15 per cent in 1970 to 23 per cent in 1993, 'the highest poverty rate experienced by children since the mid-1960s' (Hernandez 1997). Chapter 3 shows the USA (with Russia) topping the table in terms of the percentage of children in households with income below half of the median (a standard measure of relative poverty): 26 per cent compared to an average of 11 per cent across the twenty-five countries included. A dynamic perspective of family incomes and receipt of state benefits played an important part in the 1990s' reforms of 'welfare', the term used in the USA to refer to means-tested benefits received by low-income families.

The United Kingdom, Germany and Ireland are all countries in which there has recently been renewed concern over child poverty.[4] It was natural to include these countries, given the available data. The UK government elected in 1997 has placed poverty among children high on its agenda, with the Prime Minister vowing in 1999 to end child poverty within twenty years (Blair 1999). The UK comes third in the league table of relative poverty in chapter 3, with 21 per cent of children classified as poor, a figure sharply higher than twenty years earlier. Germany has had a parliamentary commission on the economic well-being of children (Kommission zur Wahrnehmung der Belange der Kinder 1997), and has a long-running household panel survey which can be exploited to investigate the issues within a dynamic framework. Ireland has a proportion of the population aged 0–17 that is higher than that of any other OECD member (with the exception of Mexico); the position of children in any debate on living standards should receive special prominence in this industrialised country. The National Anti-Poverty Strategy introduced by Ireland's government in 1997 demonstrates a commitment to combating poverty among children as well as other groups in the population. (The Strategy is discussed by Nolan 1999.)

Spain provides an example from Southern Europe to contrast with this Northern European trio. The cross-national literature on poverty among children in industrialised countries has paid relatively little attention to the Mediterranean and other Southern European countries (although see, for example, Saraceno's (1997) and Silva's (1997) discussions of Italy and Portugal respectively). Analysis of poverty within Spain has not centred on children (Cantó-Sánchez and Mercader-Prats 1998). Amongst other things, the common situation in Spain and other Southern European countries for grown-up children to live with their parents raises the question of how to define a 'child'.

The impact on children of economic and social transition in the countries of Central and Eastern Europe and the former Soviet Union is a natural subject for anxiety, leading to concerns about a 'generation in jeopardy' (Zouev 1999; see also UNICEF 1997, 1999). It is impossible for analysis of the 'industrialised countries' today to ignore those that were to the east of the former Iron Curtain. Hungary and Russia provide contrasting examples. The Hungarian economy shrank by less than 20 per cent after 1989 and has been growing slowly since 1994. Russia, however, was still in great economic turmoil at the end of the 1990s, with national income down

---

[4] The data used in chapter 3 refer to the United Kingdom of Great Britain and Northern Ireland. The UK data used later in the book only cover Great Britain ('Britain' for short), i.e. England, Wales and Scotland.

by a half since 1989 according to official figures. Both countries experienced rising income inequality (Russia much more than Hungary) during the decade (Flemming and Micklewright 2000).

An analysis of child poverty dynamics that covered all industrialised regions would in addition include countries from Australasia, Scandinavia, and the rich industrialised nations of Asia. For various reasons this has not proved possible in the current volume (no household panel data are available yet for Australia or New Zealand, for example). However, Australia, Taiwan and four Nordic countries do enter the analysis in chapter 3. We welcome the day when cross-national studies of the dynamics of child poverty can be truly comprehensive in geographical coverage.

1.3 The organisation of the book and the topics addressed

Five main topics are addressed by this book: issues of definition and measurement in the dynamic analysis of child poverty; cross-national comparisons of child poverty rates and trends; cross-national comparisons of children's movements into and out of poverty; country-specific studies of child poverty dynamics; and the policy implications of taking a dynamic perspective. The first three topics are covered in part I of the book (chapters 2–4). The country studies form part II (chapters 5–11). Policy implications and directions for further research are reviewed in chapter 12, although several of the chapters in part II also discuss policy in a national context.

The first topic (chapter 2) covers issues of definition and measurement which arise when analysing child poverty and, in particular, those that are relevant to the analysis of dynamics. Under this heading we consider, for example, the appropriate measure of living standards (and their changes), the definition of poverty and the poverty line (and movements across the line), and how to measure the dynamics of child poverty in practice, given the data that are available. Since empirical findings raise questions about causes, we also briefly review the principal explanations for the patterns of movement into and out of poverty which have been observed (related to changes over time in household income from the labour market, the changes in non-labour income, especially state benefits, and the changes in household composition).

Our second topic, the cross-national comparison of child poverty rates and trends, is covered in chapter 3. Results are provided on a consistent basis for twenty-five industrialised countries from the Luxembourg Income Study (LIS), a collection of household surveys providing data that are sufficiently comparable to allow meaningful cross-national comparisons to be made. The analysis is the most wide-ranging study of child poverty rates and child poverty trends using the LIS data that there is (at the time of writing), especially in terms of the range of countries covered. The LIS provides cross-section information, the type of data source traditionally used to analyse child poverty. These surveys provide a 'snapshot' observation of the population of children at one point in time or, for poverty trends, a sequence of snapshots, each based on a different sample. In contrast longitudinal data used to analyse income changes provide repeated observations on the *same* children. Our focus in the book on the dynamics of child poverty is not to argue that the static pictures shown by cross-section data are without interest. The invention of motion pictures did not drive still photography into obsolescence and, in the same way, cross-section and dynamic analyses of child poverty complement each other.[5]

The book's third topic is cross-national comparison of the movement – or lack of movement – by children into and out of poverty. This is the subject of chapter 4, written by the editors. We focus on the seven countries – the USA, Britain, Germany, Ireland, Spain, Hungary and Russia – that are analysed further in part II of the book. As in the analysis of the LIS data in chapter 3, the data are put on a comparable basis for each country (as far as possible). This was achieved by asking the authors of each chapter in part II to provide results for their country in a standardised format. (We are very grateful to them for their patience in this process.) This chapter substantially develops the cross-national analysis of dynamics pioneered in the paper by Duncan *et al.* (1993) that we noted above.

Chapters 5–11, forming part II of the book, focus in more detail on particular aspects of child poverty dynamics in each of seven countries (our fourth topic). Each chapter provides contextual information about child poverty and its trends in the country in question as well as original analysis of movements by children into and out of poverty. The range of issues considered is diverse, partly reflecting the lengths of time for which panel data are available in the different countries. For instance, for the two countries with long panel surveys (the USA and Germany) it has been possible to compare patterns of poverty dynamics not only in the early- to mid-1990s, but also in earlier periods. One common subject of investigation is the extent to which child poverty is persistent: how many children are found to have multiple years of poverty over an interval of five (or six) years, or not to experience poverty at all over the same interval? The chapters also investigate the heterogeneity of poverty persistence among children with

---

[5] One might ask if one could use individual frames from the panel data movie as stills, i.e. using panel surveys for their cross-section data as well as their longitudinal data. This is indeed sometimes done, but cross-section surveys tend be better for this: they are more representative and yield larger samples for a given budget than single waves of on-going panel surveys.

different characteristics, for example exploring the extent to which vulnerability is greater for younger children, for children in lone-parent families and so on.

Some of the subjects that are examined are country-specific, while still illustrating wider issues. For instance, the chapters about Russia and Hungary consider the character of movements into and out of poverty in countries experiencing substantial economic transition. Spain, as noted earlier, stands out for the relatively late age at which children leave the parental home (typically in the late twenties). This raises interesting issues about the poverty of older youths compared to the under 18-year-olds focused on in the rest of the book, and about what happens to the poverty of others when they do eventually leave home. The chapter about Ireland exploits the rich data about non-monetary indicators of deprivation available in this country's panel survey (information also collected in other European panels). It considers the relationship between the dynamics of child poverty summarised in terms of income or expenditure (as in the rest of the book) and the dynamics of multiple deprivation.

The fifth topic of the book concerns the policy implications of findings about child poverty. These are considered in some of the part II country studies but are the particular focus of the final chapter, chapter 12. This picks up the policy debate, in the light of both the cross-national analysis of chapter 4 and the studies of particular issues in different countries in the part II chapters. The chapter analyses the implications for anti-poverty policy of a dynamic perspective on the issue – the fifth reason given earlier for wishing to know about movements of children into and out of poverty.

1.4 The principal findings

This section provides a brief overview of the principal findings from this book on a chapter-by-chapter basis. The discussion of conceptual and definitional issues is not reviewed here, however. By its very nature, chapter 2 is concerned more with raising methodological questions rather than with providing answers.

Child poverty across twenty-five countries

In chapter 3 Bradbury and Jäntti show that there is a large variation in child poverty rates in the 1990s across the twenty-five industrialised nations they consider, ranging from just below 2 per cent to over 26 per cent. Nordic countries and Northern European countries tend to have the lowest rates of child poverty, whereas Southern European and English-speaking countries tend to have higher rates.

These results are obtained when the poverty line for each country is half the median income of that country – a low income cut-off which is higher in real purchasing power terms in rich countries than in poor countries. If, instead, the same fixed poverty line is applied to all countries (equal to the US poverty line in 1995) then, interestingly, the same broad groupings of countries show up as having the lowest and highest child poverty rates (with some changes in detailed rankings). The broad picture of the child poverty 'league' is thus reasonably robust to the switch in definition. There is one important exception, namely the transition countries, which have much higher child poverty rates using the alternative definition of the poverty line that applies a common dollar value across countries. This is not altogether surprising given that the level of national income in transition countries is low compared to that in other industrialised countries.

Diversity of outcome is again the picture when looking at *trends* in child poverty rates over the last two decades. In fact, rates increased in some countries (Germany, Hungary, Italy, the UK and the USA) and decreased in others (Taiwan, Canada, Denmark, Norway and Sweden), regardless of the type of poverty line used. The most common pattern, however, is that relative poverty rates increased – reflecting an increase in income inequality within each country – whereas absolute poverty rates (based on the official US poverty line) decreased, reflecting an increase in real national disposable income.

Bradbury and Jäntti show that, contrary to common belief, variations in rates of lone motherhood across countries are *not* an important reason for the variations in child poverty. (This is notwithstanding the fact that children are more likely to be poor if living in a lone-mother family in all the countries considered.) Cross-national differences in 'social spending' are another factor often emphasised when seeking to explain differences in poverty rates. To investigate this, Bradbury and Jäntti decompose the average income of the poorest fifth of children in order to compare the relative contributions of market income and social transfers to their income packages. They find that cash transfers to poor families are an important contribution to children's economic well-being – as found in other studies. However, a novel finding is that market incomes play a larger role than cash benefits do in accounting for the cross-national diversity of outcomes for disadvantaged children. Thus, for example, although the English-speaking countries (with the exception of the USA) provide quite substantial income transfers to their most needy children, the living standards of these children remain relatively low because of low labour-market incomes. The higher living standards of the most disadvantaged children in the 'welfare leaders' (particularly the Nordic countries) is due to the higher market incomes received by the children's families. These results obtained with cross-section data complement those based on longitudinal surveys, since the importance of gaining or retaining work is one factor often emphasised in the dynamic approach to poverty.

The dynamics of child poverty in seven industrialised nations

Chapter 4, written by the editors, presents a substantial body of new evidence on the patterns of income mobility and the movements into and out of poverty among children in Britain, Germany, Hungary, Ireland, Russia, Spain and the USA. The data used for these seven countries vary in several respects, most notably the period of time for which children can be followed. However, the analysis puts the data on as comparable a basis as possible, while at the same time exploiting that information which is available for only a sub-set of the countries. The results that are obtained both extend what is known about the dynamics of childhood deprivation in each country and, critically, place this in a cross-national perspective, allowing the situation in one country to be compared with that in others.

It is clear that persistence in child poverty is a widespread phenomenon. In most countries about 60 per cent of the children found in the poorest fifth of the income distribution in one year are still in the poorest fifth the next year. Among the four countries for which the period that can be studied is five years or more – Britain, Germany, Hungary and the USA – the proportion of children in the poorest fifth in each of five consecutive years ranges between 6 and 9 per cent. Many more children are in the lowest fifth at some time, rather than persistently. Depending on the country and income definition concerned, between 33 and 43 per cent of all children were in the poorest fifth at least once during a five-year period. Over a ten-year period, 5–6 per cent of all children in Germany and the USA were in the bottom fifth in each and every year while 41–44 per cent were there at least once.

These results emphasise the similarities across countries in patterns of childhood poverty, in contrast to chapter 3 which emphasises the differences. In part this is because the results just mentioned are obtained by 'standardising' across the countries, by focusing on the poorest 20 per cent of children in each case. Other results in the chapter use a conventional definition of poverty based on half median income (as in chapter 3) and here differences in patterns of dynamics are more notable. For example, while 15–20 per cent of children in Germany and Hungary are found to be in poverty on the 'half median income' basis at least once over five years, the figure is 38–45 per cent in Britain and the USA.

The analysis also looks at the issue of whether movements into and out of poverty are typically just short moves around the poverty line. The strong conclusion emerges that the great majority of entries and exits by children on most income definitions do *not* merely involve movement either way between 'near poverty' and being 'just below' the poverty line – the movements into and out of poverty in the seven countries typically involve sizeable changes in income. Other results provide intriguing cross-national comparisons of movements into and out of poverty by children in lone-parent families. The discussion in chapter 4 draws attention to the contribution to their poverty of their rate of entry *to* low income, in contrast to much discussion of policy that focuses on their exits *from* low income.

The cross-country comparisons in this chapter highlight the positions of two countries in particular. First, the most obvious exception to any picture of similarity in dynamics is Russia, where rates of exit from and entry to the poorest fifth of all children were noticeably higher than those for the other six countries, reflecting the turmoil of the transition years that have followed the fall of communism. Second, no evidence is found that the USA has greater mobility among children across the income distribution or mobility into and out of poverty. Indeed, in some respects movements in the USA appear to be fewer than in countries such as the UK and Germany, challenging common perceptions about mobility and opportunity in this the richest of the world's large industrialised countries. It is with the USA that part II of the book's studies of individual countries begins.

Income mobility and exits from poverty of American children

In chapter 5 Gottschalk and Danziger start by noting that child poverty rates in the USA have increased over the last two decades, even though economic growth was greater in the 1980s than in the 1970s. This result was largely due to the increase in income inequality that accompanied the economic growth, combined with the use of a poverty line defined as half average income in each year. As the authors point out, the resulting high poverty rates could, however, have been accompanied by an increase in income mobility which would have reduced the probability that a given child would remain poor. It is this issue that is the focus of the chapter, which provides an analysis exploiting the longest-running panel survey used in the book.

Gottschalk and Danziger analyse the extent of children's income mobility, and its changes over time, using both absolute and relative mobility concepts. Roughly half of the children who were in poor families at the start of each decade remained poor ten years later. (Poverty is assessed in most of the analysis on the basis of incomes averaged over three years, but the authors inspect the sensitivity of the results to the use of a one-year period.) Besides providing results for all children taken together, the analysis also distinguishes black and white children, children in lone-parent households, and children in households receiving 'welfare' (means-tested benefits). Some important results on differences in exit rates among American children are established. ~~Exits out of poverty (whether relative or absolute) are found to be considerably lower for black children, children in lone-parent households and children in households receiving welf~~are. For example, 47 per cent of white children in the poorest fifth of all children at the start of the 1980s were poor again at the start of the 1990s, but the figure was as high as 78 per cent for black children.

As far as the main issue addressed in the chapter is concerned, a clear result emerges: the authors conclude firmly that there was no significant change in the degree of mobility between the 1970s and the 1980s. They argue, therefore, that there is no evidence that the increase in inequality in the USA during the 1980s, which contributed to the rise in child poverty, was offset by an increase in children's mobility out of poverty.

Child poverty in Germany: trends and persistence

Chapter 6 by Schluter begins by pointing out the new interest in Germany in the issue of poverty, and the controversy in this debate over what 'poverty' really means. He notes that information on the dynamics of childhood deprivation in Germany is scarce, despite a household panel that has been in existence for a substantial length of time. Also the debate on any aspect of poverty in the country has not been marked by a focus on children.

Schluter explores the evolution of child poverty in Germany from the early 1980s to the mid-1990s, showing how the changes in the numbers of poor children were driven by the entries into poverty and the exits out of poverty from year to year. He then shows how the persistence of poverty over a five-year window changed between three periods, 1983–7, 1987–91 and 1991–5, thus exploiting the long existence of the German survey. His analysis distinguishes various different groups of children in the population: young children aged 0–6, children in lone-parent households, those in households where the head does not work and those in households receiving social assistance (means-tested benefit). In addition, two features of poverty of particular relevance to Germany are addressed, namely the differences between former West and East Germany and the situation of children of 'guestworkers'.

In the first half of the 1990s about one sixth of all children in West Germany experienced at least one year of poverty over a five-year period – which is roughly double the percentage of children who were found to be poor in any single year. The same differential is found in the former East Germany: almost one third of all children experienced at least one year of poverty over a five-year period, compared to the average annual poverty rate of roughly half this. As these figures indicate, child poverty is, not surprisingly, notably higher in the eastern part of the country. Children in lone-parent households have a much higher probability of poverty: more than a half (of those in western Germany) were poor at least once during 1991–5, a figure higher even than that for children in households receiving social assistance (one third).

One result which contrasts with findings for most other countries considered in this book is that the poverty experienced by children is not very different from the poverty experienced by all persons in the population at large. This is true whether one looks at poverty rates at a point in time or longitudinal measures of poverty persistence.

Poverty among British children: chronic or transitory?

Chapter 7 by Hill and Jenkins highlights a distinction between chronic and transitory child poverty, using data that provide six years of observations of the same children. The authors start their analysis, however, by charting the long-term trends in child poverty in Britain. Their research shows that, using poverty lines equal to half average income, child poverty rates in Britain showed no trend during the 1960s and 1970s, but increased substantially during the 1980s before levelling off again in the early 1990s. If instead the poverty line is fixed at half 1991 average income in real terms, then child poverty rates have fallen over the last thirty years. Regardless of the type of poverty line used, child poverty rates remain several percentage points higher than the rates for all persons. Not surprisingly, therefore, child poverty is a subject of considerable topical interest in Britain.

Against this background, Hill and Jenkins examine children's experience of poverty over time by considering what poverty patterns look like if people's longer-term living standards are summarised in terms of their 'smoothed income' – the income which each person would have were everyone able to spread their income evenly over time. (In practical terms in the authors' research, this figure is the average over six years of the figures for current income in each year.) Making a distinction between current income streams and smoothed income is useful because it draws attention to the fact that some of the child poverty observed at a point in time is transitory rather than chronic. Chronic poverty is defined by the authors as poverty measured on the basis of smoothed income.

For the six-year period 1991–6, Hill and Jenkins find that both total poverty and chronic poverty are of sizeable magnitude among British children, especially very young children. If income were able to be perfectly and costlessly smoothed over time, the poverty of children would be almost halved, but a significant level of poverty (chronic poverty) would still remain. If the reduction of this chronic poverty is the goal of policy, then policymakers have a problem: it is current incomes that are observed rather than smoothed incomes. The chapter's analysis closes with a numerical illustration to show that this problem of unobservability can substantially reduce the effectiveness of transfers in cutting chronic child poverty.

Child income poverty and deprivation dynamics in Ireland

The authors of chapter 8, about Ireland, had only two years of panel data available when they carried out their research, and so extensive longitudinal analysis of child poverty was severely constrained. Instead, Nolan, Maître and Watson address a complementary issue, drawing on a strength of their survey data, namely extensive information about non-monetary indicators of household deprivation. (Examples are the lack of particular durable goods, the inability to keep the home adequately warm and a restricted diet.) The authors argue that the use of non-monetary indicators, in addition to income, reveals much more about the living standards of children. They also note that the value of these alternative measures of deprivation has already been recognised by Irish policymakers with their incorporation (together with monetary indicators) into the overall poverty reduction target in the country's official National Anti-Poverty Strategy.

Nolan, Maître and Watson begin by demonstrating that income alone, measured in a single cross-section, may mislead about which children are in the most severe poverty. They show that some children in households on the lowest incomes are not among those suffering the most deprivation as measured by non-monetary indicators. The children in greatest need at any point in time, at whom policy should be targeted, turn out to be those just below or just above a conventional income poverty line.

The authors then show that income averaged over two years has a somewhat stronger relationship with the non-monetary indicators, a result that strengthens the case for measures of child poverty based on sustained low income. However, the relationship is not a lot stronger, underlining the independent value of the non-monetary indicators. Finally, the dynamics of non-monetary deprivation between the two survey waves are analysed. One half of children in the top fifth of a summary index (i.e. the most deprived children) in one year had moved out by the next year. This degree of mobility may appear high (especially when compared with the extent of mobility out of low income shown in chapter 4), but one explanation is the general fall in measured deprivation in Ireland over the period as real incomes rose sharply.

The survey used in chapter 8 is the Irish element of the European Community Household Panel (ECHP), and the non-monetary indicators of deprivation used by Nolan, Maître and Watson are also collected in the other ECHP data sets. As the authors point out, their analysis can therefore be extended to other European countries and, as more waves of the ECHP become available, this line of research on the dynamics of childhood poverty can be further developed in a number of exciting directions to improve the identification of children in most need and the design of policy to combat the problem.

Young people leaving home: the impact on poverty in Spain

Chapter 9 on Spain tackles a theme that underlines the rather arbitrary definition of a 'child' by focusing on poverty among youth, that is young people aged 18–29. This has special relevance for Spain, as well as for other parts of Southern Europe, because of the country's distinctive pattern of living arrangements: many children do not leave their parents' home until they are 30 years old or more.

In 1994 two thirds of young Spanish men aged 25–29 were still living with their parents, and almost a half of young women – both figures sharply up from their levels in the mid-1980s. Moreover youth unemployment in Spain is very high, and if young people work they are more likely than other groups to have a temporary rather than permanent employment contract. But while the weakness of the Spanish youth labour market is well known, there has been very little work to date on poverty among young people in

Spain – and on the impact on family incomes when they do eventually leave the parental home. More generally, the literature on the dynamics of household incomes that has considered the impact of changes in household composition has focused on the impact of marital breakdown or the birth of a new child rather than that of a 'grown-up' child leaving home.

Using two different data sources, one a large cross-section survey and the other a panel survey providing observations one year apart, Cantó and Mercader-Prats show that the Spanish family plays a key role in defending its members against economic difficulties. Youth poverty rates turn out to be relatively low, lower than those for children (aged 0–17), working-age adults and the elderly. (Children have the highest rate.) Young people are protected by staying at home: poverty is substantially higher for youths who leave their parental home compared to those who remain. On the other hand, parents who have children aged 18–29 still living with them may do so at the expense of increasing their own risk of being poor, and that of their younger children. Here the employment status of the grown-up children still in the home matters: families with an employed youth have a lower risk of poverty – in this case the young person is protecting the rest of his or her family. Cantó and Mercader-Prats find that on average a young person leaving the parental home in Spain is associated with an increase in the probability of the household entering poverty.

Are children being left behind in the transition in Hungary?

In chapter 10 Galasi and Nagy consider how the incomes of children have fared in a country well at the front of the transition process in Central and Eastern Europe. They track changes in child poverty in Hungary over the years 1992–6. In contrast to the situation in other countries further behind in the transition from the planned system, this was a period of economic recovery (albeit rather weak) in Hungary. How did children fare during this period? And is it the case that economic deprivation during these years was severely concentrated on the few?

The authors begin by showing that, on average, children dropped down the income distribution. In 1992 they were under-represented in the poorest fifth of the population while by 1996 they were over-represented. This change in position contrasts sharply with that made by the elderly, whose representation in the poorest fifth of the distribution fell markedly over the period. As far as movements by individual children are concerned, one in ten were in the bottom fifth of the income distribution in every year from 1992 to 1996, and 44 per cent of children were found there at least once.

The analysis in the chapter then addresses the importance of work to avoid being poor. On the one hand, Galasi and Nagy find that an increase or reduction in the number of workers (or unemployed persons) in a household with children is often associated with a notable change in the probability of entering or leaving poverty. On the other hand, they discover that the majority of entries and exits occur with no such increases or reductions, something which underlines the importance of other explanations for movements into and out of poverty.

The authors conclude by discussing policy developments on the targeting of family benefits in Hungary, relating the debate on higher marginal tax rates that would be generated by income-testing to the evidence that their research produces on the degree of persistence of child poverty. Income-testing of social transfers is a key policy issue in Hungary where – as in other transition countries in the past – there has traditionally been a system of generous family benefits (albeit now substantially eroded). They warn that the standard discussion of the advantages of finer targeting of benefits takes insufficient notice of the impact that higher marginal tax rates might have on reducing income mobility.

Mobility and poverty dynamics among Russian children

Chapter 11 considers a very different country undergoing the transition towards a market system, and one much further behind in the process than Hungary and the rest of Central Europe. Klugman and Kolev's analysis is the first study of the dynamics of poverty in Russia that has focused specifically on children. It looks at the years 1994–6, a period during which great changes were taking place and when, in contrast to Hungary, the economy was still contracting.

Focusing on expenditures rather than incomes, the authors first develop one of the results coming out of the cross-national analysis in chapter 4: the high amount of mobility in Russia. Their analysis, however, differs from that of the Russian data in chapter 4 in several ways, including the definition of the poverty line (Klugman and Kolev take the official subsistence minimum), the longer period of time covered by the data (three years rather than two), the degree of disaggregation (for example, by age of child and type of locality), and the comparison with other groups in the population. Changes in expenditure are shown to vary across different groups of children. In particular, children in lone-parent and, especially, rural households are less likely to move out of the bottom fifth of the distribution.

Klugman and Kolev next compare the poverty experience of children with that of working-age adults and the elderly. Contrary to common perceptions of the impact of the transition process, the elderly were the least likely to experience any poverty over the three years, and children the most likely: 31 per cent of elderly are found to be poor at least once compared to 41 per cent of children. Similarly, children are the most likely among the three groups to be found to be poor in all three years – 5 per cent of all children are in this position (with the figure for rural children double that for urban children). The authors call attention to the adverse effects that this longer-term poverty may have for children's development in terms of health and schooling, especially as income has become more important during the transition in Russia to the determination of access to education and health services.

The authors conclude by noting the more limited capacity of the Russian state to mount a concerted attack on child poverty compared to the other countries covered in this book, all of which have stronger economies and institutions. Nevertheless, they argue that the Russian government's response to the problem of child poverty has been inadequate, as illustrated by their finding that child benefits are no more likely to be received by children persistently poor over three years than they are by children who experience no poverty at all.

Thinking about children in time

Good policy analysis requires several ingredients: detailed information about the nature of a problem and its consequences and what the causes are, plus, of course, knowledge of the efficacy of alternative policy programmes. Since this book is more about providing new 'facts' about child poverty than it is about the causes or programme evaluation, few conclusions about specific programmes can be drawn. This emphasis is reflected in chapter 12 which focuses on the policy implications of the dynamic perspective on child poverty.

Aber and Ellwood's chapter discusses 'what we have learnt' from the studies in the book and reflects on 'what we need to know'. From the diversity in the methods used and the countries analysed, they draw together a number of generalisations about the nature of child poverty. Their review of the book's contents is thematic, thus complementing the chapter-by-chapter review provided above. They draw out common threads but also emphasise results that vary across countries. While acknowledging the increments to knowledge that the book provides, Aber and Ellwood also point to the directions in which future research could be aimed, especially directions that would be relevant to the design of policy. They refer, for example, to more detailed information about children's (and families') 'income trajectories' over time, together with the correlates of different patterns; they draw attention to the complementary advantages of qualitative ethnographic research on child poverty dynamics; and they argue that the policy relevance of cross-national research would be enhanced by a greater systematic attention to the variation across countries in the policies which affect child poverty.

The last two sections of chapter 12 emphasise that dynamic analysis should do more than simply indicate where the problems are greatest: it ought to provide us with alternative policy ideas as well. Aber and Ellwood reflect on what those ideas might be, drawing on the analysis of this book and the previous experience of the introduction of 'dynamic perspectives' into US welfare reform policy debates and practice, contrasting this with the experience of Europe. While the dynamic perspective on child poverty clearly makes a great contribution to our understanding, Aber and Ellwood warn that it does not provide a 'magic guide' to policy.

1.5 Concluding remarks

In this chapter we have argued that it is important to study child poverty dynamics as well as child poverty rates at a point in time, and we have introduced the countries and topics that are studied in the rest of the book.

The overview of principal findings is only a taster from the feast of material provided in the following chapters. Readers who are most interested in cross-national analyses might wish to turn first to chapters 3 and 4. Those with specific country interests might begin with the relevant chapter in part II. The book is, however, intended to form an integrated whole. For example, the conclusions drawn about policy in chapter 12 are best understood in the light of the empirical results. And these, in turn, are best assessed with some understanding of a number of conceptual and definitional issues – the subject of the next chapter.

Acknowledgements
The helpful comments of Tony Atkinson, Greg Duncan, Martha Hill, Brian Nolan and Robert Walker are gratefully acknowledged.

References
Ashworth, K., Hill, M. and Walker, R., 1994, 'Patterns of childhood poverty: new challenges for policy', *Journal of Policy Analysis and Management*, 13: 658–80.

Bane, M. J. and Ellwood, D. T., 1986, 'Slipping into and out of poverty: the dynamics of spells', *Journal of Human Resources*, 21: 1–23.

Blair, T., 1999, 'Beveridge revisited: a welfare state for the 21st century', in Walker, R. (ed.), *Ending Child Poverty*, The Policy Press, Bristol.

Cantó-Sánchez, O. and Mercader-Prats, M., 1998, 'Child poverty in Spain: what can be said?', Innocenti Occasional Papers, Economic and Social Policy Series 66, UNICEF International Child Development Centre, Florence.

Cornia, G. A. and Danziger, S. (eds.), 1997, *Child Poverty and Deprivation in the Industrialized Countries, 1945–1995*, Clarendon Press, Oxford.

Department of Social Security, 1998, *Households Below Average Income 1979–1996/7*, Corporate Document Services, London.

Duncan, G. J., Coe, R. D. and Hill, M. S., 1984, 'The dynamics of poverty', in Duncan, G. J., Coe, R. D., Corcoran, M. E., Hill, M. S., Hoffman, S. D. and Morgan, J. N. (eds.), *Years of Poverty, Years of Plenty: The Changing Economic Fortunes of American Workers and Families*, Institute for Social Research, University of Michigan, Ann Arbor MI.

Duncan, G. J., Gustafsson, B., Hauser, R., Schmauss, G., Messinger, H., Muffels, R., Nolan, B., and Ray, J.-C., 1993, 'Poverty dynamics in eight countries', *Journal of Population Economics*, 6: 295–334.

Ellwood, D., 1998, 'Dynamic policy making: an insider's account of reforming US welfare', in Leisering, L. and Walker, R. (eds.), *The Dynamics of Modern Society: Policy, Poverty and Welfare*, The Policy Press, Bristol.

Eurostat, 1999, *The EC Household Panel Newsletter (3/99)*, Statistics in Focus, Population and Social Conditions, Theme 3 – 16/1999, Eurostat, Luxembourg.

Federal Interagency Forum on Child and Family Statistics, 1998, *America's Children: Key National Indicators of Well-Being*, US Government Printing Office, Washington DC.

Flemming, J. and Micklewright, J., 2000, 'Income distribution, economic systems and transition', in Atkinson, A. B. and Bourguignon, F. (eds.), *Handbook of Income Distribution*, North-Holland, Amsterdam.

Goodin, R., 1988, *Reasons for Welfare. The Political Theory of the Welfare State*, Princeton University Press, Princeton NJ.

Hancock, R., 1985, 'Explaining changes in families' relative net resources: an analysis of the Family Finances and Family Resources surveys', TIDI Discussion Paper No. 84, STICERD, London School of Economics, London.

Hernandez, D. J., 1997, 'Poverty levels', in Duncan, G. J. and Brooks-Gunn, J. (eds.), *Consequences of Growing up Poor*, Russell Sage Foundation, New York.

Hill, M. S., 1981, 'Some dynamic aspects of poverty', in Hill, M. S., Hill, D. and Morgan, J. N., (eds.), *Five Thousand Families: Patterns of Economic Progress*, Institute for Social Research, University of Michigan, Ann Arbor MI.

Jarvis, S. and Jenkins, S. 1997, 'Low income dynamics in 1990s' Britain', *Fiscal Studies*, 18: 1–20.

Kommission zur Wahrnehmung der Belange der Kinder (Kinderkommission), 1997, *Anhörung und Schlussfolgerungen aus der öffentlichen Anhörung zum Thema 'Existenzsicherung von Kindern'*, Deutscher Bundestag, Bonn.

Krause, P., 1998, 'Low income dynamics in unified Germany', in Leisering, L. and Walker, R. (eds.), *The Dynamics of Modern Society: Policy, Poverty and Welfare*, The Policy Press, Bristol.

van Leeuwen, J. and Pannekoek, J., 1999, 'To work oneself out of poverty: the Dutch experience 1989–1996', Research Paper 9910, Central Bureau of Statistics, Voorburg.

Leisering, L. and Walker, R., 1998, 'Making the future: from dynamics to policy agendas', in Leisering, L. and Walker, R. (eds.), *The Dynamics of Modern Society: Policy, Poverty and Welfare*, The Policy Press, Bristol.

Nolan, B., 1999, 'Targeting poverty. Lessons from Ireland on setting a national poverty target', *New Economy*, 6: 44–9.

Saraceno, C., 1997, 'Growth, regional imbalance, and child well-being: Italy over the last four decades', in Cornia and Danziger (1997).

Silva, M., 1997, 'Child welfare in Portugal amidst fast growth and weak social policy', in Cornia, G. A., and Danziger, S. (1997).

HM Treasury, 1999, 'Persistent poverty and lifetime inequality: the evidence', proceedings of a workshop, HM Treasury, 17–18 November 1998, CASEreport 5 and HM Treasury Occasional Paper 10, London School of Economics and HM Treasury, London.

UNICEF, 1997, 'Children at risk in Central and Eastern Europe: perils and promises', *Regional Monitoring Report 4*, UNICEF International Child Development Centre, Florence.

UNICEF, 1999, *After the Fall: The Human Impact of Ten Years of Transition*, UNICEF Innocenti Research Centre, Florence.

Vleminckx, K. and Smeeding, T. (eds.), 2001, *Child Well-being, Child Poverty and Child Policy in Modern Nations*, The Policy Press, Bristol.

Walker, R. with Ashworth, K., 1994, *Poverty Dynamics: Issues and Examples*, Avebury, Aldershot.

Zouev, A., 1999, *Generation in Jeopardy*, M. E. Sharpe, Armonk and London.

Part I

Issues and cross-national evidence

2 Conceptual and measurement issues

BRUCE BRADBURY, STEPHEN P. JENKINS AND
JOHN MICKLEWRIGHT

2.1 The range of issues

In this chapter we consider some of the important issues that arise when
one looks at child poverty from a dynamic perspective. Although some are
the same as those relevant to measuring poverty at a single point in time,
they often need to be seen in a new light when one looks at poverty longitudinally. We also draw attention to additional matters which arise from a
focus on children.

Choosing the concept of living standards and the definition of poverty is
fundamental, and is the subject of section 2.2. In subsequent chapters the
focus is typically on household income (adjusted for differences in needs)
and children are taken to be poor if their incomes fall below a low income
threshold. We consider why money-based measures are relevant and
whether it is consumption expenditure or income which is the better
measure of living standards. Additional issues addressed are the distribution of living standards within families, the choice of the equivalence scale
which is used to adjust observed money income (or consumption expenditure) to take account of differences in household size and composition, and
of course the level of the poverty line itself. The interval of time over which
money-based measures of living standards should be measured is also considered: for example, whether it should be a month or a year. This issue of
the accounting period is important in all poverty studies but is an example
of one that has additional relevance to the study of dynamics.

Even if one satisfactorily resolves the various conceptual and definitional
issues, there remains the problem of how to measure children's movements
into and out of low income in practice. This topic is the subject of section
2.3. We discuss the types of surveys one can draw on as sources of data, and
several potential sources of measurement error: for example, erroneous
moves across the poverty line.

The factors which lead to movements by children into and out of poverty are reviewed in section 2.4. In this book we are principally concerned with setting out 'the facts' about child poverty dynamics, but this naturally raises questions about what caused the patterns observed. We survey what previous research suggests about the relative importance of changes in household income from the labour market, changes in non-labour income, especially state benefits, and changes in household composition.

2.2 Income and consumption – and their changes over time

Until now we have avoided defining poverty. In reality it is a phenomenon with many faces, and the choice of definition may well affect the conclusions about poverty dynamics. The word 'poverty' can be used to describe a lack of income, a low level of consumption, bad housing or other physical living conditions, lower-quality healthcare, education and other basic social services, and so on. Applied to children, poverty, in the widest sense of 'deprivation', could even imply the absence of a range of other factors affecting an individual's well-being, for example the affection and interest of a parent or other adult with the responsibility for the child's upbringing.[1]

The definition of poverty used in much of this book is, however, considerably more restrictive. Most chapters are concerned with movements into and out of poverty defined as *low income*. Where income is not the focus, poverty measurement is typically based on data about household consumption expenditure: in other words a fairly narrow 'economic' definition of the living standards a household can achieve from drawing on current, future or past income. From a practical standpoint, a uni-dimensional approach of this type is the most feasible option given that the focus is on changes over time, although in chapter 8 (about Ireland), Nolan, Maître and Watson analyse the dynamics of deprivation among children based on a range of different indicators.

Does money matter?

Were poverty to be defined in very broad terms of deprivation in a variety of dimensions, it would be easy to believe that the longer or more often a child is poor the worse will be various outcomes in later life. But what are the implications of a definition based on income or consumption alone?

---

[1] Amartya Sen's 'capability' approach is one justification for the multi-dimensional measurement of poverty (for example, see the annexe to Sen 1997).

The causal impact on future outcomes of low family income during childhood, net of other related family background influences, has been the subject of much recent debate in the USA.[2] Two major studies, *Consequences of Growing up Poor* (Duncan and Brooks-Gunn 1997) and *What Income Can't Buy* (Mayer 1997), have received considerable attention. Both sought to isolate the independent impact of low income. To what extent do children from low-income families have worse outcomes in later life because of the low family income *itself* when a child? Or are adverse outcomes for children from poor backgrounds due to a range of factors associated with – but not necessarily caused by – low income, including some of those mentioned above as possible candidates to be included in a wider definition of child poverty? These studies show, not surprisingly, that low income during childhood does have some independent association with future outcomes. Moreover, there is evidence that sustained low income has greater adverse effects than transitory poverty: see the summaries of the US literature by Blau (1999) and McLoyd (1998).[3] (Findings for other countries could be expected to differ on account of differences in economies and institutions.)

It is important not to be diverted too much by this debate. Interest in the duration of low family income while a child should not depend only on the impact of childhood poverty on later life. Low living standards represent hardship while they last. Money certainly matters in this sense. Lower income means less opportunity to buy goods and services that may benefit children now and less opportunity to live in good housing in attractive areas. Lower income may produce a variety of other effects that impact on children: for example, greater tension in the family. As one 14-year-old girl in a UK family reliant upon state benefits said:

> for me it's about not being part of things, not having the money to live normally like other people. Everything I do or I want to do, even like really small things, is decided by money, or by not having it anyway (Roker and Coleman 1998: 17).

This situation of 'not being part of things' today is clearly a concern, irrespective of any significance it may have for what happens tomorrow. (We

---

[2] The debate is present in other countries as well, of course: for example, see the studies referred to in HM Treasury (1999) in the case of the UK. But it is in the USA where research to isolate the causal impact of low income in childhood on outcomes in later life is most advanced (largely because more data have been available). The child outcome variables studied are diverse. They include measures of cognitive development, scholastic achievement, mental health, pre-marital fertility and labour market success.

[3] This is not to claim that income effects are the *major* family background influence on child development outcomes. Blau's overview of the US evidence points out that 'income effects are small compared to the effects of race, gender, and some characteristics of the mother and household' (1999: 263).

leave for the moment on one side its empirical implementation in terms of absolute or relative measures of poverty.) The longer that situation continues the greater the concern should be.

Changing income or changing consumption?

There is a strong argument that low *consumption*, rather than low income, is the better economic measure of poverty, especially if being poor is defined in relation to a minimum standard of living rather than a minimum right to resources (Atkinson 1998). Consumption will be higher than income in the case of borrowing and dissaving and lower in the case of saving and repayment of earlier loans. Income represents the flow of resources from which families may choose to spend or save, and these opportunities are the basis for the minimum rights approach to poverty measurement. However, spending and saving choices are largely made by parents and not children. Children do not benefit during their childhood from parental savings that are locked up for retirement rather than for use when the family faces a financial crisis. From the perspective of children, the family's current consumption seems in principle the better measure on which to base a definition of who is poor.

The implications for the measurement of movements into and out of poverty of the distinction between the two concepts are easy to appreciate. Suppose that family income dips below the poverty line for a short period, then rises back above it. This represents a movement into and then back out of poverty on the basis of income, but if the household is able to borrow or to draw on savings to finance its consumption while its income level is reduced, then consumption can be 'smoothed' and expenditure maintained above the poverty line throughout.

The key issue is whether families *are* able to smooth consumption in this way. For the USA, Rodgers and Rodgers have reported that 'there is increasing evidence that some poor people can, and do, save and borrow' (1993: 34). Nonetheless it is fair to say that not enough systematic quantitative information is available about the extent to which families do maintain their consumption during periods of low income. (Important qualitative studies include the work by Kempson (1996) on Britain.) Families most prone to poverty are unlikely to have significant financial savings on which to draw. This is particularly true of families with children, whereas the elderly on low incomes are more likely to have accumulated wealth. Ruggles and Williams (1989) investigated spells of poverty in the

USA, defined on the basis of low monthly income. They found that if families were to have run down their financial assets during the time spent on low income, there would have been a fall of a quarter in the number of children entering poverty during the year. (For the elderly the figure would have fallen by a half.) As the authors point out, the implication is that savings in the majority of cases could not have been used to maintain living standards above the poverty line.

For those people with few savings to draw on as living standards threaten to drop, it is the ability to borrow that may be crucial. There is even less known about borrowing by poor families. Those prone to low incomes may be unable to provide the necessary collateral to formal lending institutions. Kempson's (1996) research on Britain points to the use made by low-income families of both licensed and unlicensed moneylenders. But borrowing can take place in a variety of forms, including informal loans from relatives and friends and by delaying payment of fuel bills.[4]

In addition, many families facing a fall in income will 'cope' (they usually have little choice in the matter) by delaying expenditures on items such as consumer durables and home maintenance. To the extent to which they continue to derive services from durables purchased prior to their low-income spell, they will have a higher consumption level than their income suggests, even in the absence of access to savings or borrowing. However, this will only apply to some areas of consumption – having a good refrigerator is of little benefit unless you have the money to fill it.

Obviously, the longer the period of low income, the harder it is to draw upon savings or to go further into debt.[5] The longer low income lasts, the less likely it is that consumption can be maintained above the level of a poverty line and that the use of income will lead to misleading results about the dynamics of family living standards. The same is true the further below the poverty line that income falls and the higher above the line that it rises on leaving poverty. Ruggles and Williams (1989) noted that it was the

---

[4] Some indirect clues on the extent to which borrowing takes place when living standards are threatened come from a British survey of persons entering unemployment. (We report results based on our own analysis of microdata from the survey, which is described in Heady and Smyth, 1989.) Three months into unemployment, the median value of the stock of all forms of debt (including delayed payments of bills) held by families with children had risen from about one week's worth of unemployment benefit to about three weeks' worth. (Median savings had fallen from about one week's benefit to zero.) Two thirds of the families reported having cut down on food expenditure since entering unemployment – with the average fall in savings and rise in debt being larger for those families that said their consumption had not changed.

[5] In the survey described in the preceding footnote, the median value of debt among those families still unemployed after fifteen months was unchanged from that at the three-month point.

families with monthly income close to the line who could have filled their income shortfalls by liquidating assets.

Finally, although in principle consumption may be a more meaningful concept of living standards for children than family income, this does not resolve the question of the best empirical indicator to use from a practical point of view. It is not uncommon to equate household *expenditure* with consumption, but the two measures often differ, as the discussion above has already illustrated. In wealthy countries, a large proportion of the household budget is spent on infrequently purchased items such as clothing and consumer durables. This means that expenditure measured over the time periods typically used in expenditure surveys, such as a month, may be a less adequate indicator of consumption than the cash income of the family.[6] Moreover, repeated observations over time on households' expenditures are even less common than on incomes. The typical household panel collects much more information about income than about expenditure. However, our cross-national analysis of movements into and out of poverty in chapter 4 is able to draw on data for both measures in the cases of Spain and Russia.

Finally, we should note that the measures of income and consumption used in this book are restricted to money (or near money) income and commodity consumption expenditure. In particular, we do not analyse the impact on child well-being of government social expenditures (for example, on health services or education). This is an unavoidable limitation arising from the data available to us. Bradbury and Jäntti (1999) review research on the impact of these non-cash benefits and conclude that, at least in terms of comparing poverty rates across nations at a point in time, the inclusion of non-cash benefits would be unlikely to make much difference. This is because benefits to these services are spread reasonably evenly across all children, and countries that spend a large amount on social assistance benefits also tend to spend more on non-cash services.

Patterns of child poverty over time

Child poverty looked at from a dynamic perspective has multiple features. These include the timing of movements into and out of poverty, the length

---

[6] As Atkinson notes, 'we need to distinguish between the question as to *what we want to measure* and the issue of how far *we can measure* what we want to measure' (1998: 31, emphasis in original).

Figure 2.1. *Patterns of poverty spells for children: examples*

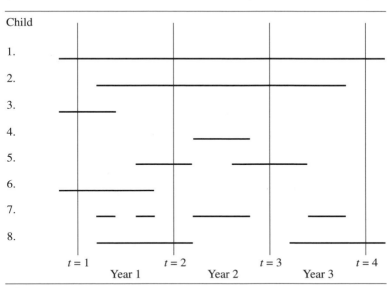

Note: for each child, the dark line shows the timing and duration of each poverty spell.

of each poverty spell, the extent of spell repetition, and the total amount of time spent in poverty over a given period.

To appreciate the many features of the dynamics of child poverty, look at figure 2.1 which shows, for each of eight hypothetical children, the poverty experienced over a three-year period. Calendar time is measured along the horizontal axis and the duration of each poverty spell is represented by the length of a line. These lines indicate the months in which monthly income is below the poverty line. The diagram refers only to children that *do* experience a spell of poverty. One could imagine there also being children 9–16 off the bottom of the diagram who never experienced poverty during the years in question. (Of course in practice the number of such children relative to those who do experience poverty might be rather more or less than in this example, and could also be expected to differ with the length of accounting period chosen.)

We should emphasise at the outset that the diagram summarises the experience of *children* rather than of *families*. Although the measurement of poverty is to be based on the income of the family or household, the unit of analysis remains the child. (In this chapter we use the terms 'household' and 'family' interchangeably, though in practice there are important differences: a household may contain more than one family.) From a longitudinal perspective the concept of the family is a slippery one, as Duncan and Hill (1985b) have forcefully argued. Families form, grow, shrink and split apart over time. Duncan (1983) noted that in the thirteenth year of the US Panel Study of Income Dynamics (PSID), only 12 per cent of the originally sampled families had not changed composition and as many as 57 per cent were headed by someone other than the original family head. A quarter of children in two-parent households interviewed in the first year of the British Household Panel Survey (BHPS) had a change of household head by the time of the sixth annual interview and a half were in households in which there had been some form of demographic change (Jenkins 1999: table 6). It is the *children* that we wish to observe over time and not the families that they may or may not still be members of.

How then may the experiences of children differ? Child 1 is in poverty throughout the three years, with the spell starting before the three-year 'observation window' and continuing after it finishes. Child 2 also has one long spell but in this case the starting and finishing dates are within the three-year window. Children 3 and 4, on the other hand, have one short spell each. Children 5–8 have two spells or more, some long, some short, some entirely within the three-year window and some straddling one end of it.

One key feature revealed by the diagram is the *repetition* of poverty, experienced by children 5–8. A substantial part of the period may be spent in poverty even if each individual spell is quite short (as is the case with child 7). A focus on an overall entry rate to or exit rate from poverty would fail to capture this phenomenon of multiple spells experienced by the same children. A high turnover among the poor does not mean the experience of poverty is being shared equally if the same children keep coming back into poverty. (Estimating the average duration of poverty spells is an alternative to calculating the exit rate that suffers from the same problem of failing to measure the recurrent nature of poverty.)

One straightforward way of accounting for repeated poverty spells would be to focus on the total number of months spent poor during some fixed period (for example 'childhood'). From this perspective child 5 and child 7 are counted as having had the same experience during the three years shown. However, their cases also illustrate that very different patterns of entry and exit are consistent with the same total poverty experience.

The fact that patterns of poverty may vary greatly has led some authors, notably Ashworth *et al.* (1994), to attempt to summarise experiences of the type shown in figure 2.1 with a poverty taxonomy. Ashworth *et al.* classified poverty during childhood into categories such as 'transient' poverty, 'persistent' poverty, 'occasional' poverty, etc. They also compared the severity (i.e. depth) of poverty across children in these different groups as well as looking at child deprivation measured with a range of other indicators (thus checking the validity of their classification).[7]

Figure 2.1 indicates nothing about the severity of poverty while poor – the shortfall of income below the poverty line – or how much income is above the poverty line during periods that are not spent poor. As far as the latter is concerned, one might wish to distinguish time spent in 'near poverty' as well as in poverty itself.

The accounting period for income

Over what period and how often should incomes be measured? The distinction between income and consumption is more important the shorter the period of time over which the two are assessed. One reason, therefore, for looking at income assessed over longer periods is that long-term income is likely to provide a better indicator of consumption at each point in time (because of consumption smoothing).

It is rare for longitudinal surveys to yield month-by-month sequences of monthly income (as in figure 2.1) from which one could also calculate measures of annual income. However, one source that does have such information is the US Survey of Income and Program Participation (SIPP) which yields a monthly income sequence about four years long from interviews carried out every four months (more about data sources below).

The SIPP data illustrate the fact that, because monthly incomes are more volatile than annual incomes, the use of a monthly accounting period will lead to more measured movements into and out of poverty. Ruggles and Williams (1989: 230–1) report that, of those persons in the USA with a poverty spell entry in 1984, the number counted as starting a spell using an annual income measure is only about 20–25 per cent of the number of persons recorded starting a spell using a definition of poverty based on low monthly income. With the same data, Ruggles (1990: table 5.1) showed that 24 per cent of children in two-parent families were poor in at least one month during the year but only 3 per cent were poor in every month. Among children in single-parent families the figures were 61 per cent and

---

[7] There is also a related literature which discusses the different sorts of income trajectories which might be associated with poverty transitions: see, for example, Gardiner and Hills (1999).

26 per cent. Clearly, use of a monthly rather than annual accounting period results in a lot more short poverty spells being counted.

It is therefore unsurprising that many income-tested cash benefits in industrialised countries are assessed on the basis of income over a month, or a shorter period (for example, eligibility for the main social assistance benefit in the UK is on the basis of weekly income). This reflects the view that smoothing of consumption is very difficult for households at the bottom of the income distribution, even over fairly short periods.

In practice the measures which are available to researchers from the vast majority of household panel surveys are rather different from those in the SIPP, not least because the interview frequency is lower – typically once per year (see the vertical lines at $t = 1$, $t = 2$, $t = 3$, and so on, in figure 2.1). There are two main types of household income variable available from each interview (some surveys have one measure or the other; some have both). *Annual income* refers to the total amount received over the year between each interview: this measure takes no account of sub-annual income variation, which is, in effect, averaged out over the year.[8] *Current income* is the total income received in the period (usually one month) just prior to the interview (i.e. just to the left of one of the vertical lines in figure 2.1). In this case information exists only on whether the child is in poverty at particular points in time rather than continuously. Clearly, current income provides an incomplete picture of incomes over the year as a whole.

What, then, are the consequences of using a current income rather than annual income definition for the measurement of poverty rates at a point in time and for the various dimensions of poverty dynamics?

First, there are consequences for estimates of the number of children who are 'currently poor'. The greater variability in monthly income means that more people will be found below the poverty line using a current income measure than would be found using an annual income measure (see Böheim and Jenkins 2000 for elaboration of this argument). The size of the difference between the two estimates of the poverty rate is not necessarily large however. Ruggles (1990: table 5.1) shows for the USA in 1984 that the annual poverty rate among persons in married-couple families with children was 7.4 per cent, whereas the average of the monthly rates was 10.2 per cent. For persons in lone-parent families, the corresponding figures were 40 and 43 per cent. Böheim and Jenkins (2000) show that, for Britain in the

---

[8] In fact the reference period for annual income is usually not coincident with the twelve months between interviews (partly because interviews are rarely exactly one year apart), but refers to the twelve months up to a date during the year of the panel interview which is the same for all respondents to the survey. The essential point is that consecutive annual panel interviews then provide a consecutive sequence of observations on annual income for each person.

early 1990s, the differences between current income and annual income estimates of the proportion of the population with low income differ by at most one or two percentage points.[9]

Second, the choice of an annual or current income measure also has implications for the estimates of income mobility between one year and the next and the corresponding poverty transition rates. One might expect that the estimates derived from data on current incomes from two consecutive interviews one year apart would be greater than estimates based on consecutive observations on annual incomes, on the grounds that there is more variability in the short-term measure. However, this is not the full story. Consider, for example, the annual poverty exit rate. This is defined as the ratio of the number of movers out of poverty between this year and last year divided by the number of persons who were poor last year. The earlier argument suggests that current income measures provide higher estimates of the number of movers (the numerator of the exit rate calculation), but the previous paragraph indicated that current income measures also provide higher estimates of poverty rates at a point in time (the denominator). Hence it is not obvious that the poverty exit rate calculated on the basis of current income is necessarily higher than the corresponding estimate based on annual income. Empirical work is required to resolve this issue.[10]

Our cross-national analysis of children's movements into and out of poverty from one year to the next in chapter 4 provides results derived from both annual incomes and current incomes for each country where the surveys used permit it. The chapters in part II follow a variety of practices.

Are start and end dates observed?

Inference about poverty spells is compromised because the start date and end date of every spell in progress at the time of interview are not observed.[11] With data about current income from four annual interviews,

---

[9] They also point out that this result may arise because the British Household Panel Survey definition of current income already incorporates an element of smoothing: the labour earnings that are included in current income are respondents' 'usual' earnings rather than those most recently received.

[10] Analysis by Böheim and Jenkins (2000), using the British Household Panel Survey, suggests that estimates of annual poverty exit rates are indeed higher for current income measures, but by only a few percentage points compared to the ones based on annual income measures.

[11] In the statistical literature on the measurement of events, the lack of information about when a spell started is known as 'left censoring' while 'right censoring' is the term applied when the end date is not observed.

one could not tell whether child 1 in figure 2.1 had been poor for several years when found in poverty at $t = 1$, or whether he or she had been poor for just a month. There would be no way of distinguishing child 2, with one long poverty spell, from child 5, who has two spells rather than one and who has much less total time in poverty over the three-year observation window: each is in poverty when interviewed. Many poverty spells will not be observed at all. Children 4 and 7 will never be seen in poverty. It is the short spells that are most likely to be missing – any spell that lasts at least twelve months during the time the observation window is in progress will be observed by definition.

Moving to an annual income concept does not solve the problem. By definition, a poverty measure based on annual income does not take account of all within-year poverty transitions either. And unknown start and end dates will again be a feature of the data. A child found at his or her family's first participation in a panel survey to have been in poverty during the previous twelve months, on the basis of the family's annual income, could have been poor for just one year – or for two, three or four or more years.

If one wishes to estimate how long poverty spells are, then inference made using the information about current income at the time of interview will provide different estimates from the case when one could observe all the entry and exit dates on a monthly basis. The reason is that the poverty spells observed in progress at each interview are a non-random sample of the population of poverty spells which occur. Longer spells will be disproportionately represented; short spells are more likely to have start dates which are not observed. It is therefore important to make a distinction between the expected length of poverty spells for the children who are observed poor at any one time and the expected length of poverty spells for all children who begin a poverty spell. Both types of statistic are of policy interest, but one should be aware that if the desired focus is on the latter type, then 'length-biased' samples derived from spells currently in progress provide estimates of exit rates which are too low and of spell lengths which are too long. These issues are discussed further in Bane and Ellwood (1986).

The income unit and adjustment for differences in family 'needs'

We have been implicitly assuming so far that we have a suitable measure of living standards for each person, and in particular for each child. This measure is based on the income (or consumption) of the family to which they belong. In all the empirical analysis in this book it is assumed that the economic well-being of each person is measured by the income (or consumption expenditure) of the family to which they belong where that income is adjusted for the family's needs. In effect it is being supposed that all family members pool their money incomes and that all family members (adults and children) have the same standard of living. There is needs adjustment (or 'equivalisation'), since a monthly income of £2,000 provides much lower living standards for a family of four than it does for a single person living alone. It is therefore conventional to adjust each household's money income by an equivalence scale factor to take account of the effects on living standards of differences in household size and composition. We now consider in turn the equal living standards assumption and the choice of the equivalence scale.

The assumption about equal living standards within a family is used almost universally in the analysis of income distribution. But it is also likely to be only an approximation to reality, and has stimulated much recent research. (For a review of the issues, see, for example, Jenkins 1991.) A number of empirical studies using innovative methods have highlighted the existence of within-household inequalities.

Lazear and Michael (1986, 1988), for example, developed a model of how parents allocate income between themselves and their children, and fitted it using US expenditure survey data.[12] They compared the distribution of income derived using this method with the one derived using the equal living standards assumption and found important differences:

On average a child receives about 40% as much as an adult in the same household. Taking these rough estimates into account, the distribution of consumption income among a population tends to locate children much further down the scale than is the case when income is assumed to be apportioned equally on a per capita basis.

Children probably require less income than adults for their consumption . . . Thus our conclusion . . . does not necessarily indicate that [children] are deprived or that their utility is dramatically less than that of an adult. But since adults tend to determine the allocation of resources within the family, there is no certainty that the utility of children and the adults are equalized (Lazear and Michael 1986: S257).

A different approach to revealing inequalities within families is represented by the qualitative research of Middleton et al. (1997) whose innovative survey of British children interviewed principal carers (almost all mothers) plus children over the age of 5 years. The authors report that 'parents are more likely to go without than children; one half of parents who are defined as "poor" themselves have children who are found to be

---

[12] They exploit the fact that some goods may be classified as exclusively adult goods. Assuming that the share of these goods in total family expenditure does not depend on the number of children present, one can estimate the adult–child expenditure split from data on childless families, and then apply it to families with children.

"not poor"' (1997: 5). In particular a large percentage of mothers, especially lone mothers receiving social assistance benefits, claim that they often or sometimes go without items or activities in order to provide things for their children. This research draws attention to potential inequalities between mothers and fathers, as well as between parents and children. This matters because the impact on children's living standards of higher family benefits may depend on which parent the extra resources are paid to. Recent research suggests that payments to mothers are more effective in raising expenditures on children's goods and services: see, for example, Lundberg *et al.* (1997) and Phipps and Burton (1998).

Although studies such as these have provided important new information, they provide little systematic guidance about how to take account of inequalities within families in analyses of income and poverty of the type routinely undertaken by national statistical agencies and in this book. The fundamental problem is that the 'true' within-household distribution is unobservable. (The problem is further complicated if one recognises the distinction between families and households.) It is difficult to characterise it in universally accepted ways which could be routinely applied in analysis. For these reasons, the conventional equal living standards assumption continues to be widely used, including in all the analysis reported in this book.

The choice of equivalence scale factors with which to adjust household money incomes is also a tricky issue. Although the assessment of the 'cost of a child' (or the cost of an adult, for that matter) has a substantive factual core, there are important matters of normative judgement inevitably involved in the assembly of this information to produce an equivalence scale which can be applied across families of different types. Hence there is no single correct way to estimate an equivalence scale which is free of normative judgements. As a result, a variety of methods have been used to derive them. Coulter *et al.* (1992a), for example, distinguish five types of equivalence scale: 'econometric scales (based on what people buy), subjective scales (based on what people say), budget standard scales (based on what experts say), social assistance benefit scales (based on what society pays), and pragmatic scales (which are precisely that)' (1992a: 79).[13] For

---

[13] For several of the methods, equivalence scales are often discussed with reference to the 'costs of children', but this is not necessarily the best way to consider them in a child-focused analysis. From the point of view of parents, children not only cost much more than the money spent on them (because there are also time costs and forgone leisure), but also usually bring more benefits than they cost. From the perspective of a child's welfare, the 'joys of parenthood' are not relevant, and the loss of parents' leisure is not a direct welfare cost to their children. However, the need to stretch the family budget further caused by the arrival of a sibling is of direct relevance to child welfare – providing support for our focus upon money income needs.

extensive surveys of equivalence scale derivation and related income distribution issues, and some comparisons of scale relativities, see Coulter *et al.* (1992a) and Citro and Michael (1995).

A mixture of equivalence scale types is used in this book. For example, chapter 5 about the USA and chapter 11 about Russia use budget standard scales. However, the most commonly used scales are the 'pragmatic ones'. In particular, several chapters use the so-called 'square-root' scale, in which each household's equivalence scale factor is given by the square root of household size. This scale is becoming widely used in cross-national research on income distribution, and has been popularised by Atkinson *et al.*'s (1995) influential study. This is an example of the Buhmann *et al.* (1988) family of equivalence scales in which the scale factor is equal to household size raised to the power e, where e is a number between zero and one. The square-root scale is the case when $e = 0.5$.

According to the square-root scale, a single-person household with a money income of £10,000 per year has an equivalent income of £10,000, but a two-parent, two-child household with the same money income would have an equivalent income of £5,000. For a per capita scale ($e = 1$), the figure for a family of four would be £2,500. In this case each additional child is assumed to be more 'costly' in living standards terms than in the square-root scale case. (Put another way, the per capita scale assumes lower economies of household size.) One might also suppose that the 'cost' of an additional household member depends on whether that person is an adult or a child. The equivalence scale used extensively in chapter 3 recognises this, assuming a household's scale rate is equal to the number of adults plus 0.7 times the number of children, with the sum raised to the power 0.85. In this case a two-parent, two-children household would have a scale rate of 2.83 (rather than 2.0 as with the 'square-root' scale) and an equivalent income in this case of £3,534.

Equivalence scales based on household size or the numbers of adults and children are clearly very simple, and one might ask about the implications of using more sophisticated scales, for example ones which take account of children's ages. This is relevant to the study of dynamics in particular, as children grow older between survey interviews. More generally, the diversity of equivalence scales in use naturally raises questions about whether conclusions are sensitive to the choices made. For the majority of topics that we address in this book we are confident that the use of simple parametric equivalence scales rather than more sophisticated ones is not a significant problem. Research suggests that even relatively sophisticated scales can be approximated well by parametric scales (see, for example, Coulter *et al.* 1992b, Jenkins and Cowell 1994). The more relevant issue is the choice of equivalence scale generosity.

Most previous research has considered the impact of changing the equivalence scale on estimates of poverty rates and the composition of the poor at a point in time (see, for example, Buhmann *et al.* 1988, Coulter *et al.* 1992b, Jenkins and Cowell 1994). It is now well known, for example, that large families (usually families with children) will be more likely to be found amongst the poorest groups if one uses an equivalence scale that assumes that additional children are relatively 'costly' in terms of living standards (i.e. a relatively high value of *e*). By contrast, little research is available about the impact of using different scales on measures of poverty dynamics such as entry and exit rates or time spent poor. A rare study is by Cantó-Sánchez for Spain (1998), who investigated the sensitivity of estimates of the proportion of the population always poor (on the basis of successive observations on quarterly income over a two-year period) to variations in the scale parameter *e*. She found that as *e* is varied between zero and one, the never-poor rate first fell and then rose – the 'U-shape' result which is also commonly found when looking at variations in the poverty rate at a point in time as *e* is changed (see the references above). However, this result does not tell us whether cross-national comparisons would be altered by variations in equivalence scale generosity (since the same U-shape relationship may hold for each country being compared). Investigation of this issue is a task for future research.

Choosing the poverty line

Measuring a movement into or out of poverty requires a line dividing the poor from the non-poor to be specified. There is of course a huge literature on defining a poverty line, and it is not our purpose to review it (see, for example, the surveys in Callan and Nolan 1991, Citro and Michael 1995 and Ruggles 1990). Nonetheless there is an important distinction between 'absolute' and 'relative' poverty lines to be made.

An absolute poverty line is a level of low real income (or expenditure) which is fixed in real terms. A relative poverty line is a low income (or expenditure) cut-off which may vary in real income terms with the time periods and countries being compared: an example is the real income corresponding to one half (or some other fixed fraction) of a country's contemporary average income. Using this definition, estimates of the child poverty exit rate in Britain would be based on half last year's average British income to identify the children who were poor last year, and half this year's average income to identify who was poor this year. And the corresponding study for the USA would use half the US average income in each of the two years.

The four cut-offs – once expressed in a common currency using a suitable exchange rate – would all differ in value. By contrast, were an absolute poverty line to be used (for example, half the US average income in 1995), estimates would be based on the same real income cut-off in each case.

The real incomes corresponding to our relative poverty lines change over time, for example rising with secular economic growth. For short intervals (or zero growth periods), these variations will typically be small. However, over longer intervals the change in real income value of a relative poverty line can be substantial. For example, in the UK between 1979 and 1995/6, average real income rose by some 40 per cent (Department of Social Security 1998), and thence so too did poverty lines defined as fixed fractions of average income. Changes in the value of a relative poverty line may also be large if economic growth – or contraction – is particularly rapid. The former case is illustrated by Ireland in the 1990s (as discussed by Nolan 1999), and the latter case by New Zealand in the late 1980s (see Statistics New Zealand 1999: chapter 6). The case of particular relevance for this book is Russia, which has experienced both large declines in income and high inflation. This discussion reminds us that, in the case where relative poverty lines are used, movements into and out of poverty are generated by different real income changes at different times. Put another way, one needs to be aware that estimates are influenced by changes in value of the low income cut-off as well as changes in incomes.

The additional element of a poverty line definition that concerns us most here is the setting of a line relevant to poverty among *children*, especially in the context of a cross-national study. The definition of an absolute poverty line has often started with consideration of the cost of subsistence for a family with children. This is true both of Rowntree's (1901) work in England at the beginning of the twentieth century and Orshansky's (1965) analysis which underlay what became the official US poverty line in the 1960s, as well as other later 'budget standards' approaches. In this sense, children have featured prominently in attempts to define critical levels of living standards in absolute terms. However, discussion of relative poverty lines has not had a child focus. The comment of Adam Smith (1776) often quoted in discussion of relative poverty – that a person would be ashamed to appear in public in late eighteenth-century Britain if he did not sport leather shoes and a silk shirt – is more a remark about parents' living standards than about those of their children.

If children are excluded from social participation by low living standards, the most important form of this may be exclusion from the lifestyle typically enjoyed by other children. (On this interpretation, the 'things' that the UK teenager, reported earlier in this section, said that she was 'not being part of' would be things being done by her peers.) This suggests the use of a poverty line defined with reference to the average living standards of children in society.

Part of the cross-national analysis in chapter 4 leans for support on this idea of defining child poverty in relation to the living standards of all children. In the first part of the chapter we classify children as having low income if they are in the poorest 20 per cent of the *distribution of children* by equivalised household income. This has the advantage that the poverty rate among children at any one time is exactly the same in each country – one fifth of children are found below the line in every case. This provides for easy comparison of poverty exit and entry rates (and of the time spent poor) across countries independently of differences in the degree of income inequality across the countries. We elaborate on this issue in chapter 4. In the rest of that chapter we then use a more conventional relative poverty line, one based on a fraction of the median of equivalised income in the population as a whole for the country concerned. This is also the approach followed in most of the chapters in part II of the book. For the most part we use *one half* as the relevant fraction of median equivalised income, but higher and lower fractions are also employed to check the sensitivity of conclusions and to reveal further details about the nature of children's income movements over time.[14]

2.3 Measuring the dynamics of child poverty

What information on the dynamics of child poverty is needed? And what can be measured given the available data?[15]

Setting aside the potential attractions of information on consumption, the ideal data set would contain, for each child, information about income in each and every month of childhood – from birth to the age of majority – and then beyond into adulthood. In this way, the short-term changes in family incomes would be revealed. One would be able to observe the movement – and lack of movement – into and out of low income from month to month. Information would be obtained on the dynamics of deprivation over periods of, say, two to three years, and within each year, which is especially relevant to the design of state transfer schemes to support family incomes.

---

[14] Contrast the Eurostat Task Force's (1998) report which recommended low income thresholds be set at 60 per cent of median equivalised income (and no longer at 50 per cent of mean equivalised income).

[15] Our discussion of the issues is in part influenced by that of Duncan (1997) who considers the longitudinal measurement of child poverty and welfare dependence in the USA.

Longer periods could also be focused on, consistent with the view that it is lengthy periods of deprivation that have a negative impact on later life. For example, the total amount of time during childhood spent in poverty could be determined – a summary statistic that is of obvious appeal. This could be calculated on the basis of monthly or annual incomes (aggregating over the months in each year), the latter catering to the concern that short-term movements may be 'noisy' indicators of changes in living standards. One would be able to distinguish between different periods of childhood: for example, the critical time of the early years of life versus the teenage period. And the continuation of the data into adulthood would allow the association between childhood poverty and that in later life to be investigated.

Needless to say, such an ideal is never realised in practice. Even in the USA, where longitudinal data on family incomes are most abundant, elements are missing. The long-running PSID, which provided the evidence cited in chapter 1 on the distribution of numbers of childhood years spent poor, provides only partial data on incomes during periods within the year. Information on incomes, month by month, is contained in a different source (the SIPP) which observes any given family's income over about four years in total. The combination of these two sources, however, represents a very rich source of information and provides the basis for the longitudinal indicators of child poverty and welfare dependence suggested for the USA by Duncan (1997). Duncan discusses a large number of useful indicators but he concludes that, if forced to condense these to just a handful of indicators, he would opt for a 'Fab Five', as follows: (1) short-run poverty (average monthly child poverty rates); (2) longer-run poverty (total time spent in poverty over a multi-year period); (3) short-run benefit dependence (average monthly social assistance recipiency rates); (4) longer-run benefit dependence (total time spent on social assistance over a multi-year period); and (5) intergenerational benefit dependence (correlations for parents' and children's receipt).

Types of longitudinal data

In reality complete information about the path of family incomes over childhood (and beyond) is not available. How then can the available data be used to measure the patterns of experience represented earlier in figure 2.1?

Longitudinal data of various sorts exist that contain information on the family incomes of children. These include:

(a) household panel surveys, such as the BHPS, the PSID, the German Socio-economic Panel, the Hungarian Panel, and the new European Community Household Panel (ECHP), which aim to track all members of the original sampled households together with their offspring (typically with annual interviews);
(b) birth cohort studies that follow a specific group of children through childhood into adulthood (typically with infrequent interviews);
(c) 'residence-based' panel surveys, such as the Spanish Encuesta Continua de Presupuestos Familiares (ECPF), where interviewers return to the same physical dwelling irrespective of who lives there (typically with a fixed number of quarterly interviews);
(d) administrative records of income tax returns;
(e) administrative records of income-tested benefits.

Each source has its merits. Buck *et al.* (1996) provide a review of the issues, although they do not take a child-focused perspective. Only sources of types (a) and (b) allow children to be followed properly over time.

Household panel surveys (type (a)) collect detailed information about the incomes (annual or current, as discussed earlier) of all household members, their personal characteristics, familial relationships, and about the household itself. Every individual in the original panel (adult or child) is followed over time and data collected about them, even if the household to which they belong splits up or if they move house. Children are interviewed in their own right when they become adults. Interviews are conducted annually with no limit on the total number (by contrast with fixed-length panels such as the SIPP or the ECPF, where the number of interviews is set in advance, after which respondents are 'rotated out' of the panel). It is this design feature which allows the PSID (which began interviewing in 1968) to build up a picture of children's incomes from birth through childhood to adulthood.

Cohort studies of children (type (b)) cover all of childhood but usually collect data at only a few selected points in time (which may not be evenly spaced) and the information on incomes may not be consistent over time. The British National Child Development Study (NCDS) is an example. Information has been collected at ages 0, 7, 11, 16, 23 and 33. But no income data were collected at birth and merely a binary indicator of 'financial difficulties' at ages 7 and 11. The interview sweep at age 16 was the first time that any attempt was made to measure total household income – an attempt that met with limited success (see Micklewright 1986).

Residence-based panels (type (c)) are a potentially useful source about income dynamics, especially since samples are often relatively large, and they may provide information about sub-annual income changes (though not as frequently as the SIPP).[16] Interviews are typically conducted quarterly, for up to six or eight quarters. One disadvantage of such surveys is that some detailed information about household composition and familial relationships may not be available (because the survey focuses on other topics). And, of particular relevance for studies of dynamics, persons who leave the household are not followed and interviewed (as in household panel surveys of type (a)). Since residential mobility is not independent of income mobility, this may limit analysis of some interesting questions (see chapter 9).

Panels may be constructed using survey types (d) and (e), and sometimes a combination of them. This practice has been followed especially in the Nordic countries where information from public registers of many kinds is more readily available and can be combined (see, for example, Pedersen and Smith 1998). However, the identification of children within these types of surveys is not without problems, especially when parents split and re-partner.

Studies of the dynamics of benefit receipt using data of type (e) alone are of considerable interest but it should also be understood what they cannot show. Being 'on benefit' is only a rough proxy for being in poverty: income thresholds for benefit eligibility may or may not correspond with the poverty line one might wish to set and there is also the question of take-up of entitlement. One knows nothing about income in periods 'off benefit'. And, importantly, since benefits are claimed by adults rather than children, it may or may not be possible to trace individual children through time in such records, as opposed to adult claimants.

This brief discussion illustrates why household panel surveys of type (a) are the ones most commonly used to examine income and poverty dynamics. In what follows we therefore focus on the problems arising from using longitudinal data of this type to examine child poverty dynamics. Several points concerning survey design need to be borne in mind.

First, many household panel surveys in industrialised countries are currently short in length. Although a few began during the mid-1980s (in Germany, the Netherlands and Sweden), many only began in the 1990s (for example, the BHPS, the Hungarian Panel and the ECHP). The number of interview waves conducted to date is thus typically less than ten. Hence one cannot examine patterns of poverty over an interval spanning the whole of childhood with most of the panel surveys that are currently in existence.

---

[16] For example, from analysis of the Spanish ECPF (the same survey as used later in this book), Cantó-Sánchez (1998: table 4.10) reports that 20 per cent of households containing two parents and children were below the poverty line in at least one quarter during a year of survey participation, whereas only 4 per cent were in every quarter.

Second, the majority of household panel surveys conduct interviews with households just once a year and, to minimise respondent burden and recall error, many collect less detailed information about incomes in each one of the preceding twelve months. For example, the BHPS collects very detailed information about types of income and the amounts received for the period just prior to the interview. By contrast the retrospective monthly calendar covering the period back to the previous interview focuses on the types of incomes received but not the amounts (with the exception that data about the initial earnings of people beginning a job during the year are also collected). Thus the BHPS has a current income focus in the sense discussed earlier. Annual income measures have to be derived by combining information about current income at this year's interview (and last year's) together with the less-detailed within-year information. Other panel surveys such as the PSID have an annual income focus. As discussed earlier, using a current income or annual income measure has a number of important implications for estimates of different dimensions of child poverty dynamics.

A third feature of household panel surveys is that they are small in size, and may become smaller over time. Sample sizes of around 2,000 to 5,000 households are common, figures that include those households that have no children at all.[17] As a result it may be impossible to establish with precision the different patterns of poverty over time for particular groups of children of interest, such as those in lone-parent families, or children in particular age groups. Sampling errors may be large.

Attrition – the dropping-out over time from the survey of households that no longer wish to participate or that can no longer be traced and interviewed – is a factor which reduces sample size over time (by a maximum of about 5 per cent per annum in mature panels).[18] In addition, attrition may not be random. For example, sample drop-out may be linked to events that bring on child poverty, such as family break-up because of divorce.[19]

[17] The main reason for samples being smaller than cross-section income and expenditure surveys is that panel surveys are expensive: there are additional costs associated with panel maintenance and tracking of respondents.

[18] If there were no attrition, the size of the panel would remain much the same from year to year or gradually increase: it depends on the rules about which respondents are followed. Each year there are new interviewees (for example, children turning 16, new partners of original panel members), and also persons no longer interviewed (for example, those who have died since the last interview, and spouses of original panel members who have left the household and who are not original panel members themselves).

[19] It may also be the case that one of the partners from a partnership which dissolves is retained as a panel member, and it may not necessarily be the one with custody of any children. This arises if the panel survey has a 'following rule' according to which only original sample members are tracked over time, and one of the partners joined the panel after the initial interview wave.

Sample weights are often used to adjust the data for such differential attrition. Fitzgerald *et al.* (1998) report that although there are differential rates of attrition in the PSID – it is higher amongst persons with lower socio-economic status, or unstable earnings and marriage, for example – the proportion of the total attrition which is explained by factors such as low income is relatively small and, in any case, the effects of attrition are moderated over time. They conclude that 'despite the large amount of attrition [since 1968], we find no strong evidence that attrition has distorted the representativeness of the PSID through 1989, and considerable evidence that its cross-sectional representativeness has remained roughly intact' (Fitzgerald *et al.* 1998: 251).[20]

These problems are faced to differing degrees by all the household panel surveys used in this book. They limit what can be discovered, sometimes severely, but they do not completely confound a dynamic perspective of child poverty. For example, one may count the number of interviews in which a child is observed in a poor family during the observation window, even if this is just on the basis of current income in the month of each interview. The resulting statistics will understate the overall prevalence of poverty – the short spells within each year will be missed – but the distribution of the number of times observed poor will still be informative about the unequal burden of the problem. For all its faults, one is better off with that information than without it.

Counting moves across the poverty line

Once a poverty line has been selected, there remains the issue of identifying when it has been crossed. This might seem an entirely trivial matter – either income remains above or below the line or it switches to the other side. But the issue is whether we are prepared to count very small income changes as genuine entries into or exits out of poverty. Crossing the poverty line, it could be argued, should 'mean something', in the sense that a child moves from being poor, with the deprivation that this entails, to being free of poverty with appreciably higher living standards. Without this, observed movements into and out of poverty may simply result from fluctuations in income that are not associated with any genuine change in living standards or from measurement error.

Of course, the analogous problem also exists in the measurement of

---

[20] Similar sentiments were expressed in other papers that appeared in the same journal issue which was devoted to 'Attrition in longitudinal surveys'.

poverty at a point in time. There are the children who are 'near poor', in households with income just above the line. And among the poor there are those children in deep poverty with incomes well below the line, others with income just beneath the line – hence the use of a variety of statistics such as the 'poverty gap' that take account of the size of income shortfalls below the poverty line.

One solution is to require that an exit from poverty entails a certain distance travelled. For example, a poverty line could be set at 50 per cent of the median and with an exit recorded only if income rises from below this cut-off to at least 60 per cent of the median. Similarly, an entry could require going from above 50 per cent to 40 per cent or below. This is the procedure adopted by Duncan *et al.* (1993) in their cross-national study. Of course, the thresholds chosen to ensure a significant movement are arbitrary. We have calculated some estimates using this approach but we find that, in practical terms, the pattern of variations across nations is not very different from the more straightforward definition.

Measurement error

The previous paragraphs may be interpreted as referring to uncertainties in identifying where the cut-off between poverty and non-poverty lies. But even if one were confident about the poverty line, errors in the measurement of income itself could lead to erroneous counting of movements into and out of poverty and provide an over-estimate of the degree of income mobility more generally.

Measurement error may arise for several different reasons. Survey respondents may not know income levels with great precision or be unwilling to divulge them (and provide interviewers with rounded values, for example), or simply forget that they received a particular type of income.[21] This problem may be exacerbated in household panel survey designs in which one household member provides information about the incomes of all household members (as in the PSID) rather than each adult reporting about his or her own income (as in the BHPS). Interviewers and data coders may record information incorrectly. Some data may be changed intentionally by the survey agency due to, for example, reasons of confidentiality. An

---

[21] Also a particular income source may be reported as falling within a given band rather than exact value. To aggregate incomes across income sources in order to derive a total income value may require imputation of an exact value which may – or may not – correspond to the unobserved 'true' value.

example of this is 'top coding', where there is an upper bound set for the value to be recorded for some income source, and all higher values are set equal to that upper bound.

Arguably measurement error is a more important issue for income dynamics than it is for the dynamics of wages, the focus of most research to date (see Atkinson *et al.* 1992, for a useful survey). The reason is that household income is the aggregate of a number of different income sources, not only employment earnings but also income from self-employment, cash benefits, income from savings and investments, etc. The measurement error in the combined total is likely to be greater than the measurement error of any single source.[22]

At each point in time the direction of the measurement error may vary from income source to income source too. For example, wages may be overestimated by as many people as under-report them, but other sources such as income from self-employment or from savings and investments are most often under-reported. This may of course affect estimates of poverty at a point in time. But from a dynamic perspective what is particularly important is whether the measurement errors of each person's income in different time periods are correlated or not. The more random they are, the more false poverty transitions will be observed.

Most evidence about the size of the measurement error problem for incomes refers to employment earnings rather than household income. For example, there has been a special validation survey in the USA based on a sample of workers in a large manufacturing company (see, for example, Duncan and Hill 1985a, Bound *et al.* 1994). Earnings reported in response to PSID-type earnings questions were compared with the earnings recorded in the company's payroll files (assumed to be error-free). These studies have found that errors in estimates of the *change* in earnings over time were somewhat larger than the errors in the level of annual earnings. The latter were relatively low, which can probably be attributed to the great care which panel survey administrators take in designing and conducting their surveys and in processing their data. Also the repeated nature of a panel survey can build trust between respondents and interviewers and encourage more complete and more accurate responses. Nevertheless it must be acknowledged that there has been little examination of measurement errors in household income data. This will probably remain the case as long as there remain substantial difficulties in gaining access to, for example, administrative records on benefit receipt or income tax for survey respondents. This is an important topic for future work.

---

[22] Unless measurement errors for some sources are negatively correlated with errors from other sources – which is implausible.

Another way in which measurement error has been accounted for has been via model-based approaches. Researchers have assumed that the relationships between earnings – it is earnings which have been the focus rather than income – and its determinants are summarised by a statistical model. This specification includes assumptions about measurement error: for example, whether it arises via the dependent variable (earnings) or one or more of the explanatory variables (which may include previous earnings), and the correlation between measurement error and the other variables in the model. For some questions, panel data allow one to derive answers 'controlling' for measurement error. However, for topics such as the degree of earnings mobility itself rather less progress has been made. The fundamental problem is that measurement error is unobserved and its impact must be summarised by simplifying assumptions in order to make the model tractable. These assumptions may not be realistic: for example, the earnings validation studies have found that measurement errors are correlated over time, rather than uncorrelated as most of the models assume. It is also difficult to identify measurement error variation separately from transitory variation (genuine inter-temporal fluctuations in income away from a long-run trend value). See Atkinson *et al.* (1992: section 5.4) for further discussion of these issues.

2.4 What moves children into and out of poverty?

What causes the observed movements by children into and out of poverty? In this section we provide a brief overview of the literature on the determinants of household income and poverty dynamics. Although the principal goal of this book is to document the patterns of dynamics *per se*, the explanations for what is observed are of obvious interest.

The simple fact of birth is one cause of entry – children may be born into households that are already poor. Bane and Ellwood (1986: table 4) estimated, using PSID data covering the period 1970–81, that 8.6 per cent of all the persons beginning a spell in the period 1970–81 were children born into a poor household. The corresponding estimate for Britain is about 6 per cent according to Jenkins' (1999: table 11) estimates based on BHPS data covering 1991–6.

Birth aside, three groups of causes of entry (and exit) can be identified: changes in household income arising from the labour market, changes in other incomes in the household (notably benefit income from state transfers), and changes in the size and composition of the household itself.

Changes in labour income

Changes in labour income may occur for a variety of reasons, including changes in hours worked, changes in wage rates, and changes in whether a job is held at all. The labour market provides – or potentially provides – the major part of total income for most households below pension age. Not surprisingly, therefore, changes in labour income are observed to have a great impact on the probability of a household with children moving into or out of poverty.

Duncan *et al.* in their eight-country study of poverty among families with children reported that labour-market events were 'by far the most frequent cause of exits' (1993: 224) and 'clearly the most important correlates of entries' (1993: 226). For Canada, Picot *et al.* (1999) found that changes in parental wages and hours worked were associated roughly equally with family composition changes in the flows of children into and out of low income between 1993 and 1994. For Britain (not covered by Duncan *et al.*'s work) Jenkins has shown that a rise in labour income accounted for 80 per cent of exits from poverty by children in households with both parents present and 65 per cent of exits by those in single-parent households (1999: table 10). Looking at movements into poverty, it is notable that falls in labour income, while also an important driver of movements into poverty, accounted for a lower proportion of transitions, 60 per cent and 39 per cent respectively. Indeed, among children in single-parent families, changes in household composition accounted for a greater proportion of exits than did changes in labour income.[23]

One feature of his results for Britain that Jenkins drew attention to was the importance of changes in labour income of persons other than the household head. If attention is restricted to the head alone, a rise in labour income accounted for only 45 per cent of exits for children in two-parent households and a fall in labour income for only 40 per cent of entries. (The British source used by Jenkins is the same as that drawn on in chapters 4 and 7.)

The existence of different earners, or potential earners, within households underlines how misleading it can be to infer much about poverty transitions from the large literature on earnings mobility. Earnings refer to a particular person, but poverty also depends on one's household context.

---

[23] Both Duncan *et al.*'s results and those of Jenkins are derived from all observed poverty spell endings, regardless of whether the spell beginning is also observed. Spell endings from short spells are likely to be under-represented – the issue of 'length bias' discussed earlier.

That said, some findings of this research are certainly useful, particularly the evidence on persistence of low pay and on cycles of 'low pay and no pay'.[24] This helps explain patterns of poverty over time, including the phenomenon of repeated experience of low income.[25] It also serves as a reminder that exits from poverty may not be to levels of income that are a great deal higher than the poverty line.

Changes in non-labour income

We restrict discussion under this heading to benefit income in the form of transfers from the state. Income from assets is not likely to be important for the great majority of those at risk of poverty, although this is not to say that a stock market crash would throw no child into poverty.

One of the functions of state benefits (although not the only one) is to maintain household living standards when they fall sharply. (State benefits of course come in various forms and conditions for eligibility vary enormously, but this general remark applies to them all.) If the benefit system is well designed and functions smoothly, state benefits should *prevent* many falls into poverty (for example, if there is a system of child benefits offsetting lower incomes for families with children). In this case, benefit income should be an important reason for children *not* entering poverty – its main role should be in reducing entries, and changes in benefit income should not be a significant explanation for any observed movement into or out of poverty. Benefit income may thus be an enormously important determinant of the static picture of poverty but not of its dynamics, in the sense of observed movements.

Of course, the reality is more complicated for at least two reasons. First, the administration of benefits is likely to be subject to delays and errors. By the time that benefit is granted a family may have experienced a period of very low income, with the result that the start of benefit receipt does in fact

---

[24] Quite a lot of the evidence on earnings mobility refers only to individuals who are *always* employed, thus missing those who move into and out of 'no pay' – a key reason for a change in labour income. This is the case in much of the cross-national analysis of earnings mobility by the OECD (1997: chapter 2). However, results for Germany and the USA that include the 'intermittent workers' show that in both countries those workers in the bottom 20 per cent of annual earnings in 1986 averaged less than two years in the rest of the distribution over 1986–91.

[25] Stewart (1999) concludes from British evidence that the overlap between low pay and poverty at any one time is not large but that the association is 'much more important' when a dynamic perspective is taken.

result in a transition out of poverty. Rises in benefit income will in this case be one of the explanations for exits. (Obviously the likelihood of this happening will vary with the length of the accounting period that is considered.) On the other hand, the researcher may choose a poverty line above the level of benefit payments. The start of benefit will then reduce the severity of poverty being experienced but will not lift the family out of poverty altogether.

Second, some benefits have fixed entitlement periods. Unemployment insurance is a notable example that exists in almost all the industrialised world in some form. The ending of a time-limited spell of receipt of benefit may be followed immediately by receipt of an income-tested assistance benefit that is sufficient to prevent entry to poverty, but in many cases this may not happen. Assistance benefit levels may be below the poverty line, or there may be no entitlement to assistance despite household income being sufficiently low.[26] Duncan *et al.* (1993: table 6) report that the termination of social insurance benefits is associated with between 7 and 19 per cent of the poverty entries for families with children in their eight-country study, with average figure about 10 per cent.

Changes in household structure

We noted earlier that the 'household' or the 'family' is not a concept that is fixed over time. Households and families change in size and composition, with important consequences for movements into and out of poverty. Duncan has argued forcefully on the issue: 'an understanding of dynamics of family economic well-being rests upon an understanding of the dynamics of families themselves' (1983: 205).

Two aspects of the phenomenon can be identified. First, we have defined children's poverty in terms of *household income*, an aggregate of the incomes of all household members. These incomes may change as a result of an alteration in household structure, pushing the child into poverty or pulling him or her out. The most obvious example is the separation or divorce of the child's parents, involving the loss of income from one parent, typically the father, and the re-partnering by a lone parent, leading to an increase in income. The child's own birth or the birth of a sibling are other

---

[26] Where turnover among the unemployed is high, the majority of recipients of unemployment insurance (UI) may return to work before exhausting their entitlement to benefit. This is the case in the USA, for example. In Hungary, by contrast, the most common way to leave the UI register in the mid-1990s was not by getting a job but by running out of benefit (Micklewright and Nagy 1999).

events that may lead to the onset of poverty on account of the child's mother giving up work.

Second, changes in household structure *per se* also have an impact on the probability of entering or leaving poverty separately from the effect on income. Poverty, as measured by low income, implies a low level of household income relative to 'needs', where the latter are usually taken as a function of the size and composition of the household. Any change in household structure that affects the household's needs (however these are measured) can push a child into or out of poverty even if the total amount of money income is unaffected. The examples given above of separation and re-partnering and of birth to a mother who previously worked involve changes to both income and needs. Another would be the death of a co-resident grandparent who had a pension. In other cases there may be a change in the needs alone: for example, birth to a mother who did not previously work, or when a sibling leaves the household on reaching adulthood.

The system of classifying the causes of entries to and exits from poverty developed by Bane and Ellwood (1986), and followed by Duncan *et al.* (1993) and Jenkins (1999), treats a change in the head of household as a sufficiently important event to warrant classification as a 'demographic change', irrespective of the extent to which labour income (or any other form of income) changes when this occurs. The estimated fractions of poverty exits and entries accounted for by variations in labour income which we cited earlier do not include those movements into and out of poverty that follow from a change in head of household.[27]

Bane and Ellwood, using PSID data covering the period 1970–81, report that 43 per cent of all poverty spell beginnings could be classified as demographic events (including the 8.6 per cent begun by children being born into poverty that was mentioned earlier). The figure was much higher, some 66

---

[27] The sequential allocation procedure for identifying poverty spell beginning and ending events is as follows. First, one determines whether there was a change in household headship concurrently with the poverty transition. Amongst those with no change in household head, one checks whether the change in household 'needs' (as summarised by the household equivalence scale rate) is proportionally greater than the concurrent change in household net money income. All the events identified so far are labelled demographic events. All remaining poverty transitions are classified as income events. Event types can be further sub-divided by type of demographic event (a birth or a divorce, say) and type of income event (whether labour earnings changed or else some component of non-labour income, say). One weakness of such a typology is that it ignores (by construction) the fact that income and demographic events may occur simultaneously. For example, a lone parent may both re-partner and take on a job at the same time, but the Bane and Ellwood event typology gives priority to the former event.

per cent, for female household heads of families with children, which underlines the impact of marital separation. By contrast, only 13 per cent of all poverty spell endings were classified as demographic events. The proportion was almost twice as large among people belonging to female-headed households with children in the last year of the poverty spell (pointing to importance of re-partnership for this group). This asymmetry in the importance of demographic events for exit and entry transitions has also been found by Jenkins (1999) in his analysis of BHPS data covering 1991–6. He found that 38 per cent of all poverty spell beginnings but only 18 per cent of poverty spell endings were accounted for by demographic events. The asymmetry is not so clear in Duncan *et al.*'s (1993) analysis focusing on families with children (although the event classification differs from the Bane and Ellwood and Jenkins studies). They found that marriage accounted for as many as 10 per cent of poverty exits in three countries (Canada, Germany, Sweden) and less for the other countries considered, but the proportion of poverty spell endings accounted for by separation and divorce was generally only slightly lower than for the corresponding proportion for spell beginnings.[28]

Family formation and dissolution can thus have a notable association with poverty spells, and noticeably more with poverty spell beginnings than endings. Marital breakdown, as measured by divorce, varies substantially across industrialised countries, suggesting that the importance of parental separation as a cause of children's entry to poverty may display significant cross-national variation. In the European Union as a whole in 1995, there were 35 divorces for every 100 new marriages, with the figures varying widely from zero in Ireland (where divorce was prohibited) and between 10 and 20 in Italy, Spain, Portugal and Greece, to 53 in the UK, 59 in Finland, 68 in Sweden and 69 in Belgium; across the Atlantic the figures were 48 in Canada and 49 in the USA (Eurostat 1997: 68). In the two Eastern European countries included in this book, the numbers of divorces per 100 new marriages were 47 in Hungary and 62 in Russia (UNICEF 1998: 107). Of course, these figures give only a rough guide to cross-national differences in parental separation among couples with children. On the one hand, many divorces do not involve children, and, on the other, parental separation may not involve divorce either because the marriage is not formally ended or because the couple were never married.

---

[28] Picot *et al.* (1999) found for Canada that, for a given child, parental divorce and (re-)marriage each had large impacts on the probability of transition into or out of low income between 1993 and 1994. On the other hand, the demographic events were much less frequent than changes in labour-market factors.

2.5 Concluding remarks

This chapter has raised a large number of questions about concepts and definitions and has provided conclusive answers to a rather smaller number. We have provided a framework which readers may use to assess the analysis in subsequent chapters of this book and other research about poverty and poverty dynamics published elsewhere. We would be pleased if the chapter were to provide a stimulus to further work on these questions.

To point out that some issues remain to be resolved is not to concede that nothing substantive can be said. As we show in this book, there is a solid core of findings which stand out. In the remainder of part I, we first provide a cross-national analysis of child poverty rates and poverty trends in twenty-five industrialised countries. Then we turn to documenting and comparing the nature of children's movements into and out of poverty in seven nations.

Acknowledgements

The helpful comments of Tony Atkinson, Brian Nolan, Greg Duncan, Martha Hill and Robert Walker are gratefully acknowledged.

References

Ashworth, K., Hill, M. and Walker, R., 1994, 'Patterns of childhood poverty: new challenges for policy', *Journal of Policy Analysis and Management*, 13: 658–80.

Atkinson, A. B., 1998, *Poverty in Europe*, Basil Blackwell, Oxford.

Atkinson, A. B., Bourguignon, F. and Morrisson, C., 1992, *Empirical Studies of Earnings Mobility*, Harwood Academic Publishers, Chur, Switzerland.

Atkinson, A. B., Rainwater, L. and Smeeding, T. M., 1995, *Income Distribution in OECD Countries: Evidence from the Luxembourg Income Study*, OECD, Paris.

Bane, M. J. and Ellwood, D. T., 1986, 'Slipping into and out of poverty: the dynamics of spells', *Journal of Human Resources*, 21: 1–23.

Blau, D. M., 1999, 'The impact of income on child development', *Review of Economics and Statistics*, 81: 261–76.

Böheim, R. and Jenkins, S. P., 2000, 'Do current income and annual income measures provide different pictures of Britain's income distribution?', Institute for Social and Economic Research Working Paper 2000–16, University of Essex, Colchester.

Bound, J., Brown, C., Duncan, G. J. and Rodgers, W. L., 1994, 'Evidence on the validity of cross-sectional and longitudinal labor market data', *Journal of Labor Economics*, 12: 345–68.

Bradbury, B. and Jäntti, M., 1999, 'Child poverty across industrial nations', Innocenti Occasional Papers, Economic and Social Policy Series 71, UNICEF International Child Development Centre, Florence.

Buck, N., Ermisch, J. F. and Jenkins, S. P., 1996, 'Choosing a longitudinal survey design: the issues', Occasional Paper 96–1, ESRC Research Centre on Micro-Social Change, University of Essex, Colchester.

Buhmann, B., Rainwater, L., Schmaus, G. and Smeeding, T., 1988, 'Equivalence scales, well-being, inequality and poverty: sensitivity estimates across ten countries using the Luxembourg Income Study (LIS) database', *Review of Income and Wealth*, 34: 115–42.

Callan, T. and Nolan, B., 1991, 'Concepts of poverty and the poverty line: a critical survey of approaches to measuring poverty', *Journal of Economic Surveys*, 5: 243–62.

Cantó-Sánchez, O., 1998, 'The dynamics of poverty in Spain: the permanent and the transitory poor', unpublished Ph.D. thesis, European University Institute, Florence.

Citro, C. F. and Michael, R. T. (eds.), 1995, *Measuring Poverty: A New Approach*, National Academy Press, Washington DC.

Coulter, F. A. C., Cowell, F. A. and Jenkins, S. P., 1992a, 'Differences in needs and assessment of income distributions', *Bulletin of Economic Research*, 44: 77–124.

Coulter, F. A. C., Cowell, F. A. and Jenkins, S. P., 1992b, 'Equivalence scale relativities and the extent of inequality and poverty', *Economic Journal*, 102: 1067–82.

Department of Social Security, 1998, *Households Below Average Income 1979–1996/7*, Corporate Document Services, London.

Duncan, G. J., 1983, 'The implications of changing family composition for the dynamic analysis of family economic well-being', in Atkinson, A. B. and Cowell, F. A. (eds.), *Panel Data on Incomes*, Occasional Paper 2, ICERD, London School of Economics, London.

Duncan, G. J., 1997, 'Longitudinal measures of children's deprivation and welfare dependence', in Hauser, R. M., Brown, B. V. and Prosser, W. R. (eds.), *Indicators of Children's Well-Being*, Russell Sage Foundation, New York.

Duncan, G. J. and Brooks-Gunn, J. (eds.), 1997, *Consequences of Growing up Poor*, Russell Sage Foundation, New York.

Duncan, G. J. and Hill, D. H., 1985a, 'An investigation of the extent and consequences of measurement error in labor-economic survey data', *Journal of Labor Economics*, 3: 508–32.

Duncan, G. J. and Hill, M. S., 1985b, 'Conceptions of longitudinal households: fertile or futile', *Journal of Economic and Social Measurement*, 13: 361–75.

Duncan, G. J., Gustafsson, B., Hauser, R., Schmaus, G., Messinger, H., Muffels, R., Nolan, B. and Ray, J.-C., 1993, 'Poverty dynamics in eight countries', *Journal of Population Economics*, 6: 295–334.

Eurostat, 1997, *Eurostat Yearbook '97*, Office for Official Publications of the European Communities, Luxembourg.

Eurostat Task Force, 1998, 'Recommendations on social exclusion and poverty statistics', Document CPS 98/31/2, Eurostat, Luxembourg.

Fitzgerald, J., Gottschalk, P. and Moffitt, R., 1998, 'An analysis of attrition in panel data: the Michigan panel study of income dynamics', *Journal of Human Resources*, 33: 251–99.

Gardiner, K. and Hills, J., 1999, 'Policy implications of new data on income mobility', *Economic Journal*, 109: F91–F111.

Heady, P. and Smyth, M., 1989, *Living Standards During Unemployment*, HMSO, London.

Jenkins, S. P., 1991, 'Poverty measurement and the within-household distribution: agenda for action', *Journal of Social Policy*, 20: 457–83.

Jenkins, S. P., 1999, 'Modelling household income dynamics', ESRC Research Centre on Micro-Social Change Working Paper 99–1, University of Essex, Colchester. Forthcoming in *Journal of Population Economics*.

Jenkins, S. P. and Cowell, F. A., 1994, 'Parametric equivalence scales and scale relativities', *Economic Journal*, 104: 891–900.

Kempson, E., 1996, *Life on a Low Income*, Joseph Rowntree Foundation, York.

Lazear, E. P. and Michael, R. T., 1986, 'Estimating the personal distribution of income with adjustment for within-family variation', *Journal of Labor Economics*, 4: S216–S244.

Lazear, E. P. and Michael, R. T., 1988, *Allocation of Income within the Household*, University of Chicago Press, Chicago.

Lundberg, S. J., Pollak, R. A. and Wales, T. J., 1997, 'Do husbands and wives pool their resources?', *Journal of Human Resources*, 32: 463–80.

Mayer, S. E., 1997, *What Income Can't Buy. Family Income and Children's Life Chances*, Harvard University Press, Cambridge MA.

McLoyd, V., 1998, 'Socioeconomic disadvantage and child development', *American Psychologist*, 53: 185–204.

Micklewright, J., 1986, 'A note on household income data in NCDS3', NCDS User Support Group Discussion Paper 18, Social Statistics Research Unit, City University, London.

Micklewright, J. and Nagy, Gy., 1999, 'Living standards and incentives in transition: the implications of UI exhaustion in Hungary', *Journal of Public Economics*, 73: 297–319.

Middleton, S., Ashworth, K. and Braithwaite, I., 1997, *Small Fortunes. Spending on Children, Childhood Poverty and Parental Sacrifice*, Joseph Rowntree Foundation, York.

Nolan, B., 1999, 'Targeting poverty. Lessons from Ireland on setting a national poverty target', *New Economy*, 6: 44–9.

OECD, 1997, *Employment Outlook*, OECD, Paris.

Orshansky, M., 1965, 'Counting the poor: another look at the poverty profile', *Social Security Bulletin*, 28: 3–29.

Pedersen, P. J. and Smith, N., 1998, 'Low incomes in Denmark, 1980–1995', Working Paper 19, Centre for Labour Market and Social Research, University of Aarhus and Aarhus School of Business, Aarhus.

Phipps, S. A. and Burton, P. S., 1998, 'What's mine is yours? The influence of male and female incomes on patterns of household expenditure', *Economica*, 65: 599–613.

Picot, G., Zyblock, M. and Pyper, W., 1999, 'Why do children move into and out of low income? Changing labor market conditions or marriage and divorce?', Analytical Studies Working Paper 132, Statistics Canada, Ottawa.

Rodgers, J. R. and Rodgers, J. L., 1993, 'Chronic poverty in the United States', *Journal of Human Resources*, 28: 25–54.

Roker, D. and Coleman, J., 1998, 'The invisible poor: young people growing up in family poverty', paper presented at the conference to mark the centenary of Seebohm Rowntree's first study of poverty in York, University of York, 18–20 March 1998, forthcoming in Bradshaw, J. and Sainsbury, R. (eds.), *Experiencing Poverty*, Ashgate, Aldershot.

Rowntree, S., 1901, *Poverty: A Study of Town Life*, Macmillan, London.

Ruggles, P., 1990, *Drawing the Line. Alternative Poverty Measures and their Implications for Public Policy*, Urban Institute Press, Washington DC.

Ruggles, P. and Williams, R., 1989, 'Longitudinal measures of poverty: accounting for income and assets over time', *Review of Income and Wealth*, 35: 225–43.

Sen, A. K., 1997, *On Economic Inequality,* third edition, Oxford University Press, Oxford.

Smith, A., 1776, *An Inquiry into the Nature and Causes of the Wealth of Nations*, ed. E. Cannan, sixth edition 1950, Methuen, London.

Statistics New Zealand, 1999, *New Zealand Now – Incomes*, Statistics New Zealand, Wellington.

Stewart, M., 1999, 'Low pay no pay dynamics', in HM Treasury (1999).

HM Treasury, 1999, 'Persistent poverty and lifetime inequality: the evidence', proceedings of a workshop, HM Treasury, 17–18 November 1998, CASEreport 5 and HM Treasury Occasional Paper 10, London School of Economics and HM Treasury, London.

UNICEF, 1998, 'Education for all?' *Regional Monitoring Report No. 5*, UNICEF International Child Development Centre, Florence.

3 Child poverty across twenty-five countries

BRUCE BRADBURY AND MARKUS JÄNTTI

3.1 Introduction

The dynamic view of poverty and living standards over time offers a dimension of understanding that simple 'snapshots' cannot provide. However, in many countries this dynamic perspective is not available. In this chapter, therefore, we begin the book's empirical analysis with a gallery of snapshots of child poverty across the industrialised world. We present recent evidence on variations in child poverty across industrialised countries and assess the contributions of family structure, state transfers and market incomes to this variation. How much does child poverty vary across countries, and what causes this variation?

The results here are based on data from the Luxembourg Income Study (LIS) which, at the time of writing, covers some twenty-five industrialised countries, many with information for several years.[1] We use almost all these data in the results presented here. This wide focus means that we cannot do justice to specific circumstances in each country. Instead, the objective is to look at the general patterns of variation in child poverty outcomes across the industrialised world. The countries examined include most of the OECD, several of the important non-OECD economies of Eastern Europe (including Russia) and one representative of the newly industrialising countries of East Asia (Taiwan).

Our results complement those in the other chapters in this volume in several respects. Longitudinal data often differ in important ways from cross-sectional data. As noted in chapter 2, longitudinal samples are in general smaller and, as samples age, they risk becoming unrepresentative of the general population due to potentially non-random attrition. It is impor-

---

[1] The Luxembourg Income Study comprises a database of household income surveys adjusted to be as comparable as possible. For more information see http://lis.ceps.lu/

tant therefore to compare the cross-sectional estimates of levels and trends available from the two data sources where possible. There is also a pragmatic reason for looking at cross-sectional data. Longitudinal data on household incomes are available from relatively few countries and cover in most cases quite short time periods. Cross-sectional data are, by contrast, available for many countries and provide in many cases information on levels of poverty over long time periods. Finally, there remain important questions about the nature of child poverty that do not require a longitudinal focus.

From previous (cross-sectional) research on child poverty, a number of important themes emerge (Cornia and Danziger 1997). While the reduction of poverty among the aged has been one of the great success stories of the post-war welfare state, in many countries the last two decades have seen a re-emergence of child poverty. Although the labour-market deterioration and family structure changes that have driven this re-emergence have been felt in most countries, there are wide variations in child poverty rates between different countries at similar levels of development (Rainwater and Smeeding 1995).

The next section discusses our methodology and then in section 3.3 we provide new estimates of child poverty using several different approaches to the definition and measurement of poverty. Which countries have been most and least successful in combating child poverty? Data from the mid-1990s show that the Nordic countries have the lowest rates of child poverty, followed by Northern European ones. Southern European and English-speaking countries have much larger proportions of their children in poor households. The transition economies we include have very high rates of poverty when this is measured in constant international dollars, whereas their relative poverty rates vary widely. The broad groupings within the non-transition countries are fairly similar across the relative and fixed real income (constant international price) definitions of poverty. Across the whole spectrum of countries, real income poverty does tend to increase with national income. The USA, however, stands out as having a much higher level of child poverty than its level of national income would suggest. Poverty trends also vary considerably across the nations in our sample.

Explanations for the pattern of child poverty across industrialised coun-tries have focused on three broad areas: the labour market (increases in unemployment and reductions in low-end wages), family structure (partic-ularly lone parenthood), and the structure of welfare state institutions (particularly income transfer programmes). Although all of these are undoubtedly important, there remain many unresolved questions of the rel-ative importance and interaction of these different factors.

We find that children living in lone-mother families are indeed much more likely to be poor. However, even though the incidence of lone parenthood varies considerably across the industrialised world, this does not provide a significant explanation for the cross-national variations that we observe. Section 3.4 then considers the relative contributions of market income and social transfers to the living standards of poor children. Most of the previous literature has focused on variations in social policies but our results suggest that greater attention should be paid to the sources of market income variation. If we examine the living standards of the poorest fifth of children in each country we find that the most important source of variation in living standards across countries is market incomes rather than social transfers.

Moreover, many of the countries with high child poverty rates (in particular, most of the English-speaking countries) actually have quite high levels of transfers. The lower poverty rates found in many continental and Northern European countries are instead due mainly to the higher market incomes of the families of the most disadvantaged children. The more rigid labour markets of these countries appear to give a better deal to disadvantaged children.

3.2 The measurement of child poverty

Income, the sharing unit and equivalence scale

Three major decisions that must be made in any poverty study concern the measure of resources, the choice of sharing unit (for example, within nuclear families or within households) and the equivalence scale (the needs of different types of sharing units). There is a large literature that addresses these issues (see, for example, Gottschalk and Smeeding 1997, Jenkins and Lambert 1993, Jäntti and Danziger 2000, and of course chapter 2). Our choices on these matters are fairly standard, limited in part by the structure of the Luxembourg Income Study and in part by space considerations.

Our measure of resources is annual disposable income.[2] This includes market incomes and government cash transfers, and deducts income taxes and compulsory social insurance contributions. While this is not a comprehensive indicator of the resources available to the families of children (for

[2] Except in the UK and Russia, where 'current' income is used.

example, it excludes non-cash services) it remains the best available indicator of cross-national variations in living standards. These issues of the appropriate measure of resources (and the role of non-cash benefits in particular) are discussed in more detail in a longer version of this chapter (Bradbury and Jäntti 1999).

We assume resources are shared within *households* and define every person in the household to have the same poverty status. This definition is the one that is most commonly available across our countries. The exceptions to this are Sweden and Switzerland, where the source data are limited to tax units, corresponding to nuclear families of parents and their dependent children. In these two countries, adult children and lone parents living with their parents are treated as separate units.

In most of our results, we assume that needs differ according to both the number of adults and the number of children in the household according to the formula *needs* = (*adults* + *children* × 0.7)$^{0.85}$. (People aged under 18 years are defined as children.) This structure for the equivalence scale is used by Jenkins and Cowell (1994) and also recommended for use by the US National Research Council Panel on Poverty and Family Assistance (Citro and Michael 1995). The particular numerical values chosen yield a scale that is very close to the widely used 'OECD' scale. In an appendix table we also present some results using a simpler equivalence scale defining household needs as the square root of the household size (a scale used in many of the subsequent chapters of this book). In terms of cross-national comparisons, there is little difference in the outcomes produced by these two scales, though the choice of equivalence scale can be more important when comparing the poverty of children with that of other groups.

The poverty threshold and counting methods

The literature on poverty measurement has typically used two types of poverty threshold: 'absolute' and 'relative' poverty lines. 'Absolute' or, more properly, fixed real price poverty lines are thresholds which permit people living in specified family types to purchase the same bundle of goods and services in different countries or times. Families that fall below the common consumption threshold are therefore considered to be poor. 'Relative' poverty lines, on the other hand, are more closely related to concepts of social exclusion. These poverty lines are usually defined with reference to a measure of 'typical' consumption level: for example, half median income.

Arguably, a focus on child poverty also calls for a somewhat different relative poverty line, as noted in chapter 2. If children are excluded from social participation, the most important form of this may be exclusion from the lifestyle typically enjoyed by other children. Similarly, if the exclusion of children arises via the exclusion of their parents, it will most often be other parents that they compare themselves with rather than, say, the elderly. This suggests the use of a poverty line defined with reference to the average living standard of children in the society in question.

The use of the median as the anchor point can be loosely justified in terms of social exclusion, but it also has a practical basis. In household surveys, because errors in data collection at the two extremes of the income distribution are likely to be more frequent, the median is a more robust measure of central tendency than the mean.

Although the comparison of real living standards across countries requires the use of strong assumptions, many would argue that it is a more important concept than that of relative poverty. To focus only on the relative measures would be, for example, to discount entirely the poverty alleviation benefits of increases in income that were spread (proportionately) evenly across the population.

Both relative and real measures provide important insights into the way the living conditions of the most disadvantaged children vary across countries. In this chapter, we therefore employ three types of poverty lines:

1 An *overall median* poverty line. This is the 'conventional' relative poverty line. For each individual in the population we calculate their household equivalent income. The poverty line is defined as 50 per cent of the median of this variable across the national population.
2 A *child median* poverty line based on the household incomes of children. In this case the median of household equivalent income is calculated over children only.
3 The *US official* poverty line. For a couple with two children in 1995, this real poverty line is set equal to the US official poverty line for this family type in that year (US$15,299). For other family types the poverty line is adjusted using the equivalence scale described above. National currencies are converted to US dollars by using the OECD's Purchasing Power Parities (PPPs) for 1995 and national inflation rates to deflate incomes over time. These price adjustments are likely to be less robust for the transition countries, not least because of the hyperinflation experienced in many of these after 1989 (the general limitations of PPP adjustments are discussed further in Bradbury and Jäntti 1999).

We present results showing the proportions of children below all three of these poverty lines, though with an emphasis on the first (our 'base case') and the last. The child median line presents a different picture to the base case for only a small number of countries. In addition, in section 3.4, we present alternative indicators of deprivation based on the mean income of the poorest fifth of children.

3.3 Child income poverty across nations

The context

Some key characteristics of the countries we consider in this chapter are presented in table 3.1 (the countries examined further in the remainder of the book are denoted in bold). In total, 220 million children live in these twenty-five countries, comprising 10 per cent of the world's children. Just under one third of the children in our study live in the USA, and one sixth live in Russia. With the inclusion of the former socialist countries, the LIS database now extends beyond the 'rich nations' club' of the OECD. National incomes therefore vary considerably. The small country of Luxembourg stands out with a GNP of US$33,000 per capita. The USA has the highest GNP per capita among the remaining group of rich nations, (those with GNP per capita of between US$17,000 and US$26,000), followed by Taiwan, Spain, Israel and Ireland. There is then quite a gap to the richest transition country, the Czech Republic, with US$9,400 per capita. The transition countries also have higher infant mortality rates. Teenage fertility rates – a strong indicator of economic disadvantage for children – are very high in the USA and Russia, and lowest in Western, Northern and Southern Europe (excluding the UK). The share of the population under 18 ranges from 34 per cent (Israel) to 18 per cent (Italy).

Across the twenty-five countries, rates of economic growth also varied widely. Over the seven years prior to the most recent LIS survey, the Taiwanese economy had been growing at an average rate of over 7 per cent per annum. The former socialist countries, on the other hand, had all experienced downward trends in national incomes – over 10 per cent per annum in the case of Russia. In the LIS survey years, unemployment rates ranged from over 16 per cent in Ireland and Spain to only 1.5 per cent in Taiwan. Inflation rates were below 10 per cent for all countries other than the former socialist countries and Israel. Russia in particular was experiencing hyperinflation in this period. Although the Russian LIS data have been adjusted by means of price indices specific to the month in which the data were collected, some caution is required in the interpretation of income data from this period. This is particularly the case for measures of real GNP and poverty measures based on real income (i.e. the 'US poverty line' rate below).

Table 3.1. *The social and economic context, 1996*

	Mnemonic for latest LIS year	Number of children <18 yrs (millions)	Share across countries (%)	Children as % of population	Real GNP per capita per annum (US$, 1995)	Under 5 mortality rate (per 1,000 births)	Teenage fertility rate (births per 1,000)
Australia	AS94	4.6	2.1	25	18,700	6	23
Austria	OS87	1.7	0.8	21	20,500	6	17
Belgium	BE92	2.2	1.0	21	20,900	7	11
Canada	CN94	7.2	3.3	24	20,500	7	25
Czech Republic	CZ92	2.4	1.1	23	9,400	7	23
Denmark	DK92	1.1	0.5	21	20,600	6	9
Finland	FI91	1.2	0.5	23	17,100	4	10
France	FR89	13.5	6.1	23	19,800	6	7
Germany	GE94	15.8	7.2	19	20,400	6	10
Hungary	HU94	2.3	1.0	22	6,200	12	31
Ireland	IR87	1.0	0.5	29	14,300	7	15
Israel	IS92	2.0	0.9	34	15,000	9	17
Italy	IT95	10.5	4.8	18	19,300	7	7
Luxembourg	LX94	0.1	0.0	21	33,000	7	12
Netherlands	NL91	3.4	1.5	22	19,800	6	4
Norway	NW95	1.0	0.5	23	22,100	6	14
Poland	PL92	10.6	4.8	27	5,400	14	21
Russia	RL95	37.1	16.8	25	4,100	25	46
Slovakia	SV92	1.5	0.7	27	7,300	11	31
Spain	SP90	8.2	3.7	21	14,000	5	8
Sweden	SW92	2.0	0.9	22	17,800	4	8
Switzerland	CH82	1.5	0.7	21	24,900	5	4
Taiwan	RC95	6.2	2.8	29	15,100		17
United Kingdom	UK95	13.3	6.0	23	18,200	7	22
United States	US94	70.4	31.9	26	26,400	8	56
Total		220.7	100.0				

Sources: Population and under 5 mortality, UNICEF (1998); teenage fertility, US Bureau of the Census International Data Base version 971 (projections); GNP, World Development Indicators 1997 (CDROM) series NY.GNP.MKTP.CN, Appendix A and (for Taiwan) Asian Development Bank (http://internotes.asiandevbank.org/notes/tap1/28be.htm) and US Census database (with imputation).

Three measures of child poverty

Table 3.2 shows the level of child poverty for the latest available LIS years using the three poverty definitions. The countries are sorted by descending child poverty rate, using the half overall median poverty line. The first pair of columns in table 3.2 show this poverty rate, the second the poverty rate relative to the child median and the third pair the proportion of children below the US poverty line.

There is a large variation in measured rates of child poverty across countries. Taking first our base case, the poverty rate relative to the overall median, the likelihood that a randomly picked child will live in a poor family ranges from 1.8 per cent in the Czech Republic to 26.6 per cent in Russia. Northern European countries have fairly low poverty rates. The Nordic countries range between 3.4 per cent (Finland) and 5.9 per cent (Denmark). Central European countries follow, with Austria, Belgium, Luxembourg and the Netherlands having rates between 5.6 and 8.4 per cent. Italy, Australia, Canada, Ireland and the United Kingdom are all fairly high up in the poverty ranking, while Spain, France and Germany fall towards the middle of the twenty-five countries.

As noted above, the five former socialist countries in the LIS database have the lowest average incomes and this is reflected in their poverty rates based on the US poverty line. However, in terms of relative poverty, these data show wide diversity in the experience of transition from socialism. Of the twenty-five countries, Russia has the highest (overall median) child poverty rate and the Czech Republic the lowest.

Although the process of industrialisation is often associated with increased inequality, our single example of an East Asian economy, Taiwan, has a comparatively low child poverty rate – not that different from those found in Northern Europe.

For most countries, child poverty is about a third lower when measured against the child rather than the adult median. This is because the equivalent family income of the median child is somewhat lower than the equivalent family income of the median person. These relativities between children and others are sensitive to the equivalence scale, and so this particular result is of limited interest. More interesting is the fact that the overall ranking across countries on the two measures is very similar.

There are three countries where the general tendency for child poverty to fall by about a third does not apply. In Russia there is little difference in the poverty rate, while in both the UK and Ireland, the drop in poverty is greater. This is because the median income of children compared to others

Table 3.2. *Child poverty rates*

| Country | Year | Poverty rate using different poverty lines (%) | | | | | |
| | | 50% of the overall median | | 50% of the child median | | US official poverty line | |
		rate	rank	rate	rank	rate	rank
Russia	1995	26.6	(1)	25.4	(1)	98.0	(1)
United States	1994	26.3	(2)	18.6	(2)	18.5	(12)
United Kingdom	1995	21.3	(3)	11.0	(5)	28.6	(10)
Italy	1995	21.2	(4)	15.7	(3)	38.1	(9)
Australia	1994	17.1	(5)	11.0	(6)	20.7	(11)
Canada	1994	16.0	(6)	11.2	(4)	9.0	(16)
Ireland	1987	14.8	(7)	6.5	(13)	54.4	(6)
Israel	1992	14.7	(8)	10.3	(8)	45.3	(8)
Poland	1992	14.2	(9)	10.9	(7)	90.9	(3)
Spain	1990	13.1	(10)	9.7	(10)	47.3	(7)
Germany	1994	11.6	(11)	7.1	(11)	12.4	(14)
Hungary	1994	11.5	(12)	10.1	(9)	90.6	(4)
France	1989	9.8	(13)	6.8	(12)	17.3	(13)
Netherlands	1991	8.4	(14)	5.8	(14)	10.0	(15)
Switzerland	1982	6.3	(15)	3.9	(18)	1.6	(24)
Taiwan	1995	6.3	(16)	4.1	(17)	4.3	(20)
Luxembourg	1994	6.3	(17)	1.9	(23)	1.1	(25)
Belgium	1992	6.1	(18)	4.2	(16)	7.9	(17)
Denmark	1992	5.9	(19)	5.1	(15)	4.6	(19)
Austria	1987	5.6	(20)	3.3	(20)	5.4	(18)
Norway	1995	4.5	(21)	3.5	(19)	2.8	(22)
Sweden	1992	3.7	(22)	3.2	(21)	3.7	(21)
Finland	1991	3.4	(23)	2.5	(22)	2.6	(23)
Slovakia	1992	2.2	(24)	1.5	(25)	95.2	(2)
Czech Republic	1992	1.8	(25)	1.6	(24)	85.1	(5)

Notes: Children are poor if their household has an equivalent disposable income less than 50 per cent of the overall or child median or less than the official US poverty line. Countries are sorted by the overall median rate. The rank correlations between the different child poverty rates are 0.951 for overall and child median rates, 0.454 for child median and US official line rates, and 0.480 for overall median and US official line rates.

is relatively high in Russia and relatively low in the UK and Ireland. It is this overall disadvantage which leads to the high poverty rate of children in the UK according to the conventional overall median definition. If, on the other hand, we are concerned with those children who have living standards much lower than those of the average child (i.e. the child median poverty concept), then child poverty in the UK is of a similar magnitude to that in Australia and Canada.

We now turn to our third definition of poverty: that based on the US poverty line and PPP-adjusted incomes. For some countries, the poverty ranking using this 'real' standard of living definition is quite different from the ones obtained using relative definitions. The transition economies now all have very high poverty rates. For instance, in the Czech and Slovak republics (which had the lowest poverty rates using both relative definitions) almost all children are now counted among the poor. There is no doubt that absolute poverty rates are very high in these countries but we would not like to ascribe too much importance to the precise estimates shown in the table as it is very difficult to estimate accurate PPPs for countries with widely different income levels.

Turning to the wealthier countries where we can better measure differences in prices between countries, we find that a large proportion – almost a fifth – of US children are poor, compared to the low of 1.1 per cent in Luxembourg or 1.6 per cent in Switzerland. The Northern European and Nordic countries with low levels of relative child poverty also have low levels of poverty measured against the US poverty line. These are countries for which there is little change in ranking. For instance, in Sweden 3.7 per cent and in Belgium 7.9 per cent of all children are poor. Italy, Ireland and Spain all have very high levels of child poverty using this measure. In Australia and the UK, more than a fifth of all children have a standard of living that is lower than the US official poverty line.

In figure 3.1, we compare these poverty estimates with the aggregate national incomes of each country (in the relevant years). As would be expected, countries with higher national income levels are able to ensure that fewer of their children live in families with incomes below the US poverty line. The most important exception to this general relationship is the USA itself. Despite having the highest national income after the small country of Luxembourg, it has a real child poverty rate that is in the middle of these twenty-five countries, and in the bottom half of the OECD countries included here. The key exception in the opposite direction is Taiwan (labelled RC95), which has a national income only slightly higher than Spain and Israel, but one of the lowest child poverty rates. Other countries with low poverty rates but with incomes only slightly higher than Taiwan are Finland, Sweden, Austria and Denmark.

The other two outliers, Luxembourg and Italy, are perhaps of less substantive interest. In the first case the poverty rate is close to negligible. The results for Italy, on the other hand, may be a reflection of the large informal economy in this country. While estimates of the informal economy are incorporated into the measures of income in the national accounts, this is more difficult to do at the household level.

Figure 3.1. *National incomes and the proportion of children below the US official poverty line*

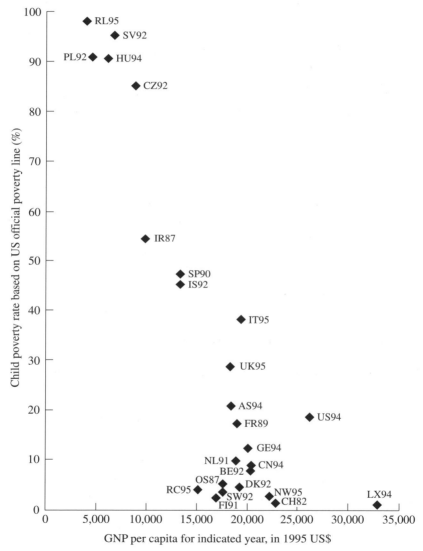

Sources: poverty rates, table 3.2; GNP per capita, as for table 3.1 (though here for the same year as the poverty estimate). See table 3.1 for country/year codes.

Trends

To summarise the changes in child poverty observed in the LIS, we estimated for each country and each of the three poverty definitions the slope
coefficient in a regression of poverty rate against year. When only two years
are available, this is the same as the annualised percentage point difference
in poverty rates. In figure 3.2 we show these estimates for the two relative
poverty measures, while figure 3.3 shows results for the 'US official' poverty
estimates.

Across the twenty countries in figure 3.2, the dominant trend is one of
increasing relative child poverty, with the most dramatic increases in
Russia, Hungary, Italy and the UK.[3] The Nordic countries figure strongly
among those with decreases (or negligible increases) in child poverty,
together with France, Canada, Spain, Israel and, most prominently,
Taiwan. In general, poverty outcomes for the child median are more favourable than the overall median (particularly in the UK and Hungary). This
implies that that median income of families with children has fallen relative
to the overall median.

In figure 3.3, we show the corresponding trends when poverty is measured using the US official poverty line. Growing average real incomes mean
a more favourable outcome in many cases. However, we exclude from this
graph those countries that had experienced extremely high rates of inflation
over the period (Russia, Poland and Israel) because of the difficulties in
accurately measuring changes in purchasing value over time.[4] Increases in
real poverty occurred in Italy, Germany and the UK (though note that
Germany expanded its borders to include East Germany over the period,
and that these percentage point changes need to be considered in the light
of the widely differing levels of real poverty shown in table 3.2). Falls in
absolute poverty were found in countries with high rates of income growth
such as Taiwan, the Netherlands, Spain and Norway.

For many countries, the direction of poverty change is uniform across all
three poverty definitions. Child poverty *decreased* using all three definitions
in Taiwan, Canada, Denmark, Finland, Norway and Spain. Poverty
increased in Germany, Hungary, Italy, the United Kingdom and the United
States. For the rest of the countries, the direction of change varied between
the three definitions. The most common pattern, however, is that relative

---

[3] We are aware of changes to the survey methodologies of the Italian, Russian and Australian
surveys over this period, but the direction of potential bias is not known.
[4] Other studies show absolute child poverty to have increased dramatically in Russia (see
Klugman and Kolev 2000).

Figure 3.2. *Child poverty trends using the half median poverty lines*

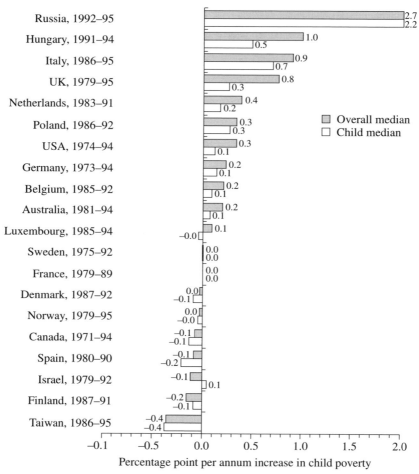

The numbers shown are the slope coefficients of regressions of the two child poverty rates (based on overall median and child median) against time using all available LIS data points for a country. Countries are sorted by the rate of increase in the overall median child poverty rate. The bars for Russia are truncated.

poverty increased – reflecting an increase in inequality – and poverty based on the US official line decreased – reflecting an increase in real disposable income. For instance, poverty in the Netherlands increased by 0.4 percentage points per annum by the overall median definition but decreased by 2.6 percentage points per annum using the US poverty line definition.

Figure 3.3. *Child poverty trends using the US official poverty line*

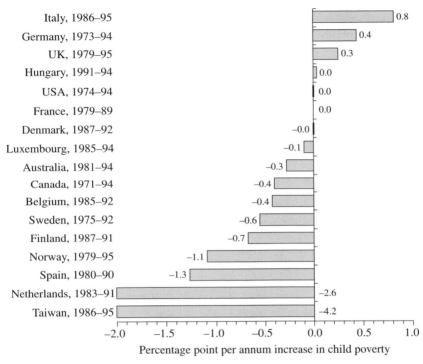

Percentage point per annum increase in child poverty

The numbers shown are the slope coefficient of a regression of the child poverty rate based on the US official poverty line against time using all available LIS data points for a country. Countries are sorted by the rate of increase in the child poverty rate. Countries which have experienced hyperinflation over the period are not included. The bars are truncated for the Netherlands and Taiwan.

It is possible, however, that the average change in poverty over time shown in figures 3.2 and 3.3 could conceal as much as it reveals. For instance, a country with a U-shaped time series of poverty will be registered as having almost no change over time. For many of the LIS countries there are very few data points. We show, for the countries for which LIS enables a longer time span, the actual data series for poverty calculated using half the overall median and the US official poverty line (figures 3.4 and 3.5).

The general flavour of the summary measure of trends remains. Both relative and real poverty decline in Canada over time and increase in the United States, albeit moderately in both cases. Relative poverty in Sweden is fairly flat, whereas it declines fairly sharply for the real definition.

Figure 3.4. *Child poverty trends using the US official poverty line: selected countries*

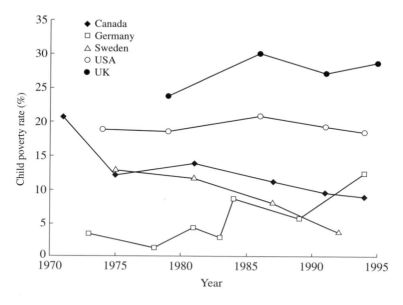

Figure 3.5. *Child poverty trends using the half overall median poverty line: selected countries*

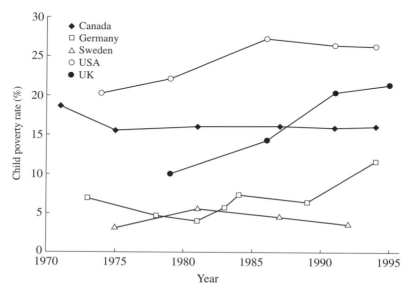

While the German poverty rate increases for both definitions (even prior to unification), poverty as measured by the US poverty line has a more variable pattern over time. Finally, poverty increased in the United Kingdom using both definitions, although the timing of the increase differs. Relative poverty accelerates in the late 1980s after a modest increase earlier, whereas real poverty increases steeply early on and then levels off.

The key conclusion to be drawn from the overall pattern of the levels and trends in child poverty is that there is wide diversity of outcomes for countries at similar states of development (as measured by GNP per capita). This is, in itself, an important, although not entirely surprising finding. Clearly there are factors other than the overall level of development that affect the prevalence of low income among children in different countries. One such factor is the different demographic compositions of the different countries, in particular the extent to which children live in two-parent or lone-parent families. Do these demographic factors explain any of the variation in poverty rates across countries?

Lone parenthood and child poverty

Learning which groups of children are poor or whether or not children face greater poverty risks than, say, the elderly provides us with a richer picture of the nature of child poverty. Looking into the structure of child poverty is also one way to approach the question of what accounts for child poverty and its variations across countries.

We examine here the poverty rates of children in lone-mother, two-parent and 'other' households. For children in each of the three household types, we show in table 3.3 the proportion of children and the poverty rate in each type using the base case definition of the poverty line. A lone-mother household is defined as a household with a female head with at least one child but no other adults present (adults are persons aged 18 or over). Our two-parent households are restricted to two-adult families, that is, there must be both a head and a spouse and there must be exactly two adults present.

As noted earlier, the household definition is narrower in Sweden and Switzerland, which leads to few households of type 'other'. At the other extreme, there are some countries where high proportions of children live in these larger households. This is particularly the case in Taiwan, Spain, Russia and Hungary where between 41 and 28 per cent of children live in households other than the lone-mother and two-parent types identified above. In many cases, these are households where lone mothers are living

Table 3.3. *Child poverty rates by family type*

Country	Year	Population shares			Poverty rate (%)		
		Lone mother	Two parents	Other	Lone mother	Two parents	Other
Russia	1995	0.08	0.60	0.32	31.0	26.0	26.5
United States	1994	0.15	0.60	0.25	59.6	16.7	29.1
United Kingdom	1995	0.19	0.70	0.12	40.3	17.5	13.9
Italy	1995	0.02	0.73	0.25	20.2	20.9	22.3
Australia	1994	0.09	0.73	0.18	38.3	14.7	16.6
Canada	1994	0.11	0.69	0.20	45.3	12.3	13.4
Ireland	1987	0.03	0.73	0.24	29.8	16.7	7.1
Israel	1992	0.03	0.71	0.25	26.6	14.0	14.8
Poland	1992	0.05	0.72	0.24	4.9	13.7	17.5
Spain	1990	0.02	0.62	0.36	25.2	12.4	13.5
Germany	1994	0.09	0.77	0.14	43.3	8.5	7.3
Hungary	1994	0.06	0.66	0.28	12.0	10.9	12.9
France	1989	0.07	0.75	0.17	25.4	7.7	12.6
Netherlands	1991	0.08	0.82	0.10	29.6	6.8	4.2
Switzerland	1982	0.07	0.88	0.05	21.2	4.8	12.5
Taiwan	1995	0.02	0.57	0.41	15.2	5.1	7.5
Luxembourg	1994	0.06	0.76	0.19	30.1	4.4	6.8
Belgium	1992	0.07	0.78	0.14	11.8	6.1	3.0
Denmark	1992	0.13	0.76	0.10	10.5	5.5	2.8
Austria	1987	0.10	0.73	0.18	33.2	2.9	2.0
Norway	1995	0.14	0.73	0.14	10.4	3.4	4.4
Sweden	1992	0.15	0.82	0.03	4.5	3.6	2.6
Finland	1991	0.09	0.79	0.13	6.2	3.0	4.1
Slovakia	1992	0.05	0.73	0.22	7.6	2.1	1.4
Czech Republic	1992	0.07	0.75	0.19	8.9	1.3	1.4
Average[a]		0.10	0.66	0.24	37.9	15.5	19.8

Notes: [a] Weighted by the number of children in 1996 (see table 3.1). Poverty defined with the half overall median poverty line and countries sorted by the all-child poverty rate on this basis.

with their parents, though this category also includes many other common household types, such as those where adult children remain at home.[5]

Across the twenty-five countries, the proportion of children living in lone-mother households varies widely. In many countries (for example, Ireland, Italy, Israel, Spain and Taiwan) the proportion of children in lone-mother households is negligible. The highest proportions are found in the UK (19 per cent), the USA (15 per cent), Sweden (15 per cent), Norway (14 per cent) and Denmark (13 per cent). It is noteworthy that the first two of

---

[5] See Motivans (2000) for more information on the Russian family type distribution.

these are also the two countries, after Russia, which have the highest child poverty rates.

The last three columns of table 3.3 provide information on the relationship between child poverty and lone parenthood. In almost all countries, lone-mother children have greater poverty risks than children in two-parent households. The two exceptions are Italy (where only 2 per cent of children are in lone-mother households) and Poland.[6] The poverty rate of USA lone-mother children is the highest. At 59.6 per cent, it exceeds by more than fifteen percentage points the next highest rate, Canada (45.3 per cent). In both countries, children in lone-mother households are around three and a half times more likely to be below the poverty line than children in two-parent households. Australia, Germany and the UK have poverty rates for children in lone-mother families close to 40 per cent. Sweden has the lowest rate (4.5) followed by Poland and Finland.

The association between lone motherhood and poverty is quite clear. Is this association responsible for any of the cross-national variations in child poverty rates? Some of the evidence presented above would suggest that lone motherhood might play an important role. The USA and the UK, in particular, have both high rates of lone motherhood and also high child poverty. One way to address this question is to make some counterfactual estimates of the national poverty rates that would exist if every country had the same family type distribution.[7] If only 10 per cent of UK and US children lived in lone-mother families (instead of 19 and 15 per cent) their national child poverty rates would be 2.3 percentage points lower in both cases. However, if this counterfactual estimate were made for all countries, the cross-national ranking would not change to any great extent. The correlation in poverty rates between this counterfactual and the actual poverty rate is 0.993, and the only ranking changes are relatively minor adjustments between countries with similar poverty rates.

These counterfactual calculations suggest that lone motherhood explains only a negligible component of the child poverty 'league table'. Although the USA and the UK have high rates of child poverty and lone motherhood, this relationship does not hold generally. Norway and Sweden, in particular, have high rates of lone motherhood but low rates of child poverty. This is the case even though lone mothers in Norway, in

---

[6] It should be noted that, in 1986, lone-mother households in Poland had a particularly high poverty rate. It is possible, therefore, that this result in 1992 represents a sampling or data coding error.

[7] These calculations are detailed in Bradbury and Jäntti (1999), where we also include an estimate of the alternative counterfactual of constant within-family type poverty rates across nations.

particular, are still significantly worse off than couples and larger house-holds.

3.4 Social transfers, market incomes and child poverty

Why is there so much variation in child poverty across nations? Since we define child poverty as low income relative to needs, the income sources of families of children provide the natural starting point for the answer to this question. Most research on patterns of poverty in rich nations has, not surprisingly, focused on public income transfers, as these are the policies which are most directly charged with providing incomes to disadvantaged families. As might be expected, there is an association between welfare effort and low rates of (relative) child poverty. Countries with a higher share of national income devoted to welfare transfers and services also tend to have lower child poverty rates.

And yet, paradoxically, this relationship is much weaker when attention is focused on those welfare state activities that should have the most direct impact on poverty. There seems to be little correlation between national poverty rates and the social transfers received by those below the median. We examine this issue by decomposing the variation in the living standards of low-income children across different countries.

Welfare effort

What are the implications of the variations in welfare state effort on child poverty? Figure 3.6 shows the association of these indicators of welfare effort with the overall median child poverty rate. In general there is a qualitatively significant relationship – countries with a high share of GNP spent on social expenditure have lower relative poverty rates. For the OECD countries, the correlation is −0.70 for workforce-age expenditures. This relationship diminishes when the transition economies – denoted by open diamonds – are included (in part because of the less reliable measurement of social expenditures in these countries).[8]

---

[8] It should also be noted that, though the social expenditure data are for 1993, the poverty rates are calculated for different years. In particular, the Swiss result is for the early 1980s. The work-force social expenditures are expenditures on family cash benefits, family services, active labour market programmes, disability and sickness benefits, unemployment benefits, housing benefits and other contingencies (social assistance).

Figure 3.6. *Child poverty rates by workforce-age social expenditure*

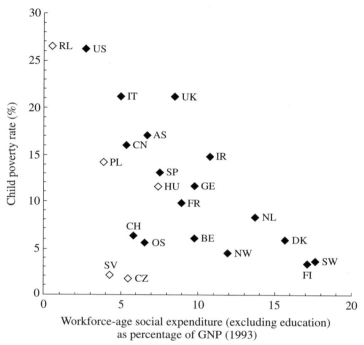

Sources: most countries, OECD Provisional Social Expenditure Data Base (March 1998); Hungary, Poland, Russia and Slovakia, UNICEF (1997) based on data provided by national statistical offices. The child poverty rate is that based on the half overall median poverty line (and the values are those given in table 3.2).

Much of this social expenditure, however, is spread more broadly across the population rather than only being targeted at those likely to be poor. In particular, most countries (the USA being a prominent exception) spend substantial amounts on programmes that provide cash transfer support to all or most families with children (Bradshaw *et al.* 1993).

It would be reasonable to expect that the link with poverty would be stronger if we could identify income transfers going to families likely to fall into poverty. However, previous research on this issue has found the opposite. Atkinson *et al.* (1995) compare poverty rates for the working-age population with the levels of transfers received by the population with below median incomes. Though their ranking of poverty rates for all the non-elderly is similar to our ranking of child poverty rates, they find a much weaker relationship between poverty and below median transfers. Norway, for example, has low poverty but also low transfers, while the UK and Ireland have high transfers but also relatively high poverty rates.

The reason for this weaker relationship must lie in the other sources of income available to households. In particular, even for the families of the most disadvantaged children, market incomes often comprise a major component of their 'income package'. What is the relative importance of market and transfer incomes for the living standards of poor children? Are social transfers or labour-market policies likely to be more important for their living standards?

Counterfactual poverty rates

The simplest disaggregation of family incomes relevant to this question is the decomposition into (net) social transfers and market incomes. Which of these contributes the most to the observed variation in child poverty across nations?

A commonly used method for addressing this question is shown in figure 3.7. This figure shows child poverty calculated using two definitions of household income. The shorter bars in the graph show our 'base case', overall median, child poverty rates (as in table 3.2) and countries are sorted by this poverty rate. The longer bars show the 'counterfactual' poverty rates that would occur if households received market incomes only (with an unchanged poverty line). The difference between the two poverty rates is often used as an index of the effectiveness of the tax and transfer system in reducing poverty.

There is a tendency for the gap between market and disposable income poverty to increase as we move down the graph (especially if we exclude Taiwan).[9] That is, low poverty rates tend to be associated with tax/transfer systems that have large impacts on poverty rates. This suggests that income transfers may be an important part of the reason why child poverty rates vary across countries.

However, they are only part of the story. One problem with this approach is that it is not symmetric; it shows the effect of excluding transfers, but does not show the complementary possibility of households living on transfers alone. Moreover, any counterfactual assumptions are just that – counter to

---

[9] Excluding Taiwan, the correlation between the difference in the two poverty rates and disposable income poverty is -0.57. See Atkinson *et al.* (1995), Smeeding (1997) and Smeeding *et al.* (1997) for similar calculations.

Figure 3.7. *Child poverty rates before and after taxes and transfers*

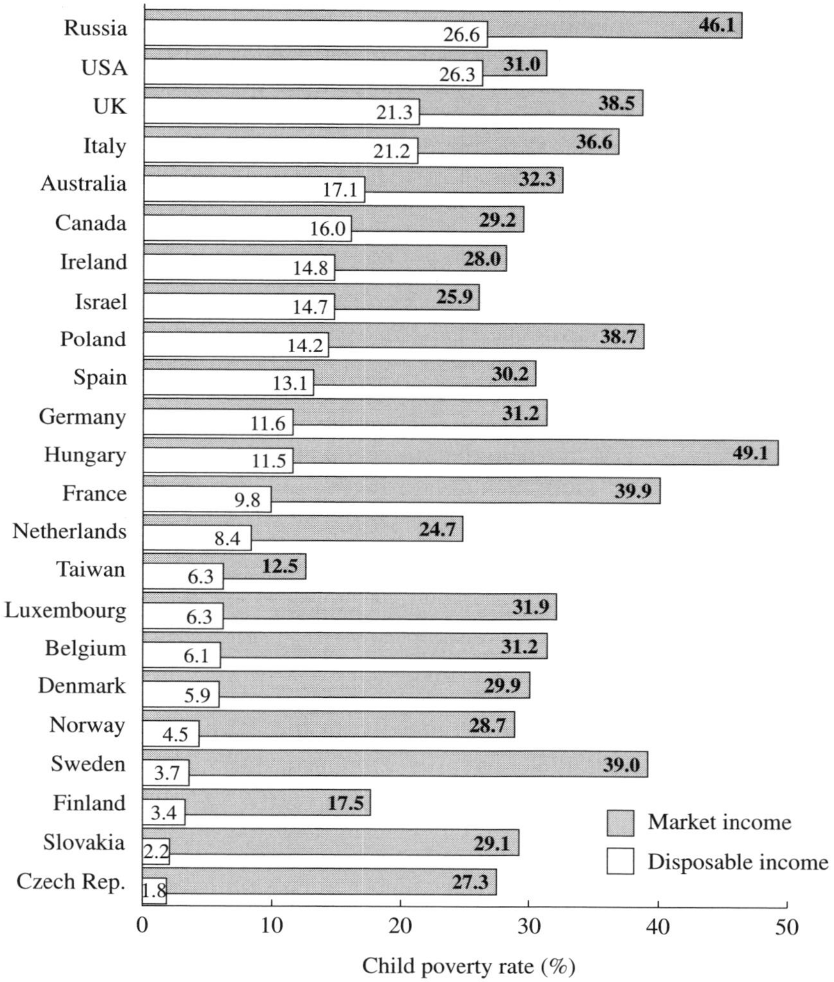

Country	Disposable income	Market income
Russia	26.6	46.1
USA	26.3	31.0
UK	21.3	38.5
Italy	21.2	36.6
Australia	17.1	32.3
Canada	16.0	29.2
Ireland	14.8	28.0
Israel	14.7	25.9
Poland	14.2	38.7
Spain	13.1	30.2
Germany	11.6	31.2
Hungary	11.5	49.1
France	9.8	39.9
Netherlands	8.4	24.7
Taiwan	6.3	12.5
Luxembourg	6.3	31.9
Belgium	6.1	31.2
Denmark	5.9	29.9
Norway	4.5	28.7
Sweden	3.7	39.0
Finland	3.4	17.5
Slovakia	2.2	29.1
Czech Rep.	1.8	27.3

Child poverty rate (%)

The disposable income poverty rate is the overall median poverty rate, as in table 3.2. Market income poverty is defined using the same poverty line, but only counting the market income of the household. In some countries (France, Italy, Luxembourg, Spain, Hungary, Poland and Russia) market income is measured net of income taxes.

fact. It is very likely that market incomes would change substantially in the total absence of public transfers, particularly since this counterfactual implies that large fractions of the population would have zero incomes. If there is substitution between social transfers and market incomes (for example, via labour-market or savings incentives or changes in labour demand), then this type of counterfactual over-estimates the redistributive impact of social transfers (Whiteford 1997).

Living standards and market and transfer incomes

For these reasons we introduce an alternative way of looking at the relative contribution made by social transfers and market incomes to child poverty outcomes. Instead of the poverty rate, we examine the cross-national distribution of the *relative disposable income* of the bottom fifth of children. In each country, we first calculate the mean household equivalent disposable income of the 20 per cent of children who live in the households with the lowest equivalent income levels. This is then divided by the median disposable income of children in their country to give an index of the extent to which the bottom fifth has similar incomes to the average child.[10] Across nations, this index is strongly associated with the 'child median' poverty rate, with which it has a correlation of -0.98 (the correlation is -0.95 with the overall median child poverty rate).

Rather than focus only on children below the poverty line, we therefore examine a closely related question: how do the one fifth of children who are most disadvantaged in each society fare? In particular, we are interested in the variation in the living standards of these different groups of children across nations. Does the variation in living standards stem from variations in social transfers or from different levels of market incomes?

For the poorest one fifth of children in each country, we calculate the elements of the identity:

$$\frac{\text{Average disposable income}}{\text{Median}} = \frac{\text{Average market income}}{\text{Median}} + \frac{\text{Average net social transfers}}{\text{Median}}$$

where all incomes are in equivalent terms and the median is the median equivalent disposable income across all children in the country (the

---

[10] In Bradbury and Jäntti (1999) we also examine the corresponding real measures (divided by the PPP index rather than the median income) and provide information on the relative contribution of transfers and taxes to net social transfers.

Figure 3.8. *Income package of the poorest fifth of children*

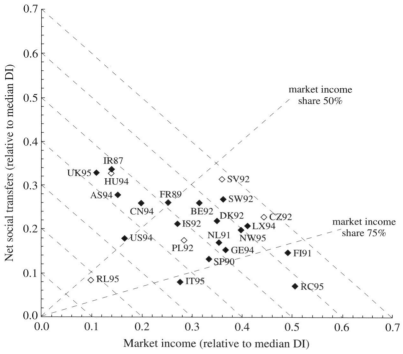

The graph shows mean incomes of the poorest fifth of children relative to the national median disposable income of all children (DI).

equivalence scale is the same as that used elsewhere in the chapter.[11] These different income components are shown in figure 3.8 for each of the twenty-three countries with recent LIS data (excluding Austria, where we cannot separately identify market incomes). The five transition countries have been separately identified with open diamonds.

[11] This equation is used at the household level to calculate net social transfers as a function of market and disposable income, and so holds by definition. In the calculations of this section, we also make some adjustments to the raw income data of the LIS data files. The measurement of negative incomes and income taxation varies somewhat across the LIS data files, and because means are more sensitive than poverty headcounts to extreme values, we have adjusted the incomes of cases with negative incomes or apparently very high taxation. For most countries this means a negligible change. The most important exceptions are Australia and the Netherlands. See Bradbury and Jäntti (1999) for more details.

Since market income (horizontal axis) and net social transfers (vertical axis) are defined to add up to disposable income, the latter (relative to median income) can also be read directly from this graph. The diagonal lines running from top left to bottom right are contours showing combinations of market income and transfers that yield the same total disposable income. The further the contour is from the origin, the higher is the living standard of the most disadvantaged children relative to that of the median child in their country. The ranking of countries in this respect parallels the child median poverty results in section 3.3, with the Nordic countries joined by the Czech and Slovak republics as having relatively equal distributions of income among children.

The lines in figure 3.8 coming out from the origin (the place where the two axes meet) indicate the share of total income received from market incomes. This share varies widely, from around three quarters of disposable income (Taiwan, Italy, Finland, Spain, Germany) to as low as one quarter (the UK). In most countries, this market income is mainly wages and salaries. In Taiwan, Russia, Ireland and Finland, however, around one-third of market income is from other sources (for example, farm and other business income) and in a number of countries these sources contribute around one fifth of market income.[12]

In addition to looking at income packages, however, the graph can be used to show how the overall variation in the relative disadvantage of poor children (variation from bottom left to top right) is due to variation in market incomes (left to right variation) or variation in net social transfers (vertical variation). Even though there is substantial variation in net social transfers, there is even greater variation in the relative levels of the market incomes in the households of the most disadvantaged children (i.e. there is more horizontal than vertical spread).

There is also a substantial negative correlation between market and transfer incomes (-0.39 for all countries and -0.66 if we exclude the transition countries). In other words, in countries where the families of the most disadvantaged children have market incomes that are well below average, there tends to be a higher level of social transfers. There are at least two interpretations possible for this correlation. One is the behavioural response hypothesis: high levels of social transfers to the most disadvantaged suppress their labour supply and market incomes adjust to more than offset the patterns of social transfers. The other is that in countries where markets lead to substantial child poverty there is a policy response to alleviate this, i.e. that social transfers reduce the dispersion in poverty rates

---

[12] In France, Italy, Luxembourg, Spain, Hungary and Russia market income is measured net of income taxes. To be comparable with other countries these points should therefore be shifted slightly down and to the right.

arising from the market. Given that the former would imply an extremely (and unlikely) strong behavioural response, we conclude that the variation in social transfers across nations does reduce the cross-national variation in poverty, at least to some degree.

Whatever the cause of this correlation, the outcome is that the cross-national variation in disposable income (relative to the median) is less than the variance in market incomes. Examining figure 3.8, it can be seen that the two outliers in this correlation between market incomes and social transfers, among the richer nations, are the USA and Italy, which both have very low relative disposable incomes for the bottom fifth of their children. The other English-speaking countries provide an interesting illustration of the strength of the correlation between social and market incomes, and the wide variation in the latter. While the USA has the highest relative child poverty rate among the non-transition countries, the other English-speaking countries also have high poverty rates (see table 3.2). Yet these countries, as a group, actually have a relatively high level of social transfers going to their most disadvantaged children.

Indeed, if we use as our 'poverty' index the average income of the poorest 20 per cent of children relative to that of the median child (justifiable as an approximation in the light of the strong correlation with more conventional measures of poverty), we can use figure 3.8 to describe some results using a counterfactual simulation that is the opposite of that commonly employed. If the poorest 20 per cent of children were forced to rely only upon the social transfers that their families were receiving at the time of these surveys, then the relative poverty rates in Ireland, the UK, Hungary, Slovakia and Australia would all be *lower* than those in Sweden. In fact, however, it is the high *labour-market* earnings of Swedish parents that ensure high living standards for the most disadvantaged children in that country.

It is also interesting to contrast the distinctive pattern for the English-speaking countries found here (low market income, high transfers) with the pattern of social expenditures shown in figure 3.6 – where they have relatively low levels of social transfers. The difference is because a larger fraction of transfers are targeted to low-income families (and particularly families with dependent children) in these countries.

It has been argued by many (for example, Korpi and Palme 1998) that targeting can be counter-productive for the poor, as it may erode middle-class political support for the welfare state and hence reduce the total funds available for transfers. The higher level of poverty in the English-speaking countries could be seen as providing some support for this proposition. However, the data here also suggest a different interpretation. In the English-speaking countries, with the prominent exception of the USA, social transfers to the families of the poorest one fifth of children are quite substantial. Instead, the reason for their high level of child poverty lies in the low levels of *market* incomes received by the most disadvantaged families.

3.5 Conclusions

Child poverty, whether measured in relative or real terms, varies widely across the industrialised countries. Our analysis has shown the extent of this variation and some of its correlates using the latest available LIS data for the early to mid-1990s. Nordic and Northern European countries have low rates of child poverty, whereas Southern European and English-speaking countries tend to have high rates. While the ranking within the richer group of countries differs somewhat between the relative and 'absolute' approaches to the measurement of poverty, the broad grouping is not all that different. (The poverty ranking of most of the transition economies in LIS, on the other hand, depends very much on this distinction.) Across the whole spectrum of industrial countries considered here, those with higher levels of national income do tend to have lower real poverty rates. Important exceptions from this general rule are the USA, which has a much higher level of child poverty than its national income would suggest, and Taiwan, which has a lower than expected child poverty rate.

Besides providing more up-to-date results for a greater number of countries than the earlier cross-national literature, we have also produced new insights into the correlates of child poverty. Children are generally more likely to be poor if living with a lone mother, but we find that variations in rates of lone motherhood are not an important reason for the variations in child poverty across countries. While cash transfers to poor families are important for their living standards, market incomes are also important and our emphasis on the role of this form of income contrasts with much of the earlier literature on cross-national differences. Indeed, we find that market incomes play a larger role than state transfers in accounting for the cross-national diversity of outcomes for disadvantaged children. The English-speaking countries other than the USA, for example, actually provide quite substantial income transfers to their most needy children. The living standards of these children, however, remain relatively low because of low labour-market incomes. The higher living standards of the most disadvantaged children in the 'welfare leaders' (particularly the Nordic countries) are due to the higher market incomes in these families. Whether this is because of different labour-market and family support policies (such as childcare subsidies), because of the different incentive structures imposed by different targeting patterns, or other factors, remains to be seen.

Acknowledgements
We thank Jonathan Bradshaw, Stephen Jenkins, John Micklewright, Albert Motivans, Lee Rainwater, Tim Smeeding and seminar participants for comments on previous drafts. Most importantly, we wish to acknowledge the central role of the Luxembourg Income Study, without which the analysis in this chapter would not be possible. Thanks, in particular, to Koen Vleminckx for providing technical advice. The UK data providers to the LIS also require that we include the following statement: 'Material from the UK surveys is crown copyright; has been made available by the Office for National Statistics through the ESRC Data Archive; and has been used by permission. Neither the Office for National Statistics nor the ESRC Data Archive bears any responsibility for the analysis or the interpretation of the data reported here.'

References
Atkinson, A. B., Rainwater, L. and Smeeding, T. M., 1995, *Income Distribution in OECD Countries: Evidence from the Luxembourg Income Study*, OECD, Paris.

Bradbury, B. and Jäntti, M., 1999, 'Child poverty across industrialized nations', Innocenti Occasional Papers, Economic and Social Policy Series 71, UNICEF International Child Development Centre, Florence.

Bradshaw, J., Ditch, J., Holmes, H. and Whiteford, P., 1993, *Support for Children: A Comparison of Arrangements in Fifteen Countries*, UK Department of Social Security, Research Report 21, London.

Citro, C. F. and Michael, R. T. (eds.), 1995, *Measuring Poverty: A New Approach*, National Academy Press, Washington DC.

Cornia, G. A. and Danziger, S. (eds.), 1997, *Child Poverty and Deprivation in the Industrialized Countries, 1945–1995*, Clarendon Press, Oxford.

Gottschalk, P. and Smeeding, T. M., 1997, 'Cross-national comparisons of earnings and income inequality', *Journal of Economic Literature*, 32: 633–86.

Jäntti, M. and Danziger, S., 2000, 'Income poverty in advanced countries', in Atkinson, A. B. and Bourguignon, F. (eds.), *Handbook of Income Distribution*, North-Holland, Amsterdam.

Jenkins, S. P. and Cowell, F. A., 1994, 'Parametric equivalence scales and scale relativities', *Economic Journal*, 104: 891–900.

Jenkins, S. P. and Lambert, P. J., 1993, 'Ranking income distribution when needs differ', *Review of Income and Wealth*, 39: 337–56.

Klugman, J. and Kolev, A., 2000, 'The welfare repercussions of single parenthood in Russia in transition', in Klugman, J. and Motivans, A. (eds.), *Single Parents and Child Welfare in the New Russia*, Macmillan, London.

Korpi, W. and Palme, J., 1998, 'The paradox of redistribution and strategies of equality: welfare state institutions and poverty in western countries', *American Sociological Review*, 63: 661–97.

Motivans, A., 2000, 'Trends in family stability and structure', in Klugman, J. and Motivans, A. (eds.), *Single Parents and Child Welfare in the New Russia*, Macmillan, London.

Rainwater, L. and Smeeding, T. M., 1995, 'Doing poorly: the real income of American children in a comparative perspective', Luxembourg Income Study Working Paper 127, CEPS/INSTEAD, Luxembourg.

Smeeding, T. M., 1997, 'Financial poverty in developed countries: the evidence from LIS. Final report to the UNDP', Luxembourg Income Study Working Paper 155, CEPS/INSTEAD, Luxembourg.

Smeeding, T. M., Danziger, S. and Rainwater, L., 1997, 'Making social policy work for children: towards a more effective antipoverty policy', in Cornia and Danziger (1997).

UNICEF, 1997, 'Children at risk in Central and Eastern Europe: perils and promises', *Regional Monitoring Report 4*, UNICEF International Child Development Centre, Florence.

UNICEF, 1998, *The State of the World's Children*, Oxford University Press, New York.

Whiteford, P., 1997, 'Targeting welfare: a comment', *Economic Record*, 73: 45–50.

Appendix table. *Child poverty rates using different equivalence scales*

Country	Year	Base case (quasi-OECD scale)			Square-root scale		
		Rate (%)	Rank	Risk	Rate (%)	Rank	Risk
Russia	1995	26.6	(1)	1.2	25.5	(1)	1.2
United States	1994	26.3	(2)	1.3	24.5	(2)	1.3
United Kingdom	1995	21.3	(3)	1.4	19.8	(4)	1.2
Italy	1995	21.2	(4)	1.4	20.5	(3)	1.4
Australia	1994	17.1	(5)	1.2	16.0	(5)	1.0
Canada	1994	16.0	(6)	1.4	15.5	(6)	1.4
Ireland	1987	14.8	(7)	1.2	13.8	(7)	1.1
Israel	1992	14.7	(8)	1.2	11.6	(10)	1.0
Poland	1992	14.2	(9)	1.2	12.4	(8)	1.2
Spain	1990	13.1	(10)	1.3	12.3	(9)	1.3
Germany	1994	11.6	(11)	1.4	10.7	(11)	1.3
Hungary	1994	11.5	(12)	1.2	10.3	(12)	1.1
France	1989	9.8	(13)	1.1	8.4	(13)	0.8
Netherlands	1991	8.4	(14)	1.3	8.3	(14)	1.2
Switzerland	1982	6.3	(15)	1.2	4.3	(20)	1.1
Taiwan	1995	6.3	(16)	1.0	6.2	(15)	0.7
Luxembourg	1994	6.3	(17)	1.4	4.5	(18)	1.5
Belgium	1992	6.1	(18)	1.1	4.4	(19)	0.8
Denmark	1992	5.9	(19)	1.2	5.1	(16)	0.9
Austria	1987	5.6	(20)	1.2	4.8	(17)	0.8
Norway	1995	4.5	(21)	1.4	3.9	(21)	1.4
Sweden	1992	3.7	(22)	1.3	3.0	(22)	1.0
Finland	1991	3.4	(23)	1.0	2.7	(23)	0.7
Slovakia	1992	2.2	(24)	1.3	2.0	(25)	1.1
Czech Republic	1992	1.8	(25)	1.4	2.2	(24)	1.4

Notes: Children are classified as poor when the equivalent income of their household is less than 50 per cent of the overall median. The 'base case' uses the quasi-OECD equivalence scale (see section 3.2), while the square-root scale is simply the square root of the number of people in the household. Countries are sorted by the base case (quasi-OECD scale) poverty rate. The rank correlation between the two rates is 0.979. The column headed 'Risk' shows the poverty rate for children relative to that for other persons.

4 The dynamics of child poverty in seven industrialised nations

BRUCE BRADBURY, STEPHEN P. JENKINS AND
JOHN MICKLEWRIGHT

4.1 Introduction

The preceding chapters summarised what there is to know about child poverty from cross-sectional data for a large number of countries, established the case for taking a dynamic perspective on the subject, and discussed the methodological issues that arise with a dynamic approach. In the second half of the book, different features of child poverty dynamics are examined on a country-by-country basis for Britain, Germany, Hungary, Ireland, Russia, Spain and the United States. This chapter provides a link between the book's two parts, documenting in a common format some basic facts about the dynamics of child poverty for these seven nations.

The principal contribution of the chapter is this new longitudinal information about child poverty. Cross-national comparisons of children's movements into and out of poverty are rare, no doubt because suitable data have not been available. By contrast we do have data, though their nature guides the scope of our enquiry, as we will explain shortly. We eschew in-depth analysis of mature panel surveys with fully comparable variables but available only for a very small number of countries, in favour of a more broad-brush summary of patterns for a larger number of countries at different stages of development. Nonetheless we do exploit the longer panels where we have them and we use several measures of income in order to check the robustness of our conclusions to changes in definition. The data sets, the sub-samples we analyse, and the income variables we use are all described in section 4.2.

One of the fundamental problems in making cross-national comparisons of movements into and out of poverty by children (or any other group) is that the numbers of transitions observed depend in part on the amount of poverty there is in the first place (as we shall explain). And yet child poverty rates differ substantially across different countries, as chapter 3 has shown very clearly. In other words, there is a standardisation issue: how to identify the cross-national variations in poverty dynamics separately from the cross-national variations in poverty rates. One way in which we handle this problem is by looking at movements into and out of the *poorest fifth* of all children in each country – in this case each country has the same child poverty rate (equal to 20 per cent). This solution is not entirely satisfactory because such a poverty line is not a commonly used cut-off level: poverty status is most often summarised in terms of a threshold equal to some fixed real income value or some fraction of average (median or mean) income. We therefore also use some of these latter definitions (described below) when looking at movements into and out of poverty, recognising that interpretation is affected by standardisation issues (that we discuss).

Although our primary interest is in movements into and out of poverty, we also provide supplementary information about movements to and from other income groups throughout the whole income range (and not only the poorest one), i.e. *income mobility* as well as *poverty dynamics*. We are interested not only in how many children fall into, or leave, poverty from one year to the next, but also where in the income distribution they have come from and where they end up. To what extent are exits from poverty dominated by children with incomes just below the chosen poverty line and to what extent do entries to poverty come disproportionately from those with incomes just above the poverty line? This information is all the more valuable because exactly where the poverty line should be drawn is not clear-cut.

We look at income origins and income destinations using two types of definition. The first categorises children according to whether they are in the poorest fifth of all children, or the second-poorest fifth, third-poorest fifth, fourth-poorest fifth, or the richest fifth, i.e. by quintile groups. (A further breakdown divides children into decile groups, i.e. into tenths.) The advantage of this definition, noted above, is that it is directly comparable across countries. The second definition classifies children into four groups according to their income level relative to cut-offs equal to 40 per cent, 50 per cent, and 60 per cent of median national income. The upper and lower cut-offs straddle the income level that we take to be the poverty line.

In section 4.3 we document cross-national differences in income mobility for children and also show how these differences relate to differences in income inequality at a point in time. Are the more unequal countries those where mobility is greatest or least? We examine how many children remain in the poorest fifth of the income distribution from one year to the next, and look at the vulnerability of children in the middle of the income distribution to falling to the bottom.

The next two sections look at children's exit rates from and entry rates to poverty using a poverty line equal to half median income. Section 4.4 documents the cross-national differences in movements into and out of poverty, and shows how they relate to the differences in poverty rates that are observed at a point in time. Section 4.5 looks at two aspects in greater detail. First, by focusing on the 'near poor', we examine the extent to which poverty entry and exit involves small or large income changes. Second, we provide information about how children's movements into and out of poverty differ by household type and how these profiles differ across the countries that we study. We focus on the distinction between children who live in lone-parent households and other children, a distinction that has received much attention in analyses of poverty rates at a point in time (including the analysis in chapter 3). The final section provides a summary of what has been learned.

Our analysis complements and extends the pioneering study by Greg Duncan and others (1993) of poverty dynamics among families with children in eight nations (Canada, the Lorraine region of France, West Germany, Ireland, Luxembourg, the Netherlands, Sweden and the USA). Our analysis has the advantage of directly examining *children's* poverty dynamics, whereas Duncan and his co-authors studied *families* with children: different samples can provide different results. (The problems of following families rather than children in longitudinal data were discussed in chapter 2.) Duncan *et al.*'s data refer mostly to the mid-1980s, ours to the beginning of the 1990s. And we show the sensitivity of results to the choice of income measure. For most of our countries we have more than one income definition available, whereas Duncan *et al.*'s work was restricted to a single measure per country.

The studies are complementary because although the range of countries covered overlaps (the USA, Germany and Ireland), we also include two transition countries from Eastern Europe and one Southern European country, rather than exclusively Northern European and North American ones.[1] Duncan *et al.* concluded that 'despite the very different macroeconomic conditions, demographic structures and degree of income inequality, favourable income changes among families with children were widespread and strikingly similar across the eight countries in our study' (1993: 215). (Of course, unfavourable income changes may also be common.) One of our aims is to investigate whether their conclusion about the cross-national similarity of income changes holds true for the countries and time periods covered by our analysis.

---

[1] The panel surveys that we use are the same in the case of the USA and West Germany (although our use of 1990s' data means that we are able to provide results for both unified Germany and West Germany alone). The survey differs in the case of Ireland. The Irish data used by Duncan *et al.* were drawn from a follow-up survey of low-income families and therefore could be used to look at poverty exits but not entries.

4.2 The data and the patterns at a point in time

The data sets and measures of 'income'

The data we use are derived from household panel surveys for seven countries: Britain, Germany (both West Germany and the united Germany),
Hungary, Ireland, Russia, Spain and the USA. The unit of analysis
throughout is the child, defined as a person aged less than 18 years in each
of the years compared. We wish to compare income changes between one
year, call it t, and an earlier year, $t - s$, and so the samples we use are the
children who are present in each survey in both year $t - s$ and year t. For all
the countries we are able to compare dynamics over two years (i.e. between
years $t - 1$ and t). For four of the countries (Britain, Germany, Hungary
and the USA) we are able also to examine dynamics over five years ($t - 4$ to
t) and for two countries (Germany and the USA) over ten years as well
($t - 9$ to t). The current year (t) was chosen to be the latest year available in
each survey, and is a year in the early to mid-1990s (except in Spain where
there is a range of years – see below). Each child is attributed the income of
the household to which he or she belongs in the relevant year, adjusted for
household needs. The equivalence scale used in the adjustment for household needs is the square root of household size (see chapter 2).

A summary description of each data set is provided in table 4.1. The main
features on which we compare them are: the type of longitudinal survey, the
period to which incomes refer, the definition(s) of income available, and two
statistics summarising sample size. Further details about each of the
surveys are provided in the country-specific chapters in part II of the book.
The most obvious contrast between the surveys is in the income measures
that are available. One difference concerns whether household income is
recorded before the deduction of income taxes and employee social insurance contributions (gross income) or after their deduction (net income).
The implications for measures of poverty dynamics of choosing different
definitions are not obvious a priori. Certainly inequality of net income will
be smaller than gross income inequality at any one time, but it is not
obvious whether the tax system also dampens income mobility. Another
difference concerns the reference period for which household incomes have
been measured, whether a full year (annual income) or the period – usually
the month – just prior to the annual interview (current income). These
differences have clear implications for differences in poverty dynamics for
the reasons discussed in detail in chapter 2.

For all but two countries (Ireland and the USA) we have a measure of

Table 4.1. *The surveys*

Country	Survey	Income variables	Most recent income period	Number of households with children in two waves	Number of children as percentage of all people in two waves
Britain	British Household Panel Survey (BHPS)	Annual gross income (pounds per annum, 1996 prices)	1996 (year to end August)	1,529	21.8
		Current gross income (pounds per month, 1996 prices)	1996 (autumn)	1,529	21.8
		Current net income (pounds per week, January 1996 prices)[a]	1996 (autumn)	1,264	22.1
Germany	German Socio-Economic Panel Survey – Equivalent File (GSOEP)	Annual net income	1995 (calendar year)	2,072 (1,232)[e]	19.9 (18.7)[e]
		Current net income[b]	1996 (spring–summer)	1,971 (1,163)[e]	20.7 (18.7)[e]
Hungary	Hungarian Household Panel Survey (HHPS)	Annual net income	1995–6 (year to end March)	488	21.9
		Monthly net income	1996 (March)	488	21.9
Ireland	European Community Household Panel Survey – Living in Ireland Survey (ECHP)	Annual net income	1994 (calendar year)	1,605	32.2
Russia	Russian Longitudinal Monitoring Survey (RLMS)	Monthly net income (December 1995 Moscow prices)	1995	1,316	24.6
		Monthly expenditures (December 1995 Moscow prices)	1995	1,316	24.6
Spain	Encuesta Continua de Presupuestos Familiares (ECPF)	Estimate of current net income	1985 to 1992[c]	5,812	25.8
		Current expenditures	1985 to 1992[c]	5,812	25.8
USA	Panel Study of Income Dynamics (PSID)	Gross total income plus the dollar value of food stamps received[d]	1992 (calendar year)	1,618	24.1

Notes: [a] Only available for 'complete respondent' households. [b] Head's estimate for whole household. [c] Data pooled over the 1985–92 period. [d] Negative and zero incomes recoded to $1. [e] Numbers in parentheses are for West Germany only. All surveys are household panels with annual interviews, except for Spain's, which is a quarterly rotating panel.

current net income. For Germany, this measure refers to what the household head estimates to be the total income of all the persons in the household. For the other countries, total income is the sum of the incomes reported by each respondent within the household. (This is also the case with the German annual income measures.) For Britain, the net income measure cannot be calculated for all households, hence reducing sample sizes somewhat. For three countries (Germany, Hungary and Ireland), an annual net income measure is available. Moreover, for Spain and Russia, we have a measure of current household expenditure in addition to current household income, which makes for an interesting comparison. The availability of the expenditure data is especially useful for Russia given arguments about the greater reliability of information on expenditures relative to incomes in transition economies (for example, there is said to be less under-reporting – see chapter 11). The arguments in chapter 2 concerning the smoothing over time of consumption are also relevant here – as are the caveats we expressed about the ability of expenditure data to adequately measure consumption.

It is obvious that we have no single comparable measure of 'income' for all seven nations. But by judicious use of the various different measures, we are able to check the sensitivity of our conclusions about cross-national differences in patterns of income change. This use of multiple measures of living standards represents a further difference between our analysis and that of Duncan and his co-authors discussed earlier.

All the surveys, with the exception of that for Spain, are household panel surveys. In these surveys, information is collected about a sample of individuals (and their households) at approximately one year apart. Persons remain in the panel until the survey is discontinued (unless they die, cannot be traced, refuse to participate or enter an institution). For Spain the survey is a quarterly rotating panel in which households are interviewed each quarter for up to eight consecutive quarters and are then dropped from the survey ('rotated out') to be replaced by new households. We use the Spanish data about income and expenditure collected one year apart in the first and fifth quarters of participation for all households entering the panel over a seven-year period.

The maximum length of time for which we can follow children depends on how many rounds of interviews the panel survey has had (except for Spain where the rotating panel design sets the constraint). For all seven nations, we can examine dynamics over a one-year interval. However, our ability to follow children for longer periods is restricted; as already noted, data span a five-year period for Britain, Germany (both the former West Germany and the re-united Germany), Hungary and the USA, and ten years for West Germany and the USA.

The number of households in the analysis is between 1,000 and 2,000 for most countries (see table 4.1). Numbers are noticeably smaller for Hungary (as the survey itself is relatively small), and noticeably larger for Spain, reflecting the pooling of data for households entering the survey over a number of years. Children form between one fifth and one fourth of all persons present in the two-year samples for every country except Ireland, where the proportion of children is almost one third. (We noted the high proportion of children in the Irish population in chapter 1.)

For each data set, sample weights which account for differential non-response and sample attrition have been used.

Cross-section differences in income distribution

To place in perspective our descriptions of the changes over time in the household incomes of children, we first provide some cross-section summaries of the income distributions for the most recent wave of data for each country. We compare children's relative income levels, income inequality and child poverty rates. These statistics are similar to those reported in chapter 3, but they are not fully comparable because there are differences in the definition of the income measure, the year referred to, the sample, and in most cases even the survey (this is true in Britain, Ireland, Spain and the USA).[2]

Statistics summarising the income distribution at a point in time in each country are shown in table 4.2. How well off are children relative to all persons in each country, summarised in terms of differences in median income? In all seven nations, children are worse off on average than the population as a whole, but the range is large. For example, in Ireland median income for children is almost one fifth lower than the all-persons median, whereas, at the other extreme, in Hungary, the difference is only a matter of about 3 per cent.[3] For Britain and the USA, the median income of children is some 10 per cent lower than for all persons. In Germany the corresponding figure is smaller, a deficit of about 6 or 7 per cent. This is the differential in Spain and Russia as well, as long as income is the measure of material well-being. The use of expenditure provides a very different perspective, however. In Russia, the median expenditure for children is some 14 per cent

[2] For example, the UK figures in chapter 3 (the UK is defined as Britain and Northern Ireland) are based on the Family Expenditure Survey, while the results for Britain in this chapter are based on the British Household Panel Survey.

[3] By 'median income for children' we mean the median of the distribution of children, ranked by the value of equivalised income of their household.

Table 4.2. *Inequality and poverty*

Country	Child median ÷ population median	Overall Gini coefficient	Child Gini coefficient	Child poverty rate (half median poverty line)	Increase in child poverty waves $t-1$ to t (percentage points)
Current net income					
Britain	0.89	0.32	0.30	16.8	0.5
Germany	0.95	0.24	0.22	7.7	−0.6
West Germany	0.94	0.25	0.22	6.8	−0.8
Hungary	0.97	0.31	0.29	9.7	3.5
Russia	0.94	0.43	0.45	24.1	5.2
Spain	0.92	0.30	0.30	11.9	−1.9
Current gross income					
Britain	0.90	0.36	0.35	23.6	0.7
Current expenditure					
Russia	0.86	0.42	0.45	22.5	4.6
Spain	0.98	0.33	0.32	11.5	0.9
Annual net income					
Germany	0.93	0.27	0.24	9.3	0.6
West Germany	0.94	0.27	0.23	6.9	−0.6
Hungary	0.97	0.30	0.30	8.9	3.3
Ireland	0.82	0.36	0.34	15.6	0.7
Annual gross income					
Britain	0.87	0.36	0.36	24.5	0.1
USA	0.89	0.41	0.40	24.7	−0.4

Notes: All incomes are adjusted by the 'square root of household size' equivalence scale. Child median, Gini coefficient and poverty rates are for children in two waves. The population median and Gini coefficient are for all persons (adults and children). Unless stated, all measures are for the most recent wave.

lower than the figure for all persons. In Spain, however, the shortfall with expenditure is smaller than for income; the child median is about 2 per cent less than that for all people. For other countries where multiple definitions of income are available, there is a reassuring robustness to the picture about differentials.

Median income levels provide no guide to how incomes vary among children. For example, a high average income may disguise very low incomes for some children. It is therefore of interest to look at the degree of income dispersion among children as a whole. This is also an important preliminary step in our investigation of movements into and out of the group that forms the poorest fifth of all children – one needs to see how far the poorest fifth is adrift from the rest. We summarise the dispersion of incomes using the Gini coefficient, an index which ranges between zero (when there is complete equality of incomes) and one (complete inequality). Higher values indicate higher inequality.

Income inequality amongst children varies substantially across these seven nations, the Gini coefficient ranging from under 0.3 in Germany to over 0.4 in Russia and the USA.[4] To put these statistics into perspective, observe that this range – of more than ten percentage points – is larger than the increase in overall inequality in the USA and in Britain during the 1980s, typically cited as 'large'. The Gini coefficients for children's incomes in Britain and Ireland lie about midway between the ends of the range, and those for Hungary and Spain are towards the lower end. This finding is robust to changing the definition of income.

These relative rankings perhaps come as no surprise once we also observe that there is a close association between income inequality amongst children and income inequality amongst the population as a whole – the Gini coefficient for the distribution across all individuals is given in the adjacent column in table 4.2. Cross-national rankings according to the overall inequality typically place the USA at the top, with social democratic European countries near the bottom, and the other English-speaking countries in between (see chapter 3). The two transition countries enter this ranking in different places. Russia heads the table with the USA, the 1990s having seen a huge increase in inequality following the break-up of the Soviet Union. Hungary, where the increase has been more modest, is at around the level in Spain. That said, inequality amongst children appears slightly lower than overall inequality, except in Russia where the opposite is the case. The difference is greatest for Germany, the country with the lowest overall inequality.

---

[4] Again, these results refer to the distribution described in the preceding footnote.

We now compare cross-national differences in child poverty rates, where the poverty line used in each case is half the country's median income in the most recent wave of data for all persons in the two-wave sample. This is a relative poverty line, in the sense that it is defined with reference to contemporary income, and so differs in real terms across the countries (see chapter 2). Differences in poverty rates according to this way of looking at poverty are thus partly dependent on cross-national differences in inequality.

The countries with the lowest child poverty rates using the half national median poverty line are Germany and Hungary, in the range 7 per cent to 10 per cent. (The all-Germany rates are slightly higher than the West German rates because poverty is higher in eastern Germany than western Germany.) The child poverty rate is slightly higher in Spain, around 12 per cent, and higher still in Ireland and Britain, around 16–17 per cent. Reassuringly, the ranking corresponds with chapter 3's analysis based on the Luxembourg Income Study (LIS) data, which also used a half national median poverty line (see table 3.2). In fact the poverty rate estimates themselves are quite similar despite the different equivalence scales used. (We have noted that the surveys used in chapter 3 and in the current chapter differ in four of the countries we look at here, which is another reason for any differences in the results.)

Switching from a measure of net income to one of gross income can have a very large effect on the poverty rate, as the results for Britain show.[5] According to the gross income measure, the child poverty rate is around 24 per cent rather than 17 per cent. This is particularly relevant for assessing the US poverty rate, which is some 25 per cent on the basis of gross income. If we had had data for net incomes, one might think that the USA would show a rather lower poverty rate – perhaps more like the British figure rather than similar to the Russian figure of 23 to 24 per cent. However, the earlier results in chapter 3 based on the LIS data with more comparable income variables suggest otherwise. For example, according to the appendix table in chapter 3, the child poverty rates in Russia and the USA are very similar if a half national median poverty line is used: about 25 or 26 per cent depending upon the equivalence scale (though the US data are for a slightly later year).

The last column of table 4.2 shows the change in child poverty rate

---

[5] Moving from a net (after-tax) to a gross income measure would be expected to increase the poverty rate because this will increase the income of the median family significantly (and hence raise the poverty line), whilst having little impact on the income of poor families (who do not pay much tax).

between the first and second year of the two-wave comparisons. Since the observation period is so short, there is, not surprisingly, little change for most countries. The notable exceptions are the two transition economies, Hungary and Russia, for which there were quite large increases in both absolute and proportionate terms.

4.3 Income mobility and the dynamics of disadvantage

We now turn to the dynamics of incomes. How much do children move up and down the income distribution? We are concerned here only with the distribution of children. That is, taking children as a group (and ignoring all other persons), by how much do they change places with each other on the income ladder (assigning to each child his or her household's income, adjusted by the household's size)? We have a particular focus on movements to and from *low income*, defined as the poorest fifth of the distribution. Our discussion at the start of the chapter emphasised the practical advantage that this approach implies: there is the same fraction of children in low income in each country at any time, which aids the making of comparisons across countries. (See chapter 2 for more on why looking at children's positions relative to each other is of interest.)

Changing places on the ladder

For each year and country sample we rank the children in ascending order of their incomes and then partition them into ten equal-sized groups (so-called decile groups). For each country, each decile group contains one tenth of all children, and we therefore have a comparable definition of income thresholds across all the countries. To examine income mobility for a country, we calculate the number of children who are in a different decile group in year $t - s$ and in year t, and express it as a proportion of the total number of children in the relevant sample. (For example, this would be the two-wave sample were we to consider mobility over a one-year period.) The larger this proportion, the greater the degree of income mobility. The results are given in table 4.3.

There is a remarkable similarity across the majority of the seven countries in the extent of children's income mobility over one year. For Britain, Germany, Hungary and Spain, the proportion of children moving to a

Table 4.3. *The income mobility of children*

Country	Percentage of children in a different decile group of the income distribution of children in waves		
	$t-1$ and t	$t-4$ and t	$t-9$ and t
Current net income			
Russia	83.3		
Spain	65.9		
Hungary	65.2	79.0	
Britain	62.8	76.1	
Germany	60.8	73.5	
West Germany	59.4	73.7	76.9
Current gross income			
Britain	60.2	73.4	
Current expenditure			
Russia	81.1		
Spain	76.4		
Annual net income			
Hungary	69.2	77.4	
Ireland	59.6		
Germany	59.5	69.3	
West Germany	57.1	69.6	72.1
Annual gross income			
Britain	58.9	69.7	
USA	57.3	67.5	77.8

Notes: Countries are sorted within each income definition in descending order of the two-year mobility rate.

different tenth of the current net income distribution is between 61 and 66 per cent. Shifting to an annual income measure suggests that Britain, Germany, Ireland and the USA have similar mobility, but that mobility is rather higher in Hungary. The annual income measure yields slightly lower mobility than the current income one in the cases of Germany and Britain, as one would expect, but not for Hungary. Spain's position in the mobility ranking is dependent on whether income or expenditure distributions are used. Surprisingly, mobility is much higher in the latter case – the reverse of what one would anticipate from the argument that there is less longitudinal variability in consumption than in income (see chapter 2).

The results for income and expenditure for Russia, however, have the expected relationship: income mobility is higher, although not by much. But the most notable finding for Russia, true with either measure, is that this country is a marked outlier in terms of mobility, with a substantially higher fraction of children changing decile group compared to the other countries: over 80 per cent. Arguably there is greater measurement error in the Russian data than in the other surveys and this is reflected in the mobility measure (more children move decile groups simply because it is more likely here than in other countries that the error with which their household income or expenditure is measured changes over the twelve months). However, the Russian survey appears to be a high-quality source. A more likely explanation for the result is simply that greater mobility is associated with the turbulence of change in this transition economy (see chapter 11 for further details).

The longer the interval between the years in which we classify children into income groups, the greater the degree of mobility which we would expect to see. For example in the USA the proportion of children who are in a different decile in year 1 and year 5 (i.e. $t-4$ and t) is about two thirds, compared with 57 per cent in a different decile group in year 1 and year 2 (i.e. $t-1$ and t).[6] Although similarities in mobility across countries remain the main impression, some differences seem to be appearing as the observation window is extended.[7]

More specifically, Hungary is confirmed as having greater child income mobility after four years than Britain, Germany or the USA (though the difference with Britain is not statistically significant). Among these latter three countries, mobility over five years in terms of annual income seems remarkably similar; there is no sign of the higher mobility in the USA that is often supposed to occur. After nine years, there appear some differences between German and American mobility, as long as one uses the annual income measures: 72 per cent change decile group in Germany compared to 78 per cent in the USA. The large difference between the German current and annual net income statistics, 72 per cent versus 77 per cent, reminds us that choice of definitions can influence the results substantially. For both the German and US data, it is clear that although the proportion of

---

[6] This assessment of mobility takes no account of what happens in the intervening years. For example, the one third of American children who are in the same decile group in years $t-4$ and t are not necessarily in the same group in each intervening year. An analogous comment applies to the intervening months for the two-wave results for 'current income'.

[7] The samples of children that we use are aged less than 18 in each year. Hence comparisons of income position in years $t-9$ and t are restricted to children aged 0–8 in year $t-9$, and comparisons for $t-1$ and t refer to children aged 0–16 in the first year. Differences in results as the observation window extends may therefore in part reflect a changing age composition of the samples.

children moving decile group rises as the interval is extended, the figure levels out relatively quickly.[8]

Given the way we chose to define the income groups for children (in terms of their rank in the income distribution), the estimates of our mobility measure are not affected by differences in income levels or the degree of inequality *per se*. Nonetheless, in practice there may well be a systematic relationship between mobility and inequality. A given change in household income is less likely to move a child across the boundaries of a decile group in a country where income is more unequally distributed – where the rungs on the income ladder are further apart – than it is in a country with less inequality where the deciles are closer together. In this situation an inverse relationship between income mobility and income inequality will be observed, provided the frequency and size of changes in incomes are similar in each country.[9] If, on the other hand, we observe a similar degree of mobility in countries that have notably different degrees of inequality, then this must imply that the changes that occur to income are larger or more frequent in the country where incomes are more dispersed.

Figure 4.1 shows how inequality among children and their mobility in the income distribution (over one year) are related in practice for our seven countries. There is no obvious relationship between them. The diagram puts into perspective the comment above about mobility in the USA relative to that in other countries. The USA has a much more unequal income distribution for children than Germany, but the probability of children changing places in the ranking from one year to the next is similar in the two countries. On the argument above, this means that incomes in the USA do change more often, or by larger amounts. But because incomes are more spread out in their country than incomes elsewhere, American children are nevertheless no more likely to change places with each other than children in other countries.

---

[8] We have also calculated results similar to table 4.3, but defining movers as people who move more than one decile group away from their original group. Measured in this way, mobility is much lower, implying that many moves in table 4.3 are by children moving only a short distance in the distribution. But the differences across countries are very similar to those found in table 4.3.

[9] This argument can be formalised using a stylised theoretical model of how the income distribution evolves over time. In a simple Galtonian autoregressive model of log income, the long-run steady-state degree of income mobility is summarised by the ratio of the inequality in income shocks to the total income inequality. If the variance of the income shock is held fixed, an inverse relationship between income mobility and income inequality results.

Figure 4.1. *Income inequality and income mobility among children*

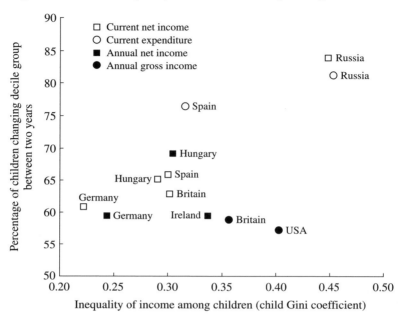

Continuing in this vein, one thing that the diagram does underline is the degree of mobility in Russia. Despite children's incomes in this country being more unequal than in the other six countries, the probability of moving within the distribution is, as noted earlier, substantially higher. Although the gaps between the rungs on the ladder are larger than elsewhere, there is a greater probability of moving up or down a rung.

Low-income persistence

Does the picture change if we focus on mobility at the bottom of the income distribution rather than the overall degree of mobility in the whole distribution? To answer this question, we look at the poorest fifth of children in each year – the bottom quintile group. We calculate the proportion of children who are found in this group *every* year over a specified number of years, and the proportion who are *ever* in the group over the

Table 4.4. *Low-income persistence of children*

Country	Percentage of children always in the bottom fifth				Percentage of children ever in the bottom fifth			
	In 1 wave[a]	2 out of 2 waves	5 out of 5 waves	10 out of 10 waves	In 1 wave	In 2 waves	In 5 waves	In 10 waves
Current net income								
Britain	19.7	14.1	4.6		19.7	27.2	41.1	
Germany	20.1	13.4	7.0		20.1	26.5	36.4	
West Germany	20.0	14.1	8.4	3.6	20.0	25.0	34.9	44.8
Hungary	19.8	13.1	5.6		19.8	26.5	42.3	
Russia	20.0	8.5			20.0	31.3		
Spain	20.0	13.3			20.0	26.8		
Current expenditure								
Russia	20.0	8.7			20.0	30.8		
Spain	20.0	11.4			20.0	28.6		
Annual net income								
Germany	19.9	12.9	6.9		19.9	27.0	38.3	
West Germany	20.0	13.5	6.4	4.8	20.0	26.4	37.5	43.7
Hungary	20.0	12.5	6.8		20.0	27.4	42.7	
Ireland	19.5	12.7			19.5	25.3		
Annual gross income								
Britain	19.8	13.9	6.4		19.8	27.1	39.0	
USA	20.0	14.2	9.3	6.2	20.0	25.6	32.9	41.3

Notes: [a] Percentages differ from 20 per cent because of the application of longitudinal weights to a cross-section from a longitudinal sample.

same interval.[10] The results are given in table 4.4, with a selection of them illustrated in figure 4.2.

The top panel of figure 4.2 shows, for different observation intervals, the percentage of children who were ever in the poorest fifth of the income distribution (of children) during each period. There is a separate line for each country, with the length of each line corresponding to the number of years of data available (for example, only two years for Russia, but up to ten years for the USA). The bottom panel is constructed similarly, except that now the summary is of the percentage of children who are in the poorest fifth of the income distribution in every year. All the lines start at 20 per cent in year 1 (with only one year to consider, the same fifth of children are 'always

[10] In the case of the five- and ten-wave results, we are therefore now considering the intervening years (see footnote 6), in contrast to the calculations of mobility given in table 4.3.

Figure 4.2 *Low-income persistence among children*

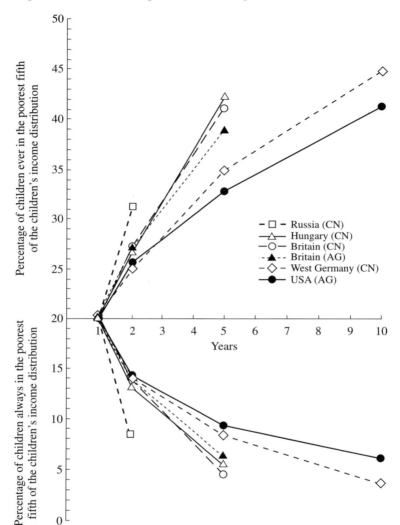

The letters in parentheses after the country name indicate the income concept: CN = current net income; AG = annual gross income. Source: table 4.4

poor' and 'ever poor'). The figures showing persistence over two years contain the same information as the exit rates from low income in the first year: the percentage of children in the poorest fifth of the distribution in the first year who leave by the second year is equal to 100 minus five times the figure for persistence in low income shown in table 4.4. For example, if 10 per cent of all children are in the bottom fifth for two consecutive years this means that the exit rate from low income is 50 per cent.

How does persistence of children in low income differ cross-nationally? When only two years are considered, the main impression given by table 4.4 is one of similarities rather than differences across the seven nations. In this sense the results are similar to those for overall income mobility described in the sub-section above. For Britain, Germany, Hungary, Ireland and the USA, between 12 per cent and 14 per cent of children are in the poorest fifth of the distribution for two consecutive years, and slightly less in Spain. (This implies that between 20 and 30 per cent of those in low income in the first year manage to escape.) Russia is again the outlier, with much less persistence in low income than the other countries. (More than half of children in the poorest fifth escape over twelve months.)

As the length of the observation window is extended for the relevant subset of countries, the degree of low-income persistence falls, as expected. But a significant number of children are found in the poorest fifth of the distribution for year after year, and differences across countries become more obvious. Taking a five-year window, the proportion varies from 5 per cent of all children on the basis of current net income in Britain to 9 per cent on the basis of annual gross income in the USA: about one in twenty and one in ten respectively. Persistence in low income is therefore higher in the USA than elsewhere. It is half as high again as in Britain, for example, when the same income concept is used.[11]

The comparison with Hungary and Germany is hampered by the differences in income definitions. On the basis of current net income the proportion of children with low income five years out of five in these two countries is 6 and 7 per cent respectively, just ahead of Britain. Over a ten-year interval, 6 per cent of American children are found with low annual income in every year and 5 per cent of West German children (gross and net income respectively). Hence one in twenty children in both countries spend ten consecutive years in low income.[12]

The proportion of children ever touched by low income – the right-hand side of table 4.4 and the top panel of figure 4.2 – rises as the observation

---

[11] The difference is statistically significant at the 1 per cent level.
[12] As with the analysis of overall mobility, it should be borne in mind that the ten-year results refer only to those children aged 0–8 in the first year.

window lengthens. Over two years the numbers are similar across countries, between 25 and 27 per cent on the basis of income, except in Russia where the greater mobility pushes the figure up to 31 per cent. Over five years one sees again that differences emerge. Hungary heads the rankings with 43 per cent of children found in the bottom fifth of the distribution in at least one year during the period on the basis of annual net income. This is ten percentage points more than in the USA, where the lowest proportion of children ever to be touched by low income in five years is found (one third). Britain comes below Hungary and ahead of Germany in the range. Over ten years, more than two fifths of children are found in low income at least once in both the USA and West Germany, with the higher of the two figures being for the German children – 44 per cent (on an annual basis) compared to 41 per cent.

Middle-class entry to low income – falling down the ladder

The incidence of low-income persistence among children is clearly of interest because of the repeated hardship this entails (with potential adverse consequences following childhood too). But one might also argue that the extent to which this influences the formation of policy depends on the perceived vulnerability of the 'middle classes' to becoming poor. An increase in their vulnerability may strengthen political support for income transfer programmes (or other policy measures) to reduce poverty. These considerations lead us to ask: how likely are middle-class children to experience poverty?

Our answer to this question is based on calculations of the percentage of children in the middle fifth of the children's income distribution in one year who are found in the poorest fifth of the distribution in a later year. This is shown in table 4.5. When we look at distributions one year apart, we find similarities across countries. The low income entry rate for those in the middle class is about 5–6 per cent, with two exceptions: Ireland and Russia. The Irish rate appears somewhat higher than this (10 per cent), and the Russian one definitely does – between 12 and 17 per cent depending on whether an income or expenditure measure is used. The higher Russian figure is in line with everything we have seen earlier concerning the greater mobility in this country. The Irish figure is a puzzle, however.

What would we judge to be a high – or a low – figure? In most countries, about one in twenty middle-class children fall down the ladder into low income the following year. Is this figure high enough for the middle class as a whole to feel a threat of a significant fall in income? This question is difficult to answer. It is not the actual figure itself that is critical; it is the

Table 4.5. *Middle-class entry to low income*

Country	Percentage of children in the middle fifth falling to the poorest fifth	
	Between years $t-1$ and t	Between years $t-4$ and t
Current net income		
Britain	4.7	13.3
Germany	4.7	9.5
West Germany	8.2	6.9
Hungary	4.9	9.4
Russia	12.8	
Spain	6.3	
Current expenditure		
Russia	17.1	
Spain	8.4	
Annual net income		
Germany	5.6	15.3
West Germany	6.1	9.5
Hungary	5.6	14.5
Ireland	10.0	
Annual gross income		
Britain	5.6	16.5
USA	4.4	9.2

perception that the fall could occur which will affect decisions, and the consequences of falling.

When the distributions being compared are five years apart, the entry rate to low income by middle-class children increases, and cross-national differences become more apparent. The higher levels are to be expected – over a longer period of time there is a greater probability that children from the middle classes will see their incomes change. Rates, for example, appear higher for Britain than for the USA (13 to 17 per cent depending on income definition compared to 9 per cent). Whether the vulnerability of Hungarian and (West) German children is nearer the endpoints of this range depends strongly on the choice of income measure: the rates based on current net income are markedly lower than the measures based on annual net income.

4.4 Poverty transitions

What fraction of children live in households that have incomes that are well below the average, how likely are they to enter this state, what are their chances of leaving, and how long do they stay there? In the previous section we defined disadvantage as being in the poorest fifth of the income distribution. In this section we return to a conventional measure of relative poverty, as used in chapter 3 and in much of the rest of the book. That is, children are classified as poor in a particular year if the income of their household (adjusted for household size) is below half the median household income of all people in their country in that year.

We noted at the start of this chapter that, in general, we expect rates of entry to and exit from poverty (and hence the lengths of poverty spells) to be related to the poverty rate itself. This provides a motivation for a focus on the poorest fifth of children in each case so as to standardise across country, as in the previous section. Throughout this section, however, we use a definition of disadvantage that results in a poverty rate which does vary markedly across our seven countries. We therefore need to justify our earlier statement. Having done this, we go on to describe how the pattern of poverty flows varies across the different countries.

Poverty rates and poverty flows

The relationship between entries and exits and the poverty rate is easiest to see in the situation where the poverty rate does not change over time and where there is no statistical association at all between incomes this year and next year (in the sense that being poor this year conveys no information about whether one is more or less likely to be poor next year). In this case, the entry rate to poverty is equal to the poverty rate, and the exit rate is equal to one minus the poverty rate. In other words, higher poverty rates mean higher chances of entry to poverty and lower chances of exit from poverty.

These relationships become more complicated when incomes in one year are associated with incomes in the next year, but the general point still holds. In countries with higher poverty rates we should expect to see the rate at which children enter poverty to be higher and the rate at which they leave poverty to be lower than in countries with lower poverty rates. Indeed, in one sense this is very obvious. To turn the argument the other way around, if the rate at which children enter poverty is higher than elsewhere and the rate at which they leave poverty is lower, then the overall proportion found to be poor at any one time is bound to be higher.

To go further with our investigation of the issue and then to inspect our data, it is useful to distinguish four measures of poverty flows:

(a) *the exit rate:* the number of children leaving poverty expressed as a proportion of the number of children who were poor;

(b) *the outflow fraction:* the number of children leaving poverty expressed as a proportion of the total number of children in the population (whether they were poor or not);

(c) *the entry rate:* the number of children entering poverty expressed as a proportion of the number of children who were not poor;

(d) *the inflow fraction:* the number of children entering poverty expressed as a proportion of the total number of children in the population (whether they were poor or not).

The rates and fractions represent alternative ways of normalising the number of movements into and out of poverty when looking at the change in the number of poor children between one year and the next. (The exit rate and the outflow fraction have the same numerator but different denominators, and so too do the entry rate and the inflow fraction.) If one assumes that the total number of children in the population remains constant, then one can say that the number of children poor this year is equal to the number of children poor last year, plus the number entering poverty between last year and this year, minus the number leaving poverty between last year and this year. If one normalises these raw numbers by the total number of children in the population, then one can say that this year's poverty rate is equal to last year's poverty rate plus the inflow fraction minus the outflow fraction. Alternatively, and restating the identity in terms of rates rather than fractions, this year's poverty rate equals last year's poverty rate multiplied by one minus the poverty exit rate, plus the poverty entry rate multiplied by one minus last year's poverty rate.[13] If the inflow and outflow fractions are equal, then the child poverty rate stays constant.

These relationships highlight why one should be interested in rates for studying the evolution of poverty. But one cannot simply compare entry and exit rates across countries as the identities might suggest. The problem is that the elements on the right-hand side of each identity are related to each other: one cannot just take the poverty rate as fixed and compare rates. The normalisations used to construct the flow rates and fractions convert the raw numbers to a comparable numerical scale. But they do not standardise for the link between the poverty rate and the exit rate and entry rate (or outflow and inflow fraction) – relationships that may vary across countries.

---

[13] This restatement uses the fact that the inflow fraction equals the entry rate multiplied by one minus last year's poverty rate, and the outflow fraction equals the exit rate multiplied by last year's poverty rate. These relationships are used to construct figures 4.3 and 4.4.

Inflow and outflow fractions will typically be higher in countries with higher poverty rates. This is because a high poverty rate usually means that the poverty line will be placed in a section of the income distribution containing more children, and so for a given amount of income movement more children will move across the line (in both directions).[14]

The exit rate is the average probability that a poor child will leave poverty. It depends on both the number of exits from poverty and the size of the poor population from which those exits must come. For a given number of exits, a higher poverty rate will mean a lower exit rate, since the size of the poor population is larger. The association between the exit rate and the poverty rate is thus governed by two opposing relationships. First, more poverty means a higher outflow fraction. Second, more poverty means that this outflow is occurring from a larger number of poor children. The second effect can be expected to dominate – with *higher* poverty rates being associated with *lower* exit rates. Now consider the entry rate. First, more poverty means a higher inflow fraction and, second, more poverty means that this inflow comes from a smaller number of non-poor children. So in this case the effects work in the same direction, and a higher poverty rate will be associated with a higher entry rate.

Cross-national differences

The discussion indicates that it is useful to examine cross-national differences in entry and exit rates within the context of differences in aggregate flows (summarised by inflow and outflow fractions) and poverty rates. Figures 4.3 and 4.4 summarise the variations across our seven nations. The horizontal axis in each diagram shows the child poverty rate. (These are the rates in year $t-1$ rather than year t as in table 4.2.) The vertical axis in each diagram shows the (normalised) number of movements by children into and out of poverty between two years. In figure 4.3 this is the outflow fraction and in figure 4.4 it is the inflow fraction. In most countries poverty rates changed little over the two years concerned and so the inflow and outflow fractions for each country are very similar (Russia and Hungary are the key exceptions).

The straight lines drawn within these two diagrams show contours of the

---

[14] This assumes that the concentration of children at points along the income range is increasing as income rises, which is usually the case at levels of income around the poverty line. It also depends on how we define a 'given amount of income movement'. In the simple Galtonian model of mobility described in footnote 9, this result will apply if we define mobility in terms of the correlation between incomes in one period and the next.

Figure 4.3. *Movements out of child poverty and the child poverty rate*

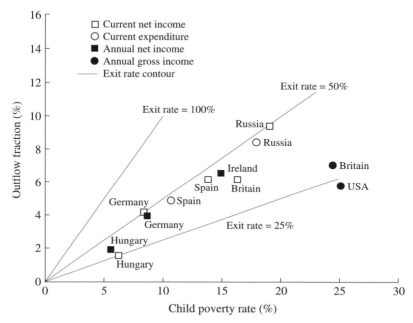

The child poverty rate = number of poor children at $t - 1$ divided by the total number of children at $t - 1$. The outflow fraction = number of children leaving poverty between $t - 1$ and t divided by the total number of children at $t - 1$ = the exit rate multiplied by the child poverty rate at $t - 1$.

entry and exit rates respectively – that is, lines along which the values of these rates are the same. The lines in figure 4.3 coming out from the origin (the point where the two axes meet) represent three different exit rates – 25, 50, and 100 per cent. Each of these contours shows the combinations of the poverty rate (horizontal axis) and the outflow fraction (vertical axis) that correspond to the exit rate concerned. Similarly, the lines in figure 4.4 drawn from the 100 per cent point on the horizontal (poverty rate) axis – well off to the right of the edge of the diagram – show three different entry rates – 5, 10, and 15 per cent. Each of these lines shows the combinations of the poverty rate (horizontal axis) and the inflow fraction (vertical axis) that correspond to the entry rate concerned.

In both Russia and Hungary, child poverty increased significantly during the survey period and this is reflected by the inflow fractions being larger than the outflow fractions. In other words, these countries come much higher up on the vertical axis in figure 4.4 than they do on the same axis in

Figure 4.4. *Movements into child poverty and the child poverty rate*

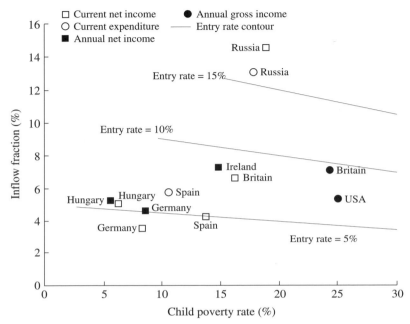

The child poverty rate = number of poor children at $t-1$ divided by the total number of children at $t-1$. The inflow fraction = number of children entering poverty between $t-1$ and t divided by the total number of children at $t-1$ = the entry rate multiplied by one minus the child poverty rate at $t-1$.

figure 4.3. Between 1994 and 1995, the Russian child poverty rate increased by five percentage points (see table 4.2). Figures 4.3 and 4.4 show that this increase arose from an inflow fraction of from 13 to 15 per cent (depending upon the income definition) and an outflow fraction of 8 to 10 per cent. The previous section showed that Russia also stood out as having a particularly high level of mobility – Russia comes highest on the vertical axis of figure 4.1 as well as in figures 4.3 and 4.4. Hungarian child poverty increased by almost as much as in Russia, but from a much lower base.

Across the other countries and income definitions, the exit rates are roughly constant in some cases – the symbols for four countries in figure 4.3 are just below the 50 per cent line coming out from the origin, implying that nearly half of poor children leave poverty each year. In other cases the symbols are lower as the poverty rate increases, with the annual gross figures for Britain and the USA being the most obvious examples (their symbols are well out to the right, near the 25 per cent exit rate line).

As discussed earlier, the switch from gross to net income measures does make quite a difference to the poverty rate in Britain. However, in terms of the number of children entering or leaving poverty as a percentage of all children (the values on the vertical axes) the definitional change again makes little difference. But since this mobility is coming from a smaller number of poor children when we measure poverty using net income, the exit rate in this case is higher. We see that the symbol for current net income for Britain lies closer to the 50 per cent exit rate line while that for annual gross income lies closer to the 25 per cent line. Although Britain and the USA have a similar child poverty rate according to annual gross income, Britain has a slightly higher exit rate (though this difference is not quite statistically significant).

For the two countries where we have both annual and current net income (Germany and Hungary) neither poverty levels nor flows seem to vary much with changes in the period over which incomes are measured. The current gross income results for Britain are not shown in figure 4.3 but are very similar to the annual gross results.

The income definition that is available for the greatest number of countries is current net income. Using this measure, the proportion of all children who leave poverty between the two years varies from under 2 per cent for Hungary to over 9 per cent for Russia. The spread of entry into poverty is even greater, ranging from over 14 per cent of all children for Russia to fewer than 4 per cent for Germany. Almost one in five (18 per cent) of those Russian children who were not poor in 1995 were below the poverty line in 1996.

Leaving the transition economies of Russia and Hungary to one side, the differences between the countries found in the movements into and out of poverty are less, but still considerable. In Germany, about 4 per cent of all children entered and 4 per cent left poverty between the two years, while in Britain 6 per cent left and 7 per cent entered. The child poverty rate in Britain was around double that of Germany, so in terms of the probability that a poor child will leave poverty over the subsequent year (the exit rate), the ranking is reversed – it is Britain that has the lower exit rate (which can be seen in figure 4.3 by comparing where the symbols lie with respect to the lines coming out of the origin). In 1995, about 8 per cent of German children were below the half median poverty line. One year later, half of these children had incomes above the poverty line. In Britain, on the other hand, even though more children left poverty as a percentage of all children, only 38 per cent of the children poor in 1995 were above the poverty line twelve months later.

For the most part, both poverty levels and poverty flows in Spain lie between those of Germany and Britain, while the situation in Ireland is similar to that of Britain (the net income symbols for the two countries are close to each other in both figures 4.3 and 4.4). In Spain, the pattern of poverty entries and exits does vary somewhat according to the income measure used. While poverty measured according to expenditure increased slightly, when measured using current income it fell by two percentage points between 1991 and 1992 (see table 4.2). This can be seen in the higher number of Spanish children leaving poverty according to this definition (figure 4.3) and the lower number entering (figure 4.4).

Child poverty entry and exit rates

The discussion above left open the question of whether it is more useful to summarise flows in terms of fractions or in terms of rates. Analysts focus on exit and entry rates because these have the closest links with the behavioural relationships that they like to model. The entry rate can be interpreted as an average probability that a non-poor child will enter poverty, and a natural development from this is to use multivariate methods to model individual probabilities of entry, allowing for heterogeneity about the average, for which the estimation sample comprises those who are not poor (rather than the population as a whole). Similarly the exit rate is the average probability that a poor child will leave poverty and a natural development from this is a multivariate model of each child's probability of exit from poverty, based on the children who are currently poor. Let us therefore focus explicitly on the estimates of child poverty entry and exit rates for our seven nations (notwithstanding the standardisation issues). See table 4.6.

There is clearly substantial cross-national heterogeneity in entry rates, regardless of which income definition is used. Obviously Russia has much the highest entry rate. Using a current net income definition, the rate, some 18 per cent, is roughly twice as large as the next highest rate, that for Britain (8 per cent). The range below this is quite large, with the smallest rate being for West Germany, about 3 per cent. The rates for the united Germany are a couple of percentage points higher, and those for Spain and Hungary slightly higher still. There is only a single entry rate estimate for the USA – that using an annual gross income definition. The rate is just over 7 per cent, a couple of percentage points smaller than the corresponding British estimate.

When we look at the estimates of child poverty exit rates, Russia is no longer an outlier. About one half of all poor Russian children leave poverty

Table 4.6. *Child poverty entry rates and exit rates*

Country	Entry rate (%)	Exit rate (%)
Current net income		
Russia	17.9	49.5
Britain	8.0	38.0
Spain	5.0	44.8
Hungary	5.3	25.1
Germany	3.9	51.8
West Germany	2.7	43.2
Current expenditure		
Russia	15.9	47.1
Spain	6.4	45.9
Annual net income		
Ireland	7.6	42.9
Germany	5.1	46.0
Hungary	5.6	34.6
West Germany	3.1	46.2
Annual gross income		
USA	7.2	23.1
Britain	9.4	28.8

Notes: The entry and exit rates refer to movements into and out of poverty between year
$t-1$ and year t. Countries are sorted within each income definition in descending order of
the child poverty rate.

between one year and the next, a rate which is of the same order as that in
Germany (using a current income definition) and Spain (using a current
expenditure definition). Now it is Hungary which stands out, in this case
for having a relatively low exit rate: 25 per cent according to the current
income definition and 35 per cent according to the annual net income one.
Arguably the USA also has a relatively low exit rate. At 23 per cent (using
annual gross income), it is markedly lower than the corresponding rate for
Britain (29 per cent), and with the other income definitions Britain's exit
rate lies between the extremes of the range.

Poverty persistence

When discussing earlier the persistence in low income (being in the poorest
fifth of the distribution) over two years, we noted that the exit rate from low
income in the first year and the proportion of all children who are in low

income in both years contain the same information. An analogous situation is true of persistence in poverty.[15] And, as with table 4.4, we can extend this concept of persistence over a longer interval by looking at the percentage of children who are poor five years out of five, or ten years out of ten. The patterns for persistence in poverty need not of course mimic the earlier ones for low income. Indeed, the cross-country picture will reflect in part the differences in poverty rates and hence, on the argument above, exit rates.

This is confirmed by the results shown in table 4.7. For example, poverty persistence appears to be relatively high in Britain and the USA, but these are the countries with the highest cross-sectional poverty rates (the 'in 1 wave' figures are the cross-sectional poverty rate in the latest wave of data). And Germany has relatively low persistence but also has a low cross-sectional poverty rate.

In one sense the table may be interpreted optimistically, for it shows that as the window of observation is extended, the number of children who are persistently poor falls quite sharply. The proportion poor in every one of five years is about one half (or smaller) of the proportion poor two years out of two for those countries where we have data. On the other hand, the sheer numbers of children in persistent poverty over the longer periods are alarming in some countries: roughly speaking one in ten children are found poor for five consecutive years on the basis of annual gross income in both Britain and the USA. These countries had virtually identical one-year poverty rates on this income measure (25 per cent), which means that the problem of comparing flows when poverty rates differ substantially does not arise. Persistence of poverty over five years was actually somewhat higher in the USA: 13 per cent of all American children were poor in every year compared to 9 per cent of British children.[16]

A much more positive picture is found in those countries with lower cross-section poverty rates. In both West Germany and Hungary only around 2 per cent of children were poor for the full five years.

The right-hand side of table 4.7 reinforces the pessimistic view of the sit-

[15] The proportion of all children who spend two out of two years poor is given by one minus the exit rate multiplied by the reciprocal of the poverty rate in the first wave. This proportion can also be read off figure 4.3, since the number of children who are poor two out of two years is equal to the number poor in year $t - 1$ minus the number who leave poverty the next year. Hence, lines drawn parallel to the 100 per cent line in figure 4.3 represent contours (lines where the value is unchanged) of the two-out-of-two rate, with values read off from the intersection of these lines with the horizontal axis.

[16] The difference is significantly different at the 1 per cent level. Indeed, the average poverty rate across the five years was slightly lower for the USA (24 versus 25 per cent) reinforcing the conclusion that the difference is due to the different mobility patterns in the two countries.

Table 4.7. *Poverty persistence among children*

Country	Percentage of children with household income always below half median income				Percentage of children with household income ever below half median income			
	In 1 wave	2 out of 2 waves	5 out of 5 waves	10 out of 10 waves	In 1 wave	In 2 waves	In 5 waves	In 10 waves
Current net income								
Britain	16.8	10.1	3.3		16.8	22.9	39.3	
Germany	7.7	4.1	1.5		7.7	11.9	15.6	
West Germany	6.8	4.3	1.7	2.2	6.8	10.0	14.5	21.3
Hungary	9.7	4.6	2.1		9.7	11.2	19.5	
Russia	24.1	9.6			24.1	33.5		
Spain	11.9	7.6			11.9	18.1		
Current expenditure								
Russia	22.5	9.5			22.5	31.0		
Spain	11.5	5.7			11.5	16.4		
Annual net income								
Germany	9.3	4.7	0.7		9.3	13.2	17.9	
West Germany	6.9	4.1	2.0	0.4	6.9	10.4	16.3	21.5
Hungary	8.9	3.6	2.2		8.9	10.8	17.5	
Ireland	15.6	8.3			15.6	21.3		
Annual gross income								
Britain	24.5	17.4	9.3		24.5	31.5	43.0	
USA	24.7	19.3	13.0	6.8	24.7	30.4	37.6	44.7

uation: the proportion of all children who are 'touched' by poverty at some time increases sharply as one considers a longer interval of time. For example, the proportion of children in West Germany experiencing poverty at least once over five years is more than twice the proportion of children poor at a point in time. The percentage touched by poverty at least once over ten years is three times larger than the cross-section rate. In those countries with five years of data, the number experiencing poverty is never less than one in seven on any definition of income and is as much as 40 per cent or more in Britain. Over ten years, even in Germany the figure rises to one in five and it is double this in the USA.

The comparison of the annual gross income figures over five years for Britain and the USA shows Britain to be the country where more children are in poverty for at least one year. This is the corollary of the larger fraction of US children who are poor in all years over a five-year period shown in the left-hand side of the table. While it is not logically necessary that the two patterns be linked, if mobility is generally less in the USA we would expect to find fewer children experiencing poverty. Given some fixed level of poverty in each year, the concentration of poverty among a smaller group does mean that the remaining children will be less likely to experience poverty.

For all countries, the figures in the right-hand side of table 4.7 are a reminder of the much larger numbers of children that are likely to have been helped by benefits targeted at families with low income if one takes a longer timeframe than one year.

4.5 A closer look at dynamics

In this section we examine two aspects of child poverty dynamics in greater detail for our seven countries. First, we focus on the 'near poor' – those children just above the poverty line – and examine the extent to which movements into and out of poverty involve this group. Second, we provide information about how entry and exit rates differ between children in lone-parent households and those households where both parents are present.

'Near poverty' and movements around the line

We are interested in the extent to which movements into or out of poverty involve small or large changes in income. If the majority of income changes over the poverty line are small, then the exits and entries that we have been counting are less likely to involve the discrete changes in living standards which the zero/one measure of poverty ('out' or 'in') suggests. Viewed another way, if a large number of entries and exits involve those just above the line, then many children may be thought of as 'hovering' near poverty. An exit from poverty, for example, may well not represent a genuine escape from low living standards.

Table 4.8 shows the share of entries and exits to and from poverty over a one-year period that involve those children that come just above the poverty line – the 'near poor'. We use the same poverty line of half national median income used earlier, and define 'near poverty' to be having an income between 50 and 60 per cent of the median. The near-poverty estimates may be contrasted with the child poverty entry and exit rates that were given in table 4.6. The countries are sorted in table 4.8 within each income definition in descending order of the child poverty rate, an order-

Table 4.8. *Entry from and exit to 'near poverty'*

	Children entering poverty		Children exiting poverty	
	Share of entries coming from 'near poverty' (%)	Share of entries coming from 'near poverty' and going to 'just below' the line (%)	Share of exits going to 'near poverty' (%)	Share of exits going to 'near poverty' and coming from 'just below' the line (%)
Current net income				
Russia	10.4	3.5	19.9	6.7
Britain	57.2	40.3	43.9	20.7
Spain	38.1	22.4	36.9	17.1
Hungary	56.6	48.4	33.8	23.0
Germany	53.7	36.2	37.3	30.7
West Germany	39.1	26.1	29.5	27.2
Current expenditure				
Russia	17.5	6.6	21.8	11.3
Spain	29.7	19.6	30.8	19.2
Annual net income				
Ireland	33.2	25.9	47.3	44.8
Germany	41.7	13.1	29.5	12.6
Hungary	44.1	35.9	47.3	21.9
West Germany	21.3	7.5	37.0	8.9
Annual gross income				
USA	38.9	16.9	28.9	18.9
Britain	29.1	15.6	33.2	14.8

Notes: 'Near poverty' is defined as income in the range 50–60 per cent of the median; 'just below' the line is defined as income in the range 40–50 per cent of the median. Countries are sorted within each income definition in descending order of the child poverty rate.

ing that corresponds quite well to that given by the entry rate, as our reasoning at the beginning of the last section would lead one to expect.[17]

There is no particular reason to expect the share of entries that come from children in near poverty to correspond to the share of all exits to the same income range. It may be that small increases in income, for example those that come from annual wage increments, are more common than small reductions, with falls in income, when they happen, being more likely to be large. (On the other hand, it is easy to think of many examples when

---

[17] The child poverty rates are those for all children in the data in both sampled years and are the same as those displayed on the horizontal axes in figures 4.3 and 4.4.

rises in income could be large too, for example when a parent gets a job or a lone parent re-partners.) In this case, the profile of income changes over time may be a series of small rises punctuated by occasional sharp falls. If this were the general pattern of income change we would typically observe a larger share of exits from poverty going to near poverty – as families moved from just below to just over the poverty threshold – than the share of entries coming from the same income range, reflecting the larger income falls that those entering poverty were experiencing.

Looking first at the results for current net income, we see that, if anything, with this income definition the opposite pattern is found. In all but one case, Russia, the share of entries from near poverty is higher than the share of exits that go to near poverty. In three cases, Britain, Hungary and Germany, the entry share is a lot higher. In Hungary it is over twenty percentage points higher. Child poverty rose sharply between the two years in question in this country (see the final column of table 4.2) and it may be that this is the explanation, the rise in poverty being driven by a fall in income among households with children that were hovering near the poverty line. But the figures for Russia, where poverty among children rose even more over the twelve months concerned, show that no such general rule applies.

According to the current net income measure, about a third (or rather more) of all exits are to near poverty in most cases, but with a notably larger share than this found in Britain (44 per cent) and a lower share (20 per cent) in Russia, where we have emphasised that recorded income mobility is greater than elsewhere. A notable minority of children who leave poverty are therefore not seeing their family incomes improve by a great deal. But viewed another way, the majority of exits in all countries do involve increases in income that take previously poor children a significant distance (in percentage terms) away from the poverty line.

Staying with the current net income measure, the same sort of statement that has just been made does not apply to entries to poverty. In the case of the three countries mentioned above, Britain, Hungary and Germany, a minority of entries are coming from above 60 per cent of median income. In these countries the majority of entries come from the near-poor children. (It is notable, however, that the figures for Germany as a whole and West Germany are rather different.) Russia, with its greater mobility, is the real exception – here only one in ten entries are from among the near-poor children.

Turning to other income measures, the pattern of results changes somewhat, emphasising the danger in telling a general story based on a particular measure. In the case of current expenditure, the shares of entries from and exits to near poverty in Spain are lower than for current net income, reflecting the (surprisingly) greater mobility of children on the basis of expenditure that we noted earlier in section 4.3. The annual net income figures show only one country, Germany, to have a higher share of entries from near poverty than exits to this state, so the general pattern seen with the current net income figures is not repeated. The larger share in the case of exits is particularly notable for Ireland – only a third of entries are from near-poor children but nearly a half of exits by children are to near poverty. In the case of Hungary, the switch from current to annual net income leads to the share of entries from near poverty falling, from 57 per cent to 44 per cent. In contrast to the situation with current net income, the use of the annual net measure means that there are no countries where the majority of entries come from among the near-poor children.

The figures for annual gross income for Britain show notably lower shares for the entries from and exits to near poverty than for current net income, especially for entries. The share of entries by British children from near poverty on the basis of annual gross income is only half that found for current income – 29 per cent compared to 57 per cent. The figure for the USA for exits is similar to that for Britain, with both showing somewhat more (Britain) or less (USA) than 30 per cent of exits going to near poverty. These two countries' annual income figures clearly show that the majority of both entries and exits do not involve near-poor children.

Finally, we look at the share of all entries that involve movement, not only from near poverty but that also go to an income range just below the poverty line, namely 40–50 per cent of median income. Similarly, in the case of exits we measure the share of children that both go to near poverty and also start from 40–50 per cent of the median range. The percentage shares in each case are given in the second column under each of the 'Children entering poverty' and 'Children exiting poverty' headings. These are the movements over the poverty line that involve smaller income changes than others, although it should be noted that they include moves that are both very small, for example from 51 to 49 per cent of the median, and those that are considerably larger, for example from 60 to 40 per cent. While the former implies a very small change in living standards (and might be due to merely a change in the error with which income is measured from one wave of a panel survey to the next), the latter will be associated with a more appreciable fall.

These figures show great diversity, but the patterns naturally reflect those for all entries from and exits to near poverty. Whereas only 4 per cent of all entries to poverty in Russia on the basis of current net income involved a movement from 50–60 per cent of the median to 40–50 per cent, the figure was as high as 48 per cent in Hungary. For exits, only 9 per cent of the total in West Germany on the basis of annual net income involved movement from 'just below' the line to near poverty above the line, whereas this was the case in 45 per cent of all exits in Ireland. A general result coming out of the table is that the great majority of entries and exits by children on most income definitions do not involve movement between 'near poverty' and being 'just below' the poverty line.

These last results in table 4.8 can be seen as strengthening our confidence in much of what we are measuring. Most movements across the poverty line are the result of income changes that are not insignificant. But the other results in the table tell us that a significant minority of movements into and out of poverty in most countries do involve incomes that are not a great deal higher than the poverty line. This is a reminder that children experiencing poverty at some time in their childhood may often be close to being poor at other times.

Children in lone-parent households

We now turn to explore the movements into and out of poverty by children in lone-parent households. It is well known from cross-section studies (see chapter 3) that children in lone-parent households suffer higher poverty rates than other children. What does this higher poverty risk imply about these children's entry and exit rates?

In table 4.9 we show a number of indicators comparing the poverty status of children in lone-parent households with that of all children, taking, as before, a poverty line of half the national median income (adjusted for household size). For pragmatic reasons our definition of 'lone-parent' households is a restricted one. Children are defined as being in a 'lone-parent' household if their household contains one, and only one, adult, and this is true in both the most recent survey wave and in the previous year. This definition means that households comprising children plus a parent and other adult relatives will not be included among our definition of lone-parent households. Nor does our definition require the single adult to be a parent. The restriction to children in lone-parent households in both surveyed years means that we cannot describe the movements into and out of poverty associated with demographic changes such as divorce or separation and re-marriage, factors that we noted in chapter 2 as important causes of entry and exit (especially the former). Our definition means that we can only look at the movements that children in lone-parent households make into and out of poverty once they are already in such households.

As we have already seen in chapter 3, the prevalence of lone parenthood varies widely across industrialised countries, including the seven that are

Table 4.9. *Poverty and exits from poverty for children in lone-parent households*

Country	Children in lone-parent households as a share of:			Poverty rates		Outflow fractions	
	All children (%)	Poor children (%)	All poverty exits (%)	Lone-parent households (%)	All children (%)	Lone-parent children (%)	All children (%)
Current net income							
Britain	15.0	41.2	33.5	44.7	16.3	13.8	6.2
Russia	6.4	11.7	7.8	35.0	19.0	11.5	9.4
Germany	7.7	31.2	19.5	33.6	8.3	10.6	4.2
Spain	2.2	5.6	5.0	35.7	13.8	14.2	6.2
Hungary	7.0	6.5	17.1	5.8	6.2	3.9	1.6
Current expenditure							
Russia	6.4	10.7	9.3	30.0	17.9	12.3	8.4
Spain	2.2	4.9	6.2	23.8	10.6	13.7	4.9
Annual net income							
Ireland	2.9	12.6	3.1	65.2	14.9	7.0	6.5
Germany	7.7	31.5	19.7	35.1	8.6	10.1	4.0
Hungary	7.0	11.6	16.2	9.3	5.6	4.5	1.9
Annual gross income							
Britain	12.7	37.6	23.8	72.2	24.4	13.2	7.0
USA	22.3	56.9	35.9	63.9	25.1	9.3	5.8

the focus in this chapter. The figures in the first column of table 4.9 differ somewhat from those for the same countries in table 3.3 (there are differences in the data sources and in the particular samples drawn from them), but the basic picture is the same. In Spain and Ireland only 2 to 3 per cent of children are in lone-parent households, while over one fifth are in such households in the USA. Britain also has a high lone-parenthood rate, while the remaining countries have between 6 and 8 per cent of children in lone-parent households.

In all countries, except for Hungary (where there are only thirty-six lone-parent households in our sample), the poverty rate for children in lone-parent families is higher than for other children, so that their share of poverty (given in the second column in the table) is greater than their population share. In Spain, about a quarter to a third of lone-parent children are poor, in Russia and Germany about a third, and in Ireland, Britain and the USA the figure is around a half to two thirds. These comprise over half of all poor children in the USA, around 40 per cent in the UK, and a third in Germany. In Russia, Spain and Hungary lone-parent children make up a small proportion of poor children.

From our discussion in section 4.4, we expect that higher poverty rates for children in lone-parent households will mean a greater number of such children moving into and out of poverty than children as a whole. This is indeed the case here. Excluding Hungary and Ireland, where sample sizes are small, the table shows that the outflow fraction is about 8 to 14 per cent for lone-parent children. Similar fractions of lone-parent children enter poverty (not shown in the table). These are higher than the inflow and outflow fractions for all children, which are generally between 4 and 9 per cent (see figures 4.3 and 4.4).

However, these flows out from poverty need to be assessed in the context of the larger proportion of lone-parent children who are poor. For any given poor child, the probability of leaving poverty over the following year is almost always lower if he or she lives in a lone-parent household, that is the exit rate is lower for lone-parent children. This can be seen from the fact that the proportion of all exits from poverty which are made by lone-parent children (the third column in table 4.9), is, except in Hungary and in Spain (on the basis of expenditure), lower than the share of all poor children who are in lone-parent households (given in the second column).

The differences in exit rates between children in lone-parent households and other children are shown directly in table 4.10. In most cases the exit rate for lone-parent children is well below that of other children. The table also shows the differences in entry rates to poverty. Again, one can see that lone-parent children have a much higher risk of becoming poor. Indeed, the difference in entry rates is even more notable than that for exit rates in some

Table 4.10. *Poverty exit and entry rates: children in lone-parent households and other children*

	Exit rate			Entry rate		
	Lone-parent children (%)	Other children (%)	Ratio[a]	Lone-parent children (%)	Other children (%)	Ratio[b]
Current net income						
Britain	30.9	42.9	0.7	24.2	4.5	5.4
Russia	32.8	51.7	0.6	22.7	17.5	1.3
Germany	31.5	58.7	0.5	16.0	2.8	5.7
Spain	39.7	45.1	0.9	10.8	4.8	2.2
Hungary	67.3	22.7	3.0	4.0	5.5	0.7
Current expenditure						
Russia	41.0	47.9	0.9	23.3	15.3	1.5
Spain	57.8	45.2	1.3	10.1	6.4	1.6
Annual net income						
Ireland	10.7	48.8	0.2	16.9	8.3	2.0
Germany	28.8	54.0	0.5	26.1	3.1	8.4
Hungary	48.2	32.8	1.5	11.4	5.1	2.2
Annual gross income						
Britain	18.3	35.2	0.5	15.6	8.2	1.9
USA	14.5	34.3	0.4	17.2	3.0	5.8

Notes: [a] Ratio of exit rate for lone-parent children to exit rate for other children.   [b] Ratio of entry rate for lone-parent children to entry rate for other children.

cases. Lone-parent children have an entry rate that is six or eight times the rate for other children in Germany (depending on the definition of income that is taken) and, on the basis of current income, twice as high in Spain and five times higher in Britain. In the USA, lone-parent children have an exit rate that is less than half that of other children but their entry rate is nearly six times as high. However, comparison of the different British results based on current net and annual gross incomes shows that the results can be sensitive to the income measure taken. In contrast to the results with current net income, the annual gross figures show lone-parent children in Britain to suffer the same disadvantage on both entry and exit rates – they are twice as likely as other children to enter and half as likely to exit.

Discussion of lone-parent poverty is often framed in terms of the policy required to move lone parents out of poverty. In other words, the focus is on increasing the exit rate. Our results in table 4.10 show that addressing the problem is as much, or more, a case of preventing lone-parent children from becoming poor in the first place – a case of taking action to reduce the entry rate.

4.6 Summary and conclusions

This chapter has presented many new results on the movements made by children into and out of poverty in a range of industrialised countries. In doing so we have extended in several important respects what was known from the findings of the pioneering cross-national study of low-income dynamics of families with children of Duncan *et al.* (1993). We have looked at a different set of countries to Duncan and his colleagues (although with some overlap); we addressed the issue of standardising for differences in the number of poor children across countries; we have shown the sensitivity of results to different income measures; and we have focused firmly on the child as the unit of analysis rather than the family.

Our results underline that the longitudinal perspective of child poverty adds a great deal to one's view of childhood deprivation. Some of our key findings are as follows:

- Around 60 per cent of children who were found in low income (the poorest fifth of all children) in most countries in one year were still there the next year.
- Nine per cent of US children were in the poorest fifth in every year of a five-year window and around 6–8 per cent of children were in the same situation in Britain, Germany and Hungary.
- Over a ten-year window at least 40 per cent of German and US children were found in the poorest fifth at least once.
- One in ten children in Britain and the USA are found in poverty (defined using a half median line) in five consecutive years.
- Between 15 and 20 per cent of children in Germany and Hungary, and about 40 to 45 per cent of children in Britain and the USA were found in poverty (below half of median income) at least once over five years.
- There are notably higher rates of entry to poverty as well as lower rates of exit from poverty by children in lone-parent households.

One feature of our results that contrasts with those in the previous chapter is the similarity in some of the patterns of income and poverty mobility among children in the seven countries we have studied. Whereas chapter 3 showed clear differences across countries in the cross-sectional incidence of child poverty, in this chapter we have seen correspondence in some aspects (although certainly not all) of the dynamic picture of deprivation. We find, for example, that longer-term indicators of poverty follow much the same pattern of variation across countries as do short-term indicators. Admittedly, this may be due to the fact that for several countries we have only been able to examine living standards over two consecutive years.

Future research that exploits a larger number of longer panels may find more clear differences between countries.

Perhaps the most interesting example of cross-country similarity, however, does not suffer from a limitation on the length of the observation window. As was emphasised in the previous chapter, the USA stands out as a country with both a high average standard of living and a high child poverty rate. In this chapter we have been able to see if the high US poverty rate among children is 'compensated for' by a greater degree of turnover – by a more equally shared experience of being poor. Exploiting the longer panels at our disposal, we have been able to compare the dynamics of poverty in the USA over a period of five years with those in three other countries and over ten years with one other. We do not find any evidence that the less-regulated US economy is associated with greater mobility by children across the income distribution or by more movements into and out of poverty. Indeed, in some respects mobility in the USA appears to be less than in countries such as Britain and Germany.

The most obvious exception to any broad conclusion of uniformity in dynamic patterns of deprivation is that of Russia. The turmoil of economic transition has led to great income mobility and large movements into and out of poverty. Russian children in the mid-1990s were much more likely to move into or out of the group forming the poorest fifth than were children in the other countries that we have studied. When the Russian economy stabilises, it is likely that the high rates of flow into and out of poverty that we observe will begin to decline to the levels seen in the other countries in our study.

The conventional cross-sectional poverty rate will be a misleading indicator of trends in social welfare under these circumstances. If the poverty rate were to remain constant while mobility dropped, this would mean that the proportion of all children experiencing long spells of poverty had continued to increase. In other words, changes in dynamic patterns can have as important an impact upon child well-being as changes in the cross-sectional poverty rate. We might derive a quite misleading picture of trends in living standards if we focus on one but not the other. Not only for Russia, but also for other countries where changes are not so dramatic, information on the dynamics of low household income is essential for obtaining an adequate picture of economic disadvantage among children.

Acknowledgements
We are very grateful to all the authors of the country studies in part II of the book for providing the statistics discussed in this chapter. Tony Atkinson and Martha Hill made helpful comments on an earlier version.

References

Duncan, G. J., Gustafsson, B., Hauser, R., Schmaus, G., Messinger, H., Muffels, R., Nolan, B., and Ray, J.-C., 1993, 'Poverty dynamics in eight countries', *Journal of Population Economics*, 6: 295–334.

Part II

Topics in child poverty dynamics

5   Income mobility and exits from poverty of American children

PETER GOTTSCHALK AND SHELDON DANZIGER

5.1 Child poverty since the 1960s

The availability of longitudinal data has had a profound influence on the way analysts view poverty in the United States. Prior to the availability of data from the Panel Study of Income Dynamics, which started in 1968, researchers and the press assumed that poverty was a relatively permanent condition from which few people managed to escape.

The pioneering work of Bane and Ellwood (1986) challenged these stereotypes by showing that a majority of spells were in fact quite short. For example, they found that 45 per cent of persons who were just beginning a spell of poverty (i.e. they were not poor last year, but were poor in the current year), would be in poverty for only one year; only 12 per cent would be poor for ten or more years. They also showed that most of those who are poor in a given year are in the midst of a long spell of poverty, that is about half of all persons identified as poor in a cross-sectional survey are in the midst of a poverty spell that will last ten years or more.

This new conventional wisdom viewed poverty (and welfare participation) as a transitory state for most, and a permanent situation for only a small percentage of the total population. Some analysts even questioned the importance of poverty as a social problem. They assumed that mobility would have two salutary effects. First, it would reduce the pain to those families who experienced a poverty spell, as their incomes would ultimately rise above the poverty threshold. Second, mobility would spread the pain across many families by ensuring that the same set of families did not bear the brunt of poverty year after year.

The view that poverty was largely a transitory phenomenon brought into question the social importance of America's high childhood poverty rates in the 1980s and 1990s. These childhood poverty rates are not only high compared to those in other advanced industrial nations (as shown in chapter 3), but are also high relative to rates achieved in the USA a quarter

Figure 5.1. *Official poverty rates in the USA, 1966–1997*

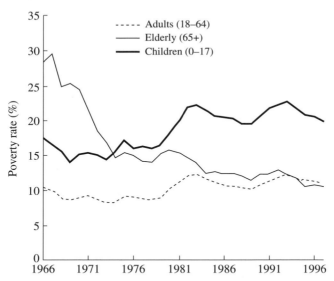

Source: Census Bureau analysis of data from the March Current Population Surveys.

of a century earlier. Figure 5.1 shows the official Census Bureau poverty rates (the proportion of persons found below the official US poverty line) between 1966 and 1997. The rates are shown for children (persons aged less than 18), adults (persons aged 18 to 64), and the elderly (persons 65 years and older).[1] Children had poverty rates that were roughly two thirds as high as the rates facing the elderly in 1966. In contrast, by 1997, children had the highest poverty rate (19.9 per cent) and this rate was roughly twice as high as that of the elderly (10.5 per cent). The poverty rate of children hit an all-time low of 14.0 per cent in 1969 and then began to increase. Over the same period, poverty among the elderly began to decline. Twenty-eight years later, in 1997, one in five children were poor.

These cross-sectional poverty rates may overstate the extent of hardship if most children do not remain in the same place in the income distribution in successive years. If a family's low income in one year is offset by high income in another year and *if* the family is able to save or borrow in order

---

[1] These poverty rates are from tabulations of the March Current Population Surveys. Tabulations of the Panel Study of Income Dynamics, which we use in this chapter, show lower poverty rates in every year, but the trends in the two sources are similar.

to cover expenses when income is low, then poverty rates based on a single year of income will overstate the problem. On the other hand, poverty rates based on yearly income may understate the extent of poverty if families cannot smooth expenses within the year. (These issues are discussed in more depth in chapter 2.) Receiving income at the end of the year may raise yearly income above the poverty line, but may do little to offset low income and serious hardship during previous months.

Even if multiple-year income is the appropriate accounting period for measuring poverty, it is still not true that the *level* of mobility is relevant to the analysis of changes in poverty. It is only *increases* in mobility that can offset the effects of *rising* yearly poverty rates among children. In other words, if the mobility rate of poverty for children did not increase in recent years, the higher child poverty rate of the 1990s means that children are worse off than they were in the late-1960s.

To address this issue, we focus on two major questions about child poverty dynamics. The first is whether long-run transitions out of poverty have changed. The second is whether the events associated with exits from poverty have changed.

Examining changes in mobility over time requires that we contrast the experiences of at least two different cohorts of children. We contrast the mobility patterns of young children over the 1970s to patterns for young children over the 1980s.[2] We also examine which poor children have higher or lower mobility prospects (i.e. children classified by their family structure and race) and whether these mobility prospects have changed over time. Then we focus on how changes in family structure and changes in receipt of welfare income are associated with exits out of poverty and how they have changed over time.

Section 5.2 describes the data we use and methods we apply to them, including our definition of poverty and our two measures of mobility (relative and absolute). Section 5.3 documents the extent of mobility – the proportion of children who made transitions and the changes in mobility – and how these transitions differed between the two cohorts. Section 5.4 focuses specifically on children who made successful transitions either out of poverty or out of the poorest fifth of the family income-to-needs distribution. We show how mobility differs among children classified by family composition (for example, whether or not they live with a single parent) and income sources (for example, whether or not they received 'welfare' (means-tested social assistance)). Section 5.5 concludes, summarising our findings.

---

[2] Our focus is on mobility status ten years apart. For discussion of year-to-year transitions, see Ashworth *et al.* (1994).

5.2 Data and methods

We use data from the Panel Study of Income Dynamics (PSID), which continues to gather longitudinal information on the offspring of the original 1967 sample of 5,000 families.[3] By properly using sampling weights, these data form a nationally representative sample of the US population at the start of the panel.[4]

Although the PSID is the most appropriate data set for the analysis of this chapter, it has weaknesses as well as strengths. Strengths include the long period covered (over twenty-five years) and the availability of income and demographic data on both parents and their offspring, even when the members of the original households form or enter new households. The major disadvantages are the availability of information only on annual money income and the potential bias introduced by the high attrition rates (less than half of the children of the original sample families are still in the panel). Attrition, however, need not lead to bias if the remaining sample is still representative of the US population. In recent work, Fitzgerald et al. (1998b) show that the characteristics of the children who have stayed in the PSID are remarkably similar to those of a corresponding cohort of children drawn from the Census Bureau's annual Current Population Survey. Even though they find that families who experienced fluctuations in earnings were more likely to drop out of the PSID, they conclude that these differences are small and are unlikely to have a qualitatively important impact on estimates of mobility.

We measure income mobility over childhood by following two cohorts of children from the time they are between the ages of 0 and 5 until they reach the ages of 10 to 15. The first cohort includes 2,068 children who were 0 to 5 in 1970–2 (and were 10 to 15 in 1980–2).[5] The second cohort includes 1,637 children who were 0 to 5 in 1980–2 (and were 10 to 15 in 1990–2). Contrasting the experience of these two cohorts allows us to see whether transitions out of poverty differed between the 1970s and the 1980s. We know from figure 5.1, for example, that the annual rate of child poverty has

---

[3] We use data from both the Survey Research Center random sample and the Survey of Economic Opportunities over-sample of low-income families. The family is defined to include all persons related by blood, marriage or adoption. The PSID treats a woman who has been cohabiting with a man for at least one year as a wife.

[4] Because the PSID follows offspring of the original sample families, it does not include immigrants who entered the United States after 1968 or their offspring. For a discussion of these issues see Fitzgerald *et al.* (1998a and 1998b).

[5] We use a three-year period to increase sample size and to eliminate transitory fluctuations in earnings.

increased over these years, but we do not know how mobility out of child poverty has changed.[6]

We classify each child according to the income-to-needs ratio of the family in which he or she resides.[7] The income-to-needs ratio for a child varies as needs (family size) and family income change. Most of our analysis classifies children according to the *three-year average* income-to-needs ratio of the family in which they reside (in 1970–2 and 1980–2 for the first cohort, 1980–2 and 1990–2 for the second cohort). This implicitly assumes a very long accounting period, as children are counted as poor only if their average three-year income is less than their poverty line. (An even longer period is taken in the analysis of chronic poverty in Britain in chapter 7.) Because low-income families are unlikely to be able to smooth consumption over such a long period, we also show results for a one-year accounting period. Shortening the period results in a greater poverty rate in each year, as some children are poor only on a one-year basis. (Low incomes are offset by sufficiently higher income in the other two years that their three-year average income is above their poverty line.) On the other hand, shortening the accounting period increases mobility, since fluctuation within the three-year period is a form of short-term mobility (which may be important to low-income people who cannot save or borrow to smooth consumption across a longer period).

For each cohort we construct transition matrices based on both relative and absolute income-to-needs thresholds. Relative measures of mobility classify children according to their position in the distribution of all children in the cohort, ranked by income-to-needs ratios. (The restriction of the distribution to just that of children is also applied in the analysis of low income in chapter 4.) For example, these transition tables show the proportion of children who move from the poorest fifth to the second, third and other fifths (quintile groups). Because each quintile group includes 20 per cent of all cohort children, any movement out of a quintile group must be matched by a movement into that group. There cannot be net upward or downward mobility under this relative measure. Relative mobility, therefore, captures the notion that children change their rank position in the income distribution (of all children). In contrast, absolute thresholds are based on income-to-needs ratios that are fixed in real terms, so it is possible for more children to move out of the lowest grouping. Absolute measures of mobility can show greater exits than entries into poverty, with the result that the net outflow leads to a reduction in poverty.

---

[6] For a discussion of the causes of the increase in child poverty, see Danziger *et al.* (1997).

[7] We use the same equivalence scales as those used as part of the official poverty lines for different family sizes in the USA.

Our two measures of mobility correspond to different theoretical conceptions. *Relative* mobility tells us the extent to which children change places in the income distribution over time. A society with little relative mobility might be labelled a static society, as there is little chance of changing relative places in the distribution of income. This measure is independent of whether there is economic growth in this society. If all incomes grow but everyone keeps the same position (or rank) in the distribution of income, then there is no relative mobility.

Absolute mobility is consistent with the concepts exemplified by the popular statement that 'prosperity brings upward mobility'. As commonly used, this implies that economic growth raises average living standards for families at all points in the income distribution. However, it reveals nothing about relative mobility because it does not tell us whether those children who started at the bottom of the distribution stayed there or whether they moved up relative to other children. Statements about absolute mobility are almost always about changes in the mean of the income distribution, not about changes in the degree of persistence in income positions. Consider, for example, how mobility would be affected if rapid economic growth produced a doubling in the real income of every family. An absolute measure of mobility would indicate that low-income families had experienced upward mobility as they moved into higher income categories. However, there would be no change in a measure of relative mobility because all families would have maintained their initial place in the distribution.

We use changes in poverty status, taking the PSID official poverty line as the cut-off, as our measure of absolute mobility.[8] Transitions out of poverty can reflect either changes in relative positions (children who escape from being the poorest are replaced by children who become the poorest children) or economic growth which increases the incomes of all children, or demographic change, where there is a net decrease in the number of children in the family.

5.3 The extent of income mobility among children

Relative mobility

Table 5.1 shows the extent of relative mobility for our two cohorts. Children are classified into five quintile groups based on their income-to-needs ratios

---

[8] The needs standard used in the PSID is based on the 1967 USDA Low-Cost Food Plan, which differs from the Economy Food Plan used in the official US measure of poverty. This needs standard is approximately 25 per cent higher than the official standard.

Table 5.1. *Relative mobility of two cohorts of children (row percentages)*

(a) *Children 0 to 5 in 1970*

Quintile groups of family income/needs in 1970–2	Quintile groups of family income/needs in 1980–2					
	First	Second	Third	Fourth	Fifth	
First	59.9	25.3	9.3	4.4	1.1	100.0
Second	25.1	32.1	21.8	16.3	4.7	100.0
Third	7.8	24.0	37.4	22.6	8.2	100.0
Fourth	4.0	15.1	19.2	33.5	28.2	100.0
Fifth	2.4	4.1	12.0	24.7	56.8	100.0

(b) *Children 0 to 5 in 1980*

Quintile groups of family income/needs in 1980–2	Quintile groups of family income/needs in 1990–2					
	First	Second	Third	Fourth	Fifth	
First	60.4	27.2	7.5	3.5	1.4	100.0
Second	24.3	40.3	20.7	9.9	4.8	100.0
Third	12.5	20.9	29.7	29.8	7.2	100.0
Fourth	3.5	10.5	31.2	29.5	25.3	100.0
Fifth	0.5	1.2	9.7	27.9	60.8	100.0

(c) *Change between cohorts*

	First	Second	Third	Fourth	Fifth	
First	0.5	1.9	−1.8	−0.9	0.3	0.0
	(4.9)	(4.5)	(2.7)	(2.1)	(1.0)	
Second	−0.8	8.2*	−1.1	−6.4*	0.1	0.0
	(4.2)	(4.9)	(4.1)	(3.4)	(2.3)	
Third	4.7	−3.1	−7.7	7.2	−1.0	0.0
	(3.1)	(4.2)	(4.8)	(4.6)	(2.6)	
Fourth	−0.5	−4.6	12.0***	−4.0	−2.9	0.0
	(2.0)	(3.5)	(4.5)	(4.9)	(4.7)	
Fifth	−1.9	−2.9	−2.3	3.2	4.0	0.0
	(1.2)	(1.6)	(3.3)	(4.7)	(5.3)	

Notes: Standard errors in brackets. *** indicates statistically significant at 1 per cent level,
** at the 5 per cent level and * at the 10 per cent level.

in each period. For example, the first row of the first panel includes those children who were in the bottom 20 per cent of the income-to-needs distribution in the early 1970s.[9] The columns in this first row show how these children (who started at the bottom of the distribution) fared ten years later. About three fifths (59.9 per cent) were still in the bottom quintile group. A quarter (25.3 per cent) had moved to the second fifth. But only a handful (1.1 per cent) had moved to the richest fifth. Likewise, about three fifths (56.8 per cent) of those children who started in the richest fifth in the

[9] Classification is based on the three-year average income-to-needs ratio in 1970–2.

early 1970s (bottom row, last column of the first panel) were still in the richest fifth ten years later. And most of the highest-income children who did change quintile groups had fallen only to the next highest quintile group.

The second panel in table 5.1 shows the comparable transition matrix for the cohort of children who were 0 to 5 in the early 1980s. The third panel shows the *change* in transition rates between the two cohorts and whether these changes are large enough to be statistically significant.

The second panel shows that about three fifths (60.4 per cent) of children in the lowest quintile group in the early 1980s were still in the lowest quintile group in the early 1990s. The 0.5 per cent increase in the probability of staying in the poorest fifth (60.4 minus 59.9) is not significantly different from zero. There was a small increase in the probability that a child who started in the poorest fifth would move into the second-poorest fifth (from 25.3 to 27.2) but this decline in mobility – like almost all others – is also not statistically different from zero. There was certainly no increase in relative mobility across the two cohorts.

Table 5.1 shows that while there is some income mobility during child-hood, children who started at the bottom of the distribution tended to remain there ten years later. And children who started at the top of the distribution seldom fell very far. For example, consider those children who started in the poorest fifth in 1980–2 (first row, all columns, second panel) – 87.6 per cent of them were in either the poorest or second-poorest fifth ten years later (60.4 plus 27.2). Likewise, among those children who were in the richest quintile group in 1980–2 (bottom row, all columns, second panel), 88.7 per cent were in the top two quintile groups ten years later.

Not surprisingly, the overall transition rates in table 5.1 differ across economic and demographic categories. This is shown in table 5.2, which focuses on the probability that children who were in the poorest quintile group when they were 0–5 years of age either remained in that group or in the two lowest quintile groups when they were 10–15 years of age. Again there are three panels. The top two show transition rates for the two cohorts, while the bottom panel shows the resulting change in transition rates and whether these changes are significantly different from zero.[10]

The differences across economic and demographic groups in each cohort are striking.[11] For example, white children who were in the poorest fifth (of all children in the cohort, black and white) in the early 1970s had a 50.7 per

---

[10] In each case the quintile groups in table 5.2 refer to the distribution for all cohort children, and not to the distribution of just the children with the characteristic concerned.

[11] The first row shows transition rates for all children and can be derived directly from the first row in each panel in table 5.1.

Table 5.2. *Probability of remaining in the lowest or two lowest quintile groups*

	Probability of remaining in lowest quintile group (%)	Probability of remaining in two lowest quintile groups (%)
a) 1971–81		
All	59.9	85.2
Whites	50.7	77.8
Blacks	77.1	94.8
Difference	−26.4***	−17.1***
	(6.3)	(4.4)
Not a single parent in 1971	55.1	82.4
Single parent in 1971	74.7	93.6
Difference	−19.6***	−11.2***
	(6.4)	(4.4)
Not receiving welfare in 1971	48.7	77.4
Receiving welfare in 1971	77.9	97.7
Difference	−29.2***	−20.3***
	(6.1)	(3.8)
b) 1981–91		
All	60.4	87.5
Whites	46.9	82.2
Blacks	77.7	92.0
Difference	−30.9***	−9.8**
	(6.8)	(4.8)
Not a single parent in 1981	51.6	87.0
Single parent in 1981	70.7	88.2
Difference	−19.1***	−1.2
	(7.2)	(4.9)
Not receiving welfare in 1981	53.2	84.2
Receiving welfare in 1981	69.1	91.6
Difference	−15.9**	−7.4
	(7.3)	(4.6)
c) Change between cohorts		
All	0.5	2.3
	(4.9)	(6.6)
Whites	−3.8	4.5
	(7.3)	(5.8)
Blacks	0.6	−2.8
	(5.6)	(3.0)
Not a single parent	−3.5	4.6
	(6.3)	(4.5)
Single parent	−4.0	−5.4
	(7.3)	(4.8)
Not receiving welfare	4.5	6.8
	(6.3)	(5.2)
Receiving welfare	−8.8	−6.1**
	(7.2)	(3.1)

Notes: See note to table 5.1.

cent chance of remaining in the poorest fifth ten years later. For black children the probability of staying in the poorest fifth was 77.1 per cent and the probability of staying in the poorest or second-poorest fifth was a full 94.8 per cent, both of which are significantly greater than for whites.[12] Thus, only 5.2 per cent of all young black children starting in the lowest quintile group managed to move into the third or higher quintile group by the time they entered their teens.

Among young children in the poorest fifth who lived in families that received welfare in the early 1970s (means-tested social assistance), only 2.3 per cent managed to escape beyond the second tenth.[13] Likewise, children living in single-parent families (and in the lowest quintile) had only a 6.4 per cent chance of escaping beyond the second-poorest fifth.[14]

While differences across demographic groups are all statistically significant for both cohorts, only one demographic group experienced a significant change between the 1970s and 1980s: children in families receiving welfare became slightly *less* likely to remain in the bottom 40 per cent of the distribution (upward mobility rises). Therefore, as in table 5.1, there was no substantial increase in mobility for children classified by race or family structure.

Absolute mobility

Table 5.3 classifies children according to fixed income-to-needs categories: less than 1, 1.0 to 1.5, 1.5 to 2.5 and over 2.5 times the (PSID) poverty line. Using these absolute cut-offs makes it possible for every child to escape from the lowest income group if his or her income increases sufficiently. We use an income-to-needs ratio of 1 to differentiate between poor children (i.e. those children in families with the ratio below 1) and near-poor children

---

[12] There is not a sufficient number of children of other races to calculate precise mobility rates.

[13] A family is classified as receiving welfare if it received Aid to Families with Dependent Children or 'other welfare' in 1971. Roughly 11 per cent of our full sample were in families receiving welfare.

[14] Single parenthood is determined by the marital status of the head of the household. A large majority of these heads are the parents of the children we study. However, in some cases the household head is unmarried, but not necessarily the parent of the child. Marital status was miscoded for some families in the early years of the PSID. The marital status variable for our sample in the years we study is consistent with other measures (based on presence of a wife) in all but a small proportion of the cases (less than 0.5 per cent).

Table 5.3. *Absolute mobility of two cohorts of children (row percentages)*

(a) *Children 0 to 5 in 1970*

Family income/needs (Y) in 1970–2	Family income/needs (Y) in 1980–2				
	$Y<1$	$1<Y<1.5$	$1.5<Y<2.5$	$Y>2.5$	
$Y<1$	56.8	24.2	17.1	1.9	100.0
$1<Y<1.5$	23.3	32.6	32.8	11.2	100.0
$1.5<Y<2.5$	6.7	12.7	43.1	37.4	100.0
$Y>2.5$	0.8	4.5	16.4	78.3	100.0

(b) *Children 0 to 5 in 1980*

Family income/needs (Y) in 1980–2	Family income/needs (Y) in 1990–2				
	$Y<1$	$1<Y<1.5$	$1.5<Y<2.5$	$Y>2.5$	
$Y<1$	48.8	18.6	26.0	6.7	100.0
$1<Y<1.5$	19.3	32.5	28.2	19.9	100.0
$1.5<Y<2.5$	7.9	8.0	44.8	39.3	100.0
$Y>2.5$	0.0	2.6	12.5	84.8	100.0

(c) *Change between cohorts*

	$Y<1$	$1<Y<1.5$	$1.5<Y<2.5$	$Y>2.5$	
$Y<1$	−8.0	−5.6	8.9	4.8*	0.0
	(6.1)	(4.9)	(5.4)	(2.6)	
$1<Y<1.5$	−4.0	−0.1	−4.6	8.7**	0.0
	(4.4)	(5.4)	(5.3)	(4.3)	
$1.5<Y<2.5$	1.2	−4.7**	1.7	1.9	0.0
	(2.1)	(2.3)	(3.9)	(3.9)	
$Y>2.5$	−0.8	−1.9	−3.9	6.5**	0.0
	(0.6)	(1.4)	(2.6)	(2.9)	

Notes: See note to table 5.1.

(i.e. those with the ratio above 1 but below 1.5). The cut-off 2.5 is used to ensure that a sufficient number of children are in the highest groups.[15]

The table shows that patterns of absolute mobility are not very different from those of relative mobility. The top row of the top panel shows that the probability of a poor young child escaping poverty between the early 1970s and the early 1980s is 43.2 per cent (100 minus 56.8). For the second cohort (second panel) the probability of escaping was 51.2, which is not significantly different from for the first cohort.

Rising real mean incomes over the decades did lower the three-year poverty rate for the first cohort of children from 13.1 per cent in the early

[15] For the 1970 cohort, 13.1 per cent were poor, 16.2 per cent were near poor, 33.2 per cent were in the next higher category and 37.6 per cent had an income-to-needs ratio over 2.5.

1970s to 11.6 per cent in the early 1980s, but this did not ensure that all children experienced real increases in income relative to needs.[16] For example, the second row of each panel shows the distribution of the near poor (children in families with income between 1 and 1.5 times their poverty lines) at the start of the decade. The first column in the top panel shows that 23.3 per cent of the near poor in the early 1970s fell into poverty by the early 1980s, despite a decline in the overall child poverty rate. Likewise, 6.7 per cent of children in households with an income-to-needs ratio between 1.5 and 2.5 times the poverty line at the start of the decade were poor by the end of the decade. This illustrates how the stock of poor children is the result of flows both into and out of poverty. The bottom panel of table 5.3 shows that absolute mobility did not significantly increase across the two cohorts for most groups of children. Of the sixteen transition rates only two show a significant increase in mobility and one shows a significant decline.

Table 5.4 shows how these absolute mobility rates differed by economic and demographic categories. Again, for each cohort, there are substantial differences across groups. For example, 67.6 per cent of poor black children in the early 1970s were also poor ten years later and 89.8 per cent were either poor or near poor. This is significantly higher than the rates for whites. Likewise, 80.4 per cent of children in poor single-parent households and 89.3 per cent receiving welfare were either poor or near poor a decade later.

Turning to the changes in mobility shown in the bottom panel we see that there was a small decline in the probability of remaining poor for the 1980s cohort relative to that of the 1970s cohort (column 1). However, the change for all children is not significantly different from zero and only one demographic group (children in two-parent families) shows a significant decline in this probability. Children in families on welfare have a significant decline in the probability of being poor or near poor (column 2), in line with the rise in their relative mobility shown in table 5.2. The probability of being poor or near poor also decreased significantly for white children and children in two-parent families.

Until now we have used a three-year average of income-to-needs ratio for each child in order to focus on changes in permanent income. This, however, eliminates mobility associated with short-run fluctuations in income that may at least give temporary respite from poverty. Table 5.5, therefore, shows absolute mobility rates based on single-year incomes. As expected, fewer children stay in poverty, but the differences between tables

---

[16] These figures for the marginal distributions are not shown in the table. For the 1980 cohort, 13.7 per cent were poor in the early 1980s and 10.9 per cent were poor in the early 1990s.

Table 5.4. *Probability of remaining poor or near poor*

	Probability of remaining poor (%)	Probability of remaining poor or near poor (%)
(a) *1971–81*		
All	56.8	81.0
Whites	50.9	73.0
Blacks	67.6	89.8
Difference	−16.7**	−16.8**
	(8.3)	(6.7)
Not a single parent in 1971	53.1	81.3
Single parent in 1971	65.3	80.4
Difference	−12.2	0.9
	(7.6)	(6.7)
Not receiving welfare in 1971	44.7	72.7
Receiving welfare in 1971	68.8	89.3
Difference	−24.1***	−16.7***
	(7.6)	(6.1)
(b) *1981–91*		
All	48.8	67.4
Whites	39.4	55.5
Blacks	62.8	81.5
Difference	23.4 **	−26.0***
	(9.7)	(9.2)
Not a single parent in 1981	35.0	58.7
Single parent in 1981	60.7	74.8
Difference	−25.7***	−16.1*
	(9.0)	(9.2)
Not receiving welfare in 1981	34.2	61.3
Receiving welfare in 1981	59.5	71.8
Difference	−25.3***	−10.5
	(8.8)	(9.3)
(c) *Change between cohorts*		
All	−8.0	−13.7*
	(6.1)	(7.8)
Whites	−11.5	−17.5*
	(10.3)	(9.8)
Blacks	−4.8	−8.4
	(7.5)	(5.8)
Not a single parent	−18.1**	−22.6***
	(8.1)	(8.2)
Single parent	−4.6	−5.6
	(8.5)	(7.9)
Not receiving welfare	−10.5	−11.4
	(8.1)	(8.7)
Receiving welfare	−9.3	−17.5**
	(8.4)	(7.0)

Notes: See note to table 5.1.

Table 5.5. *Absolute mobility: one-year income (row percentages)*

(a) *Children 0 to 5 in 1970*

Family income/needs in 1971	Family income/needs (Y) in 1981				
	$Y<1$	$1<Y<1.5$	$1.5<Y<2.5$	$Y>2.5$	All
$Y<1$	43.7	28.8	16.4	11.1	100.0
$1<Y<1.5$	23.8	31.3	27.4	17.5	100.0
$1.5<Y<2.5$	10.0	14.3	33.4	42.3	100.0
$Y>2.5$	3.7	4.0	22.5	69.8	100.0

(b) *Children 0 to 5 in 1980*

Family income/needs in 1981	Family income/needs (Y) in 1991				
	$Y<1$	$1<Y<1.5$	$1.5<Y<2.5$	$Y>2.5$	All
$Y<1$	55.8	18.9	17.4	7.9	100.0
$1<Y<1.5$	21.5	27.3	34.9	16.3	100.0
$1.5<Y<2.5$	6.6	10.7	42.6	40.1	100.0
$Y>2.5$	0.8	3.5	13.9	81.8	100.0

(c) *Change between cohorts*

	$Y<1$	$1<Y<1.5$	$1.5<Y<2.5$	$Y>2.5$	All
$Y<1$	12.1**	–9.9**	1.0	–3.2	0.0
	(5.7)	(4.8)	(4.5)	(3.6)	
$1<Y<1.5$	–2.3	–4.0	7.5	–1.2	0.0
	(5.2)	(5.9)	(6.0)	(4.7)	
$1.5<Y<2.5$	–3.4	–3.6	9.2**	–2.2	0.0
	(2.4)	(2.8)	(4.4)	(4.5)	
$Y>2.5$	–2.9**	–0.5	–8.6***	12.0***	0.0
	(1.2)	(1.5)	(3.1)	(3.4)	

Notes: See note to table 5.1.

5.3 and 5.5 are not large. Table 5.3 showed that 56.8 per cent of children with income-to-needs below 1 (based on a three-year average) were still poor ten years later. Table 5.5 shows that using a one-year measure of income reduces this to 43.7 per cent. Likewise inflows into poverty are greater, but again the differences are not large. The changes across cohorts in the rates of mobility show that the persistence of poverty increased significantly over time from 43.7 for the 1970s cohort to 55.8 per cent for the 1980s cohort. Likewise the probability that a child in the highest income category remained in that category increased from 69.8 to 81.8 per cent.

Thus, whether one uses one-year or three-year measures of income, and whether one uses absolute or relative measures of mobility, we find similar patterns. A substantial proportion of children who start at the bottom of the distribution remain there over a ten-year period. These mobility rates differ significantly across demographic groups, but they have not changed very much over time. One exception is that absolute mobility on the one-year basis has fallen.

5.4 Events associated with exits from poverty

Thus far we have focused on the extent of mobility and its changes across the two cohorts. We now turn to events associated with exits from absolute poverty for two disadvantaged groups of children – those living in single-parent households and those living in households receiving welfare. We examine the extent to which these children, a decade later, were still living in single-parent families or in households receiving welfare. We also examine how the probability of escaping poverty changed when there was a change in household headship or a change in welfare receipt.

Throughout this discussion we treat these as events *associated* with exits from poverty, not as *causes* of changes in poverty, because the latter implies causation. For example, the cause of the decrease in poverty may be the increased earnings of a family member, which may allow the family both to exit poverty and to either leave welfare or get married. The distinction between association and causation is particularly important when examining mobility. It would be inappropriate to conclude that an association between welfare receipt and escape from poverty implies that having a family leave welfare increases its probability of escaping poverty. More likely some intervening factor occurs (for example, an increase in earnings) which results in both an exit from welfare *and* an escape from poverty.

Table 5.6 shows results for the first cohort, those between the ages of 0 and 5 in 1970–2. The first row shows that 23.5 per cent of all those children living in a single-parent family in 1971 were living in two-parent households a decade later. The numbers in the first column in the next two rows show that children who moved to a two-parent family had a higher chance of escaping poverty than those who continued to live with a single parent. The probability that a poor child who moved to a two-parent family escaped poverty was 51.1 per cent, compared to only 29.6 per cent for those remaining with a single parent. The net result of these changes in family structure and different escape rates is that 34.7 per cent of all poor children living in single-parent households in the early 1970s were not poor a decade later.[17]

Comparing across columns shows substantial differences between blacks

---

[17] Note that the probability of exit is completely determined by the other three elements (i.e. $0.347 = 0.235 \times 0.511 + (1.0 - 0.235) \times 0.296$, corresponding to the rate shown in table 5.4 for children of single parents, $1.0 - 0.653$).

Table 5.6. *Events associated with exits from poverty between 1971 and 1981 (probabilities)*

	All	Whites	Blacks
(a) *Children in poor families with single parents in 1971*			
Pr (become two-parent in 1981)	0.235 (0.057)	0.481 (0.130)	0.122 (0.052)
Pr (exit poverty | became two-parent)	0.511 (0.149)	0.427 (0.202)	0.680 (0.175)
Pr (exit poverty | stayed single parent)	0.296 (0.058)	0.431 (0.174)	0.253 (0.060)
Pr (exit poverty)	0.347 (0.058)	0.429 (0.128)	0.305 (0.064)
(b) *Children in poor families with welfare recipients in 1971*			
Pr (getting off welfare in 1981)	0.598 (0.052)	0.676 (0.089)	0.532 (0.067)
Pr (exit poverty | got off welfare)	0.439 (0.077)	0.442 (0.118)	0.415 (0.109)
Pr (exit poverty | stayed on welfare)	0.123 (0.044)	0.176 (0.121)	0.070 (0.024)
Pr (exit poverty)	0.312 (0.054)	0.356 (0.091)	0.254 (0.070)

Notes: Pr = probability. Poverty is defined as having a ratio of three-year average family income-to-needs of less than 1 (i.e. equivalised three-year average income below the poverty line). Single parents are those defined as having no spouse present. Welfare recipients are those defined as those who receive AFDC or 'other' welfare. Robust standard errors in parentheses.

and whites. During the 1970s, white children had a considerably higher probability of having a change from a single- to a two-parent family (48.1 versus 12.2 per cent). If they stayed in a single-parent family they also had a greater chance of escaping from poverty (43.1 versus 25.3 per cent). On the other hand, black children had a higher chance than white children of escaping poverty if they made the transition from a single-parent family to a two-parent family by the end of the decade (68.0 versus 42.7 per cent).

The bottom panel of table 5.6 presents a comparable analysis for children in poor families who received welfare in 1971. Only 31 per cent of them had escaped poverty by 1981 (35.6 per cent of whites and 25.4 per cent of blacks), despite the fact that more than half (59.8 per cent) were not receiv-

Table 5.7. *Events associated with exits from poverty between 1981 and 1991 (probabilities)*

	All	Whites	Blacks
(a) *Children in poor families with single parents in 1981*			
Pr (become two-parent in 1991)	0.272	0.462	0.170
	(0.059)	(0.127)	(0.054)
Pr (exit poverty | became two-parent)	0.697	0.576	0.878
	(0.125)	(0.191)	(0.069)
Pr (exit poverty | stayed single parent)	0.280	0.211	0.309
	(0.067)	(0.143)	(0.076)
Pr (exit poverty)	0.393	0.380	0.405
	(0.063)	(0.122)	(0.072)
(b) *Children in poor families with welfare recipients in 1981*			
Pr (getting off welfare in 1991)	0.596	0.621	0.514
	(0.063)	(0.107)	(0.079)
Pr (exit poverty | got off welfare)	0.659	0.644	0.565
	(0.080)	(0.130)	(0.112)
Pr (exit poverty | stayed on welfare)	0.029	0.000	0.050
	(0.022)	(0.000)	(0.037)
Pr (exit poverty)	0.405	0.400	0.315
	(0.064)	(0.103)	(0.074)

Notes: Pr = probability. Poverty is defined as having a ratio of three-year average family income-to-needs of less than 1 (i.e. equivalised three-year average income below the poverty line). Single parents are those defined as having no spouse present. Welfare recipients are defined as those who receive AFDC or 'other' welfare. Robust standard errors in parentheses.

ing welfare in that year. This reflects the fact that 43.9 per cent of children whose families no longer received welfare remained poor. Thus, even though the probability of exiting poverty is much greater for those no longer receiving welfare than for those receiving welfare (43.9 versus 12.3 per cent), the events associated with leaving welfare give no assurance of leaving poverty.

Table 5.7 repeats this analysis for the second cohort. Almost all of the patterns are the same, with one major exception. For whites, the probability that a young child living in a poor single-parent family would escape poverty over the next ten years fell from 42.9 per cent in the first cohort to 38.0 per cent in the second, whereas the escape rate increased from 30.5 to

40.5 per cent for black children. This change for white children reflects both a decline in the probability that a child living in a one-parent family was living in a two-parent family ten years later (from 48.1 to 46.2 per cent), and an even larger fall in the probability of escape from poverty if the child remained in a single-parent family (from 43.1 to 21.1 per cent).

Other changes between tables 5.6 and 5.7 that are worth noting relate to the probability of exit from poverty for children in families receiving welfare. Table 5.4 showed a significant decline in the probability of remaining poor or near poor and the comparison of tables 5.6 and 5.7 sheds more light on this. The probability of exit for those children in families who get off welfare rises sharply, from 43.9 per cent to 65.9 per cent, while the exit probability for those who remain on welfare falls, from 12.3 to 2.9 per cent (with the probability for white children falling away to zero). The association between moving off welfare and moving out of poverty therefore strengthened, as did that between remaining on welfare and remaining in poverty. (Remember our warning on the distinction between association and causation.)[18]

5.5 Summary

Economic growth was more rapid in the 1980s than in the 1970s, yet child poverty in the USA actually increased. This was largely the result of the increase in inequality that accompanied the economic growth.[19] The resulting high poverty rates could, however, have been accompanied by an increase in mobility which would have reduced the probability that a child would remain poor.

This chapter has explored the extent of and change in both absolute and relative mobility among children. Roughly half of the children who were in poor families at the start of each decade remained poor. For black children and children in female-headed households, both the relative and absolute mobility are considerably lower. Our comparison of mobility during the 1970s and the 1980s shows no significant changes over time. There is, therefore, no evidence that the increase in inequality during the 1980s, which contributed to the rise in poverty, was offset by an increase in mobility.

[18] This change in exit probabilities over time may partially reflect compositional changes. The decrease in the exit probabilities among families receiving welfare may simply reflect the fact that those remaining on welfare had below average exit rates, which may not have increased.
[19] See Danziger and Gottschalk (1995).

Acknowledgements
This research was supported in part by a grant from the Ford Foundation to the University of Michigan. Nancy Collins and Kelly Haverstick provided valuable research assistance.

References

Ashworth, K., Hill, M. and Walker, R., 1994, 'Patterns of childhood poverty: new challenges for policy', *Journal of Policy Analysis and Management*, 13: 658–80.

Bane, M. J. and Ellwood, D. T., 1986, 'Slipping into and out of poverty: the dynamics of spells', *Journal of Human Resources*, 21: 1–23.

Danziger, S. and Gottschalk, P., 1995, *America Unequal*, Harvard University Press, Cambridge MA.

Danziger, S., Danziger, S. K. and Stern, J., 1997, 'The American paradox: high income and high child poverty', in Cornia, G. A. and Danziger, S. (eds.), *Child Poverty and Deprivation in Industrialized Countries, 1945–1995*, Clarendon Press, Oxford.

Fitzgerald, J., Gottschalk, P. and Moffitt, R., 1998a, 'An analysis of sample attrition in panel data: the Michigan panel study of income dynamics', *Journal of Human Resources*, 33: 251–99.

Fitzgerald, J., Gottschalk, P. and Moffitt, R., 1998b, 'An analysis of the impact of sample attrition on the second generation of respondents in the Michigan panel study of income dynamics', *Journal of Human Resources*, 33: 300–44.

6 Child poverty in Germany: trends and persistence

CHRISTIAN SCHLUTER

6.1 Background and motivation

Poverty in Germany is no longer seen by many to affect only a small group of persons on the margin of society. Widespread public concern is reflected in front-page newspaper reports about worsening social indicators and the high incidence of social assistance receipt. These are complemented by descriptions of German society which use concepts such as 'new poverty' and a 'two thirds, one thirds society' of haves and have-nots – themes which have re-emerged from the sociological literature of the 1980s.[1] At the same time this concern about poverty is not equally shared amongst Germans: a frequently encountered response is one of denial or apathy. Indeed, the former Conservative minister for the family (Frau C. Nolte) has stated that recipients of means-tested social assistance cannot be regarded as being poor – so poverty must be all but absent in Germany.

How do such soundbites square with the facts? Quite a lot is now known about poverty in the population at large, but child poverty and poverty dynamics have received only a little attention. This chapter seeks to redress some of this deficit. Using the German Socio-Economic Panel data for the years 1983 to 1995, I go beyond an analysis of child poverty snapshots and examine the motion picture of children moving into and out of poverty. I also compare the poverty incidence and persistence of children living in households headed by native Germans and by foreigners, and compare the experience in the East with that in the West.

Research to date about poverty in Germany has had three main features: it is predominantly based on cross-section surveys; the unit of analysis is the person (adult or child) rather than the child; and there is a variety of poverty rate estimates due to the use of different definitions (for example,

[1] Cf. *Süddeutsche Zeitung*, 21 August 1998, 'Die Sozialhilfe als Normalfall'. Quote in *Süddeutsche Zeitung*, 31 July 1998, 'Länder halten Bericht zurück'.

154

of the income concept, the equivalence scale, the poverty line and the sample selection rule).

An example of cross-section survey-based research is the paper by Hauser *et al.* (1981), which examines poverty in the 1960s and in 1973 using data from the Einkommens- und Verbrauchsstichprobe (EVS, Income and Expenditure Survey). Hauser *et al.* sketch a picture of poverty for this period which resembles the current picture: the poverty rate for all persons ranges between 7 per cent and 10 per cent, and lone parents and children have disproportionately high poverty risks. The principal but crucial difference between the 'old' poverty of the 1960s and early 1970s and the poverty of the 1980s and 1990s is the role of unemployment, as the 1960s were, in effect, a period of full employment. It appears that 'old' poverty was predominantly a long-term experience – the poor out of the labour market were unlikely to enter it and the working poor had little chance to improve their fortunes.

The poverty rate has changed little over the last two decades. Although poverty research has been diverse and lacks a dominant approach, recent estimates of the proportion of the population poor range from 5.8 per cent to 13.6 per cent. Habich and Krause (1995) and Krause and Wagner (1997) report poverty rates for the entire West German population ranging between 10 per cent and 12 per cent for the years 1984 to 1994, where poverty is defined as having an income below half the average income of the year in question. Using the same poverty line but a different definition of income, Hanesch (1994) found similar poverty rates. For 1984 Burkhauser *et al.* (1996) report a West German poverty rate of 6.4 per cent using a half median poverty line combined with an 'expert' equivalence scale, and a poverty rate of 5.8 per cent using the same poverty line but the social assistance equivalence scale. Increasing the poverty line to 60 per cent of the median raised the poverty rate to 12.5 per cent in the first case and to 13.6 per cent in the second.

Analysis of poverty in Germany has increasingly taken a longitudinal perspective, and important findings have started to emerge, such as the predominantly transitory rather than permanent nature of poverty. Although this information is valuable, it can shed only indirect light on the nature and extent of child poverty, since children have not been the focus of analysis. A recent meeting of the parliamentary commission on the economic well-being of children (die Kommission zur Wahrnehmung der Belange der Kinder, known as the 'Kinderkommission') recognised this lack of information, and much of the evidence presented to it was based on cross-section surveys rather than longitudinal ones.[2]

---

[2] The Kinderkommission (1997) recommended the launch of a dedicated child welfare survey to collect more adequate information. Cf. also Walper (1995) 'bislang verfügen wir

This chapter seeks to address this deficit of knowledge about child poverty and its dynamics in Germany. An advantage of the long-running German Socio-Economic Panel (GSOEP) is that some children can be followed for up to thirteen years. More details about the GSOEP and about definitions of income and poverty are provided in section 6.2. By contrast with the extensive longitudinal research on the dynamics of social assistance receipt in Bremen (see, for example, Buhr 1995, Leisering and Leibfried 1998), this chapter looks at total household income rather than one particular source, uses nationally representative data, and uses a child-focused analysis.

A longitudinal perspective on poverty is provided in section 6.3. I describe how the annual poverty rates have evolved since the mid-1980s – the conventional cross-sectional focus – and supplement this with information about trends in poverty entry and exit rates and the year-to-year changes in these. I then look at the extent of poverty persistence (section 6.4), classifying children according to how many years they spend in poverty over a five-year period, and contrast three five-year periods covering from the mid-1980s to the mid-1990s. The chapter also examines two features of particular relevance to Germany. I contrast the poverty of West and East German children, a dimension of particular interest given the profound changes associated with re-unification. Also considered, in section 6.5, is the situation of the children of 'guestworkers' (i.e. foreigners who were recruited from abroad during the economic booms of the 1960s and 1970s). Guestworkers and their families are commonly thought to be socially and economically vulnerable.

6.2 Data and definitions

The analysis in this chapter is based on the German Socio-Economic Panel (GSOEP), a large-scale representative household survey launched in western Germany in 1984 which has re-interviewed the same people each year thereafter. An eastern Germany sample was included in the panel from 1990 onwards (with income data available from 1992 onwards). I use data from all interview waves up to 1996 for West Germany and the data collected from 1992 to 1996 for East Germany. The distinction between western and eastern Germany is made using information about respondents' place of

Footnote 2 (*cont.*)
   allerdings nur über sehr begrenzte Informationen zu Armutslagen im Leben von Kinder und Jugendlichen' ('hitherto we have had, to be sure, only very limited information at our disposal about the place of poverty in the lives of children and young people', p. 182).

residence in 1991; subsequent geographical mobility between East and West is not taken into account.

By design, the GSOEP over-samples guestworkers (there are no guest-workers in the eastern sample). Children of guestworkers are included in my analysis. To account for the differences in sample inclusion probabilities due to sample design and attrition, all estimates reported below are based on weighted data. Excluded from my analysis are asylum seekers and ethnic German immigrants from Eastern Europe – groups whose children constitute a disproportionately large share of recipients of means-tested social assistance. For example, Buhr reports that, in the city of Bremen, children of ethnic German immigrants constitute 43 per cent and children of asylum seekers 16 per cent of all children in receipt of means-tested social assistance (Kinderkommission 1997: 65).

The unit of analysis is the child, defined to be a person aged less than 18 years. The 1984 sample contains 2,302 native West German children and 1,637 children of guestworker households (unweighted numbers are reported in this paragraph). The East German sample enters the analysis in 1992 with 1,358 observations. Later in the chapter, I also report break-downs for various sub-groups of children. In 1984, the West German cross-section contains 1,377 children aged less than 7 years, 209 children living in lone-parent households, 859 children in households whose head is not in full-time employment, and 342 children in households receiving some form of means-tested social assistance. The combined West and East German sample in 1991 has a similar size, except in the last two categories, in which there are 1,462 and 752 observations respectively. The composition of the sample changes over time as newborn children enter the panel sample, and others leave the sample either because they reach the age of 18 (and become adults) or because their household ceases to participate in the panel study (attrition).[3]

The income concept is annual post-tax post-benefit household income evaluated at 1996 prices and equivalised in order to take account of differences in size and composition across households. Annual income refers to the calendar year prior to the interview. Hence interviews for 1984 to 1996 provide information about incomes for 1983 to 1995. Henceforth I refer to calendar time in terms of income years rather than interview years.

The income variable was created by a Syracuse University team using a simulation model to estimate household tax payments since data about

---

[3] Retention rates are a measure of the changing composition of the sample. For the period from 1983 to 1995, the cohort of children aged less than 6 years in 1983 has a thirteen-year retention rate of 57 per cent for native Germans and 33 per cent for children of guestworker households. In the East German sub-sample, the cohort of children aged less than 14 years in 1991 has a five-year retention rate of 76 per cent.

these are not collected by the GSOEP (see Wagner *et al.* 1993). Income from all sources (with the exception of imputed rental income from owner-occupation and grouped asset income) was aggregated within each household and the household total is assumed to be shared equally amongst household members.[4] The equivalence scale rate is the square root of the household size. An alternative would have been the equivalence scale embodied in the German Social Assistance Law. This scale attributes a weight of 1.0 to the household head, 0.8 to any other adult in the household, and values ranging between 0.45 and 0.90 to each child, depending on age. Burkhauser *et al.* (1996) concluded that the economies of scale of the social assistance scale are very low, and 'out of line with other measures . . . for Germany or other countries'. My sensitivity tests show that estimates of secular trends in poverty rates are similar for the square-root and social assistance scales.

The poverty line is defined to be equal to 50 per cent of the contemporaneous median of the West German income distribution. Analysis of poverty in the East using this poverty line thus answers the question: what proportion of children in the East are poor according to the standards of the West?

The real value of the half median poverty line for each year between 1983 and 1995 (calculated from the sample) is depicted in figure 6.1. The poverty line rose in value until the early 1990s and then declined somewhat. The poverty line is of the same order of magnitude as typical social assistance levels.[5] In view of the hardship experienced by some social assistance beneficiaries (see, for instance, Buhr 1995), one might argue that the poverty threshold should exceed the social assistance benefit levels. Moreover, moving from below the poverty line to just above it – a poverty exit but only to 'near poverty' – may not mean more bread on a child's table (cf. chapter 4). Hence I also examine the sensitivity of results to raising the poverty line from 50 per cent to 60 per cent of median income.

Before moving to the analysis, it is important to describe the macroeconomic context. To this end, figure 6.1 shows the official unemployment

[4] The equal sharing assumption may not be valid in practice (see, for instance, Middleton *et al.* 1997, and Chiappori 1988), but in the absence of consumption data, sharing rules cannot be estimated.

[5] Consider three types of households: a single person, a lone parent with a 5-year-old child, and a two-parent household with children aged 5 and 15 years. Social assistance recipients are entitled to housing benefit, which typically pays all the rent. Supposing housing benefit amounts to DM550 per month for the first two households, and to DM650 per month for the last one, annual equivalised income from social assistance for the three households is DM13,056, DM11,743, and DM14,230, respectively. Sufficient contributions are required for receipt of means-tested unemployment assistance (*Arbeitslosenhilfe*), whose benefits typically exceed social assistance benefits. If they do not, the social assistance is used to top income up to the social assistance threshold.

Figure 6.1. *Unemployment rates (West and East), real GDP growth and the value of the poverty line, 1983–1995*

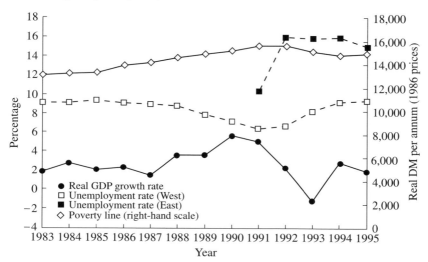

Sources: OECD *Economic Outlook* and Bundesanstalt für Arbeit. The half median poverty line was computed from the analysis sample (see text).

rate for Western and Eastern Germany, and the real GDP growth rate for each year between 1983 and 1995. During this period Germany moved through a business cycle of moderate amplitude. West German unemployment fell from 1983 until 1991 and then increased again. Unemployment is substantially lower in the West than in the East, where hidden unemployment is thought to be considerable. Real GDP growth was positive throughout the fifteen-year period (highest in the late 1980s), except for 1993 when it fell to −1.2 per cent. Average income in the East has gradually moved towards Western levels: although median income in West and East differed by 54 per cent in 1991, the difference fell to 19 per cent in 1994 and 18 per cent in 1995.

6.3 Trends in child poverty rates, entry and exit rates

In this section I examine secular trends in the annual child poverty rate and relate these to the movements into and out of poverty from one year to the next. For children escaping poverty, I also investigate how far they move.

Table 6.1. *Child poverty rates, by sub-group and five-year sub-period*

Percentages	1983–6 (West)	1987–90 (West)	1991–5 (West)	1991–5 (East)
All children	7.8	6.5	8.1	15.8
Children aged 0–6 years	9.2	7.7	9.1	20.2
Children in guestworker households	9.6	6.3	10.5	–
Children in lone-parent households	43.9	37.3	46.3	53.8
Children in households whose heads have no full-time employment	28.3	23.2	20.4	21.2
Children in households whose heads have no full-time employment but with secondary adult earners	10.0	7.6	5.7	10.8
Children in households receiving means-tested assistance	27.1	20.5	27.7	30.6
All persons	8.1	7.1	8.6	14.8

Notes: Means-tested assistance refers to the receipt of social assistance, housing benefit or unemployment assistance. Guestworkers are absent in the East. Weighted data.

For several parts of the analysis it is useful to average over several years rather than look at each year separately. In line with the broad movement of the business cycle, I have split the period between 1983 and 1995 into three sub-periods: 1983–6, 1987–90, 1991–5. The West German economy was stagnant between 1983 and 1986. Unemployment then fell between 1987 and 1990 but rose again between 1991 and 1995.

Table 6.1 reports annual child poverty rates averaged for each of the three sub-periods, and for a range of sub-groups of children. Given the macro-economic background, it is not surprising to find that the child poverty rate in West Germany fell from 7.8 per cent to 6.5 per cent and then rose again to 8.1 per cent. The poverty rates of various sub-groups of children follow a similar trend, but the amplitude of the fluctuations is larger than for all children combined (five to ten percentage points rather than two).

In the period 1991–5, the all-children poverty rate in the East was about twice as large as the corresponding rate for the West. Indeed child poverty in the East is higher than in the West for each of the sub-groups considered, especially for children aged 0–6 years and for children in unemployed households with a secondary earner. Interestingly the all-children poverty rate is broadly the same as the all-persons poverty rate in both the West and the East.

Table 6.1 also highlights some poverty patterns which were reported in earlier poverty research by, for example, Hauser *et al.* (1981). In particular children of lone parents continue to be dramatically affected: during the period 1991–5, 46 per cent of this group in the West were poor and 53 per cent of this group in the East were poor. Young children had a poverty rate which was higher than for all children – but only slightly so.

Children in households with a head who is not in full-time employment also exhibit a large poverty risk: 55 per cent in the West and 45 per cent in the East on average during 1991–5. However, this proportion is lower than might be expected because of two factors. First, social insurance unemployment benefits are often sufficiently high to prevent the household from slipping into poverty. Second, the labour earnings of household members other than the household head play an important role. Consider those children living in households whose head is not in full-time employment but in which there is at least one adult earner. For the period 1983–6 an average of 10 per cent of these children were poor in the West, with this proportion falling to 5.7 per cent for 1991–5. In the East an average of 10.8 per cent of this group of children were poor in the period 1991–5. It is important to observe, however, that these statistics also demonstrate that having an additional earner is not sufficient to prevent poverty altogether.

For some 70 per cent of children in households receiving means-tested assistance (social assistance, housing benefit or unemployment assistance), benefits combined with other incomes are sufficient to keep them out of poverty. In part this result simply reflects the poverty line used here, which does not always exceed the potential income from combinations of benefits. The effects of choosing a higher poverty line are reported below.

The picture of child poverty described so far becomes slightly more complicated when one inspects the complete year-by-year time series of poverty rates rather than the sub-period averages, since within-period movements are not always uniform: see figure 6.2. As one might expect from the business cycle timing, poverty in the West decreased until 1989 and then rose again in the following six years. The result was that in 1995 the child poverty rate was much the same as it was in 1983, around 8 per cent. In East Germany the overall trend in child poverty in the 1990s was clearly downwards, from 22 per cent to 12 per cent between 1991 and 1994. Poverty rose again in 1995, by one percentage point. This poverty rate was substantially above the corresponding West German rate.

Figure 6.2 also shows the time series of child poverty entry and exit rates for West Germany (left-hand graph) and East Germany (right-hand graph), in each case compared with the child poverty rate itself. The relationship between the various rates is as follows. The number of poor children this year consists of the children remaining poor (poor last year and poor this year), plus those who newly entered poverty this year. The child poverty rate is the number of poor children divided by the total number of children. This year's child poverty *entry rate* is the number of children who are poor this year but were not poor last year, divided by the number of children who were

Figure 6.2. *Child poverty rates, poverty entry and exit rates for West and East Germany, 1983–1995*

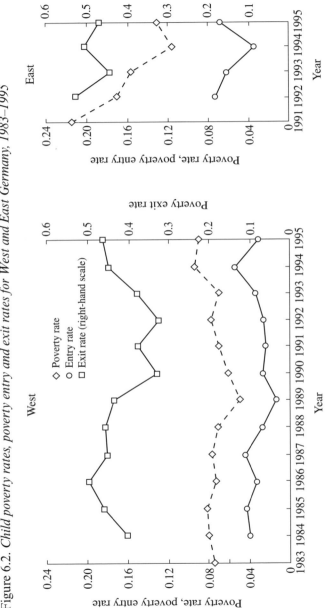

not poor last year. This year's child poverty *exit rate* is the number of children poor this year but not poor next year, divided by the number of poor children this year.[6] Thus increases in the annual poverty rate may arise via increases in the entry rate or falls in the exit rate (or both). Similarly, the poverty rate may decrease via a fall in the entry rate or a rise in the exit rate. Although the exit rate is very much larger than the entry rate, it applies to a much smaller base population (the number of poor children) than does the entry rate (for which the base is the number of non-poor children).[7]

Figure 6.2 suggests that changes in the child poverty rate track changes in the entry rate more closely than changes in the exit rate. Put another way, trends in entry and exit rates had a mutually reinforcing effect for much of the time (but not all the time), in the sense that often when the poverty rate rose, the exit rate fell and the entry rate rose (for example, West Germany 1991–2, or East Germany 1994–5). And when the poverty rate fell, the exit rate rose and the entry rate fell (for example, East Germany 1993–4). There were, however, periods when changes in entry and exit rates were in opposing directions. For example, in West Germany, in 1984–5 when the child poverty rate increased slightly, the entry rate had risen although the exit rate also rose. There was a similar pattern again in 1993–4. In East Germany prior to 1993, the poverty rate was falling even though the exit rate was also falling (the entry rate also fell). Overall, if one looks at the trends in entry and exit rates over the period as a whole rather than at the within-period fluctuations, then neither rate exhibits a clear upward or downward trend over time.

So far I have only looked at movements into and out of poverty, but not examined how far beyond the poverty line people move. This aspect should not be ignored, since moving from just below the poverty line to just above it may only imply a trivial change in living standards. Figure 6.3 summarises the extent of income improvements relative to the poverty line. Three time series are depicted. The first is the child poverty exit rate (as shown in figure 6.2 and discussed earlier). The second series summarises the exit rate from poverty to 'near poverty'. It shows the proportion of children who exited from poverty (as earlier) but whose income in the year after the exit did not exceed 60 per cent of median income. The third series shows the exit rate from poverty to 'relative affluence', i.e. having an income above 60 per cent of median income in the year after exit. The overall child poverty exit rate is the sum of the exit rate to 'near poverty' and the exit rate to 'relative affluence'.

---

[5] I estimate these rates using the children present in the sample in two successive years, i.e. the sub-sample of children aged less than 17 years this year. Newborn children are ignored in the calculations.

[7] See chapter 4 for further discussion of this issue.

Figure 6.3 shows that, in West Germany, the exit rate to 'near poverty' and the exit rate to 'relative affluence' make roughly equal contributions to the overall child poverty exit rate, except at the end of the period. In the early 1990s the rise in the exit rate reflects a rise in the latter rate rather than the former one. Thus, for this period, one might more confidently claim there was an increase in 'genuine' outflows from poverty.

Other aspects of the results could be emphasised, however. For example, one might argue that a not insignificant number of exits from poverty involved only short-range upward income mobility. While 42 per cent of children moved out of poverty annually on average, the exit rate to 'relative affluence' was about half this amount at 25 per cent. Although the exit rate exhibited no upward trend or downward trend over the twelve years between 1983 and 1995, the exit rate to 'near poverty' trended slightly downwards over time. In the East, the exit rate to 'near poverty' was about 20 per cent between 1991 and 1993, but the rise in the poverty rate in 1995 was accompanied by a drop in the exit rate to 'near poverty' and an increase in the exit rate to 'relative affluence'.

Analysis of the exit rate to 'near poverty' also sheds some light on the sensitivity of estimates of the child poverty rate at a point in time to the location of the poverty line. Increasing the poverty line from 50 per cent of median income to 60 per cent of the median should raise the poverty rate by a significant amount, since the poverty line is located in the crowded part of the income distribution. Moreover I have just demonstrated that a lot of movement from below the half-median threshold to above it is to a destination in the 50 per cent to 60 per cent of median income range. Put another way, increasing the poverty line to 60 per cent of median income raises the annual poverty rate by between 50 per cent and 100 per cent in both West and East. For instance, in the West, the 1986 poverty rate would be 13 per cent rather than 7.4 per cent, the 1992 poverty rate 16 per cent rather than 8 per cent, and the 1995 rate, 14 per cent rather than 9 per cent. In the East in 1995, raising the poverty line to 60 per cent of median income increased the poverty rate from 13 per cent to 19 per cent.

Another sensitivity check involves the use of an equivalence scale with different assumptions about household economies of scale from those incorporated in the square-root scale. Using the social assistance equivalence scale described earlier (and a half median poverty line), the annual child poverty rate was always somewhat higher than the corresponding rate based on the square-root scale, but the trends over time are similar. For instance, using the social assistance scale yields a 1995 poverty rate for West Germany of 12.5 per cent rather than 9 per cent, and 17 per cent rather than 14 per cent for the East.

Figure 6.3. *Exit rates from poverty to 'near poverty' and 'relative affluence'*

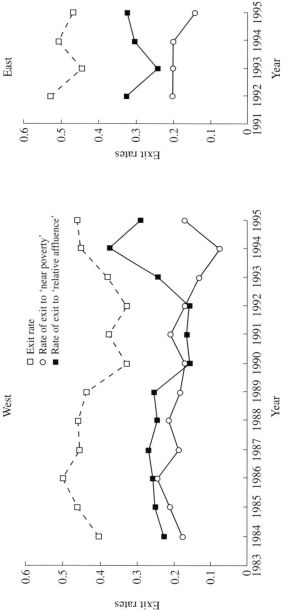

The exit rate to 'near poverty' is the rate of exit from poverty to 50–60 per cent of median income. The exit rate to 'relative affluence' is the rate of exit from poverty to an income of at least 60 per cent of median income. The sum of these two exit rates is the overall exit rate. Weighted data.

6.4 Poverty persistence

In this section I extend the observation window on income and poverty to five years rather than one year in order to investigate poverty persistence. Children are classified into three groups according to the number of years for which they are observed to be poor over a five-year period (none, one to four, or five years poor out of five).[8] The three poverty groups are broken down further into various sub-groups of children using the same classifications as in table 6.1. To provide a reference point, the corresponding figures for all persons (adults and children) are also shown.

The results are reported in table 6.2. Since a movement from just below the poverty line to just above it may not involve a significant income improvement, I have also redone the calculations using an income cut-off line equal to 60 per cent of median income (rather than 50 per cent as in table 6.1). The three 'low-income' persistence groups distinguished include the near poor as well as the poor. For brevity's sake the results are not shown, merely cited.

Four principal findings about the longitudinal nature of poverty emerge from table 6.2. First, very few children are poor for every year during a five-year period, regardless of which five-year sub-period is considered. In fact, the always-poor percentage is not statistically significantly different from zero. If we look at 'low-income' persistence rather than poverty persistence, then about 4 per cent of all children in the West and 8 per cent in the East have 'low income' every year in a five-year interval. However, this fraction is still small by international standards (cf., for example, chapter 7 on Britain).

The second principal finding is that a significant minority of children experience transitory poverty during a five-year period. The proportions of children sometimes poor during each five-year sub-period are considerably larger than the annual poverty rates. For instance, 16 per cent of all children in the West experienced between one and four years of poverty between 1983 and 1987. In the East, 29 per cent were sometimes poor between 1991 and 1995. Looking instead at low-income persistence rather than poverty persistence raises these numbers to 23 per cent and 43 per cent respectively.

A third finding revealed by table 6.2 is that the pattern of poverty persistence for all children differs little from the pattern for all persons. For example, in the West the proportion of children never poor between 1991

---

[8] Extending the observation window restricts the sample to children aged less than 14 years at the beginning of a five-year period (new births within the five-year period are ignored).

Table 6.2. *Patterns of child poverty persistence by sub-group and five-year sub-period*

Percentages	1983–7 (West)	1987–91 (West)	1991–5 (West)	1991–5 (East)
0 years poor out of 5				
All children	82.4	87.9	83.7	68.5
Children aged 0–6 years	81.4	86.1	81.6	64.4
Children in guestworker households	78.0	88.2	77.9	–
Children in lone-parent households	19.8	46.9	44.2	30.2
Children in households whose heads have no full-time employment	50.8	62.8	71.0	62.8
Children in households whose heads have no full-time employment but with secondary adult earner(s)	78.3	76.6	85.3	70.0
Children in households receiving means-tested assistance	47.4	75.2	65.3	60.9
All persons	83.9	85.9	83.5	68.2
5 years poor out of 5				
All children	1.8	2.3[a]	2.0[a]	2.3[a]
Children aged 0–6 years	2.3[a]	3.0[b]	2.7[b]	2.2[b]
Children in guestworker households	0.2[b]	0.2[b]	2.6[b]	–
Children in lone-parent households	12.8[b]	0.7[b]	14.3[b]	7.4[b]
Children in households whose heads have no full-time employment	8.6	9.5[a]	6.4[a]	2.8[a]
Children in households whose heads have no full-time employment but with secondary adult earner(s)	3.7[b]	10.1[b]	1.4[b]	1.9[b]
Children in households receiving means-tested assistance	3.9[b]	1.9[b]	8.0[b]	2.8[b]
All persons	2.1	2.6	2.5	2.5
1–4 years poor out of 5				
All children	15.9	9.8	14.3	29.2
Children aged 0–6 years	16.3	10.9	15.7	33.5
Children in guestworker households	21.8	11.6	19.5	–
Children in lone-parent households	67.4	52.4	41.5	62.3
Children in households whose heads have no full-time employment	40.7	27.7	22.7	34.4
Children in households whose heads have no full-time employment but with secondary adult earner(s)	18.0	13.3	13.3	28.0
Children in households receiving means-tested assistance	48.8	23.0	26.6	36.2
All persons	14.0	12.5	14.0	29.3

Notes: [a] Cells with fewer than twenty (unweighted) children. [b] Cells with fewer than ten (unweighted) children. Parental characteristics are measured at the beginning of each five-year period. There are no guestworkers in the Eastern sample. Weighted data.

and 1995 was 84 per cent – exactly the same as the corresponding percentage for all persons. In the East the fraction never poor was 69 per cent for children and 68 per cent for all persons. This similarity between children and the population as a whole contrasts with the results for Britain (see chapter 7), where never-poor rates (in the six-year period 1991–6) were lower for children than for all persons.

The fourth set of findings concerns the question of which children are more likely to experience persistent poverty. The answer from the longitudinal analysis is that it is many of the same groups as were identified by a cross-sectional analysis as being poor at a point in time. For example, of all children living in lone-parent households, 67 per cent had 1–4 years of poverty in the period 1983–7, and 29 per cent were poor five years out of five (but the cell size of nineteen raises concerns about the reliability of this estimate). Interestingly the poverty persistence patterns for young children differ little from those of all children.

Children in households whose head is not in full-time employment or in households receiving means-tested assistance experience a relatively high chance of having 1–4 years of poverty in a five-year interval. The numbers are again not as high as expected, which is partly due to the importance of the labour supply of other household members. Compare those children living in a household whose head is not in full-time employment with the sub-set of children who also have a secondary adult earner in the household. During the period 1983–7, 78.3 per cent of the latter group were never in poverty and 18 per cent had 1–4 years of poverty. The corresponding figures for the former group were 51 per cent and 41 per cent. In the East, there is a similar differential between the two groups of children. Having a secondary earner in the household by itself does not necessarily prevent poverty. Consistent with the substantially higher poverty incidence in the East, 28 per cent of such children had 1–4 years of poverty and 70 per cent were never poor between 1991 and 1995 (cf. 13 per cent and 85 per cent in the West).

Children in guestworker households have a greater chance of being poor for at least one year in five than native West Germans do. Comparing the East with the West, a larger proportion of each sub-group of children were poor for 1–4 years out of five or five years out of five in the former region. Consistent with their substantially higher poverty rates, children in the East are more than twice as likely to have 'low income' in all five years out of five, or to have 1–4 years of poverty (or low income). In particular, young children are disproportionately affected. The impact of unemployment is also larger in the East than the West since, given the substantially higher unemployment rate, other household members are less able to compensate sufficiently for the income missing given the lack of a main breadwinner.

The changes between each five-year sub-period in the West, although not large, correspond to the movement of the business cycle. When the macro-economic environment improved between 1987 and 1991, the poverty rate fell. Almost all the groups of children who were either always or sometimes poor shrank, and the groups of children who were never in poverty necessarily grew. Then, as the macro-economic environment deteriorated, so too did most rates of persistent poverty. Children as a group do not have disproportionately high risks of persistent poverty compared to all persons in the population.

6.5 Children of guestworkers

Children of guestworkers are commonly thought to be more vulnerable, socially and economically, than native German children. Official unemployment figures suggest this: the unemployment rate amongst foreigners was 13.9 per cent in 1985 and 16.6 per cent in 1995, whereas for native Germans it was 9.3 per cent in both years. The results of sections 6.3 and 6.4 have shown that poverty rates are higher for children of guestworkers, and they are also more likely to be poor (or have low income) at least one year in five. For instance, their poverty rates in the years 1984 and 1995, 10 per cent and 15 per cent, exceeded the all-children rates for West Germany of 8 per cent and 9 per cent (the rates for native Germans thus being slightly lower). In the period 1991–5, 20 per cent of guestworker children experienced 1–4 years of poverty compared to the West German all-children rate of 14 per cent. These differentials are likely to be explained more by economic factors rather by than demographic ones because the problem of lone parenthood is mainly confined to native Germans.

In this section I take a closer look at poverty trends and turnover using the same methods as in section 6.3, but now applied specifically to children of guestworkers. Look at figure 6.4 which shows the trends in their poverty rates and entry and exit rates. The format of the figure is exactly the same as figure 6.2, which refers to all children, facilitating comparisons of patterns.

Two findings emerge. First, the fluctuations over time in all three rates are greater for children in guestworker households than all children in West Germany, especially exit rates. This is another reflection of the fact that substantially more guestworker children are sometimes poor (table 6.2). That

Figure 6.4. *Guestworker child poverty rates, poverty entry and exit rates, West Germany 1983–1993*

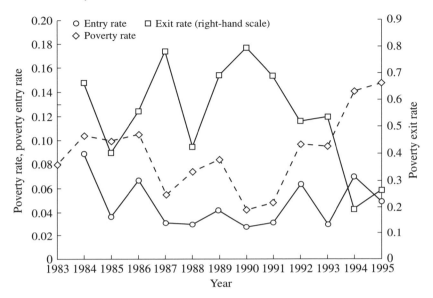

is, poverty turnover is generally larger for guestworker children. Although the poverty rates for both all children and for guestworker children fall and then rise over the period, the changes are more distinct for the latter group. Indeed the poverty rate for guestworker children is more obviously higher at the end of the period than at the beginning.

The second finding concerns the time series pattern of the various rates. Up until 1988, poverty entry and exit rates for guestworker children tended to move either up or down together, rather than in opposite directions (the case in which they would have had a mutually reinforcing effect on the poverty rate). This pattern differs from that for native children. From 1989 onwards, the time series patterns are more similar for both groups of children. The difference between native children and children in guestworker households in the earlier period might be explained by a different timing of the business cycle for guestworkers. That is, the greater amplitude in entry and exit rate variation may follow from the greater incidence and swings in guestworker unemployment.[9]

---

[9] For example, the official unemployment rate for foreigners was 10.7 per cent in 1991 and 16.6 per cent in 1995 compared to combined West German rates of 6.3 per cent and 9.3 per cent.

6.6 Concluding remarks

This chapter is one of the first studies to focus on child poverty in Germany. It has shown how the child poverty rate evolved between 1983 and 1995 and supplemented this picture with new information about the dynamics of child poverty. Using panel data from the GSOEP, I have demonstrated how the trend in poverty rate is related to changes in the annual entry rate to and exit rate from poverty, and also documented the prevalence of poverty over a five-year interval compared to a single year (and how this has changed).

Perhaps the most striking finding is the relatively low degree of persistence in child poverty in Germany. Very few children are poor for all five years in a five-year observation period; the vast majority experience no poverty at all over an interval of this length. This is not to say that transitory poverty is a trivial phenomenon. In the first half of the 1990s about one sixth of all children in West Germany experienced at least one year of poverty over a five-year period – which is roughly double the percentage of children who were found to be poor in any single year. The same differential is found in the East: almost one third of all children experienced at least one year of poverty over a five-year period, compared to the average annual poverty rate of roughly half this.

Another interesting finding, and one which contrasts with several other countries considered in this book, is that the poverty experience of children is not very different from the poverty experience of all persons in the population at large. This is true whether one looks at poverty rates at a point in time or longitudinal measures of poverty persistence. The experience of children aged 0–6 years is worse than that of all children on most poverty indicators, cross-sectional or longitudinal – but not by very much.

Several other results for specific sub-groups of children also stand out. For example, the analysis of this chapter has highlighted the continuing strong association between lone parenthood and child poverty – a feature which has persisted since at least the 1960s. I have shown that not only do children of lone-parent households have higher poverty rates, but they are also more likely to experience repeated poverty over a period of time (whether they are in the West or the East). These results should be seen against the background of a secular rise in the incidence of lone parenthood.[10]

Looking at children of guestworkers, I have shown that not only do they have higher poverty rates than native German children, but they also have

---

[10] Official statistics show that the number of single mothers with children aged less than 18 years increased from 614,000 in 1972 to 879,000 in 1992 (Datenreport 1994: 32).

more years of poverty over a given period. Guestworker children also experience relatively greater fluctuations in poverty entry and exit rates compared to other children.

Another interesting result concerns the effect of parental unemployment and secondary earners. Children in households with heads not in full-time employment have relatively high chances of being poor at a point in time or of experiencing several years of poverty over a five-year interval. On the other hand, both these risks are substantially reduced if there is a secondary earner in the household (other than the head). They are not reduced to the level of the average for all children, however. It remains the case that unemployment is associated with higher poverty rates and greater poverty persistence.

My overall conclusion is that the true picture of child poverty in Germany differs from that caricatured in the opening paragraph of this chapter. Child poverty rates may be lower in Germany than in many other countries, but the extent of poverty and poverty persistence should not be ignored – especially when one notes the existence of particularly vulnerable groups of children within the population.

Acknowledgements
I am grateful to the editorial troika and to Simon Burgess, David Ellwood and Carol Propper for comments.

References
Bieback, K.-J. and Milz, H., 1995, *Neue Armut*, Campus Verlag, Frankfurt am Main and New York.

Buhr, P., 1995, *Dynamik von Armut. Dauer und biographischer Bedeutung von Sozialhilfebezug*, Westdeutscher Verlag, Opladen.

Burkhauser, R., Smeeding, T. M. and Merz, J., 1996, 'Relative inequality and poverty in Germany and the United States using alternative equivalence scales', *Review of Income and Wealth*, 42: 381–400.

Chiappori, P.-A., 1988, 'Rational household labour supply', *Econometrica*, 56: 63–89.

Datenreport, 1994, Band 325, Bundeszentrale fuer politische Bildung, Bonn.

Datenreport, 1997, Band 340, Bundeszentrale fuer politische Bildung, Bonn.

Habich, R. and Krause, P., 1995, 'Armut in der Bundesrepublik Deutschland', in Barlösius, E. (ed.), *Ernährung in der Armut*, Edition Sigma, Berlin.

Habich, R. and Krause, P., 1997, 'Armut', in Datenreport (1997).

Hanesch, W., 1994, *Armut in Deutschland*, Rowohlt, Reineck bei Hamburg.

Hauser, R., Cremer-Schäfer, H. and Nouvertne, U., 1981, *Armut, Niedrigeinkommen und Unterversorgung in der Bundesrepublik Deutschland*, Campus Verlag, Frankfurt and New York.

Huster, E.-U. (ed.), 1997, *Reichtum in Deutschland*, Campus Verlag, Frankfurt and New York.

Kommission zur Wahrnehmung der Belange der Kinder (Kinderkommission), 1997, *Anhörung und Schlussfolgerungen aus der öffentlichen Anhörung zum Thema 'Existenzsicherung von Kindern'*, Deutscher Bundestag, Bonn.

Krause, P. and Wagner, G., 1997, 'Einkommens-Reichtum und Einkommens-Armut in Deutschland', in Huster (1997).

Leisering, L. and Leibfried, S., 1998, *Time, Life, and Poverty*, Cambridge University Press, Cambridge.

Middleton, S., Ashworth, K. and Braithwaite, I., 1997, 'Expenditure on children in Great Britain', Social Policy Research Findings 118, Joseph Rowntree Foundation, York.

Wagner, G., Burkhauser, R. and Behringer, F., 1993, 'The English language public use file of the German socio-economic panel study', *Journal of Human Resources*, 28: 429–33.

Walper, S., 1995, 'Kinder und Jugendliche in Armut', in Bieback and Milz (1995).

7 Poverty among British children: chronic or transitory?

MARTHA S. HILL AND STEPHEN P. JENKINS

7.1 Child poverty in Britain: a topical issue

Concern about child poverty in Britain has grown significantly and is currently a topic of hot policy interest. According to the Chancellor of the Exchequer, 'child poverty is a scar on the soul of Britain' (Brown 1999), and the Prime Minister has spoken of plans to end child poverty within twenty years (Blair 1999). Government programmes are now being explicitly directed at improving children's welfare (HM Treasury 1999, UK 1999). This new concern is based on evidence from official statistics and other studies which have revealed an increase in the incidence of low income among children (Department of Social Security 1998 and 1999, Gregg *et al.* 1999) and increases in their poverty relative to children in other countries (chapter 3, Bradbury and Jäntti 1999, Bradshaw 1997a). This evidence, reviewed later, is based on a series of snapshots of the distribution of income at a point in time. In this chapter we supplement the standard picture with longitudinal perspectives, in particular examining the extent to which child poverty in Britain is chronic rather than transitory in nature.

To place our research in context, we begin with an overview of long-term child poverty trends since the 1960s using data from a variety of repeated cross-section studies and evidence from cross-national research. We then concentrate our analysis on evidence about child poverty dynamics over a six-year period (1991–6) using panel data from the first six waves of the British Household Panel Survey (BHPS).

At any point in time within this six-year period, each person (child or adult) in our sample is either poor or not poor. Taking the six years as a whole, we can count the numbers of times each individual was poor, and classify them as either always poor, never poor or sometimes poor. Another way of looking at persistent poverty, and the focus of this chapter, is to calculate for each person the average, over the six years, of their income and to compare this average to a low income cut-off. Thus we define a child (or an adult) as being in chronic poverty if his or her six-year average income ('smoothed income') is below the poverty line. If an individual is poor some time during the six years but not chronically poor, she or he is classified as experiencing transitory poverty.

US research findings suggest that chronic poverty exerts more adverse effects on children than transient poverty (see chapter 2). These findings suggest that it is important to learn more about the nature of British children's poverty, particularly the extent to which it is chronic versus transitory, and how similar it is across different stages of childhood.

The paper provides information about the six-year experience of poverty for our sample in terms of the numbers of times children and adults are observed poor over the six-year interval, and also decompositions of total poverty into its chronic and transitory components (using two poverty indices). A distinctive feature of our analysis is that we compare poverty at different stages of childhood. We also compare the poverty of children with the poverty of adults.

Policy programmes aimed at reducing chronic poverty face an important practical problem: at any point in time it is only current income (and perhaps past incomes) which are observed; smoothed incomes and chronic poverty status are unknown. If the programmes are to take a means-tested approach to allocating benefits, which is frequently suggested, of necessity they must use current income (possibly along with past incomes) to identify the poor people to target. But since incomes typically vary from one year to the next, many people's observed (current-income) poverty status may not match their chronic poverty status. As a result, the aim of reducing chronic poverty is compromised when current income targeting is used. We illustrate the size of this problem by considering a stylised policy programme in which a uniform per child flat rate cash benefit is given to poor households with children.

7.2 Concepts: smoothed incomes, chronic and transitory poverty

Current income versus smoothed income

For each adult and child in our BHPS sample (described in the next section), we have six observations on current income, one for each year 1991–6. For each of these individuals we can calculate the six-year average of his or her current income, and it is this average that we label 'smoothed income'.

Smoothed income is the income which each person would have were there no year-on-year income variability or, alternatively, were everyone able to smooth income inter-temporally perfectly and costlessly. Making a distinction between current and smoothed income streams over time is useful because it draws attention to the fact that some of the poverty observed at a point in time is transitory rather than chronic. (We elaborate below on how we quantify this point.) At the heart of our empirical analysis are comparisons of the poverty patterns associated with inter-temporal streams of current income and smoothed income, inspired by previous research such as Chaudhuri and Ravallion (1994), Jalan and Ravallion (1997) and Rodgers and Rodgers (1993).

For both the current and smoothed definitions of income, measurement of poverty at a point in time requires assumptions about how to identify who the poor are (which is equivalent to defining a poverty line), and assumptions about how to aggregate each individual's poverty over all individuals. When a panel perspective on poverty is introduced, one also has to decide how to aggregate poverty over time.

Aggregating poverty over time and across individuals

For each individual, and for both definitions of income, we summarise poverty for a given year using two different indices. The first is simply a binary ('headcount') indicator of whether a person is poor or not, equal to one if the person is poor and zero otherwise. This indicates the incidence of poverty. The second measure is each person's normalised poverty gap, and takes account of the depth of poverty. For people with incomes below the poverty line, this is equal to the gap between the poverty line and income, divided by the poverty line – in other words, their proportionate shortfall in income from the poverty line. For non-poor people, the normalised gap is set equal to zero.

For each definition of the poverty line, the simplest way of summarising the poverty experience for a person over a given period of time is to count the number of times she or he is poor during the interval. The experience for a group of persons, for example, children or the population as a whole, is then described by the distribution of numbers of times poor for the relevant group. This summarises the incidence of *repeated poverty*. Following a major poverty review (completed after our research had ended), the government has announced that an indicator similar to this (though based on a three-year observation window) is to be used to monitor child poverty persistence: see UK (1999).

In order to decompose total poverty over a period into its chronic and transitory components, and also to be able to use measures of poverty such as the normalised income gap which take account of how poor someone is (rather than only whether she or he is poor), we focus our longitudinal analysis on an alternative approach.

We define *total poverty* for each person to be the six-year average of the poverty she or he experienced in each year, where poverty – whether summarised using the headcount or the normalised income gap measure – is calculated using current incomes. Analogously, we define *chronic poverty* for each person to be the six-year average of poverty in each year, but now with poverty calculated using smoothed incomes. Transitory poverty, the poverty attributable to inter-temporal variations in income, is then defined as the component of total poverty which remains after chronic poverty is removed. That is,

$$\text{transitory poverty} = \text{total poverty} - \text{chronic poverty}.$$

Measures of total poverty and its components for sub-groups of individuals or the population as a whole are defined as the average values for the relevant groups. (For example, chronic poverty among all children is simply the average among children of each child's measure of chronic poverty.) This set of definitions guarantees that total poverty equals the sum of chronic and transitory poverty at the aggregate level as well as at the individual level. It also guarantees that if poverty increases for one sub-group and does not fall for any other group, then aggregate poverty must increase. Aggregate poverty will also increase if poverty is higher in one year and no lower in all the other years during the period.

The various definitions imply that, when we use the headcount poverty measure, inter-temporal total poverty for each person is simply the proportion of the total period when she or he is poor. Inter-temporal total poverty for the population as a whole is the proportion of persons who are poor in an 'average' year during the period (which also equals the average across the population of the per-person proportions of total time poor). If instead we use the normalised gap concept, inter-temporal total poverty for the population as a whole is the average across persons and time periods of the normalised poverty gaps.

7.3 Data and definitions

This chapter focuses on panel analysis of data from the British Household Panel Survey (BHPS) covering 1991–6, but sets the stage using additional sources in order to describe cross-section trends extending further back into history than the BHPS allows.

The data sets

The BHPS's first wave is a nationally representative sample of the population of Great Britain living in private households in 1991. Original sample respondents (including both partners from a dissolved wave 1 partnership) have been followed and they, and their co-residents, interviewed at approximately one-year intervals subsequently.[1] Children in original sample households are also interviewed when they reach the age of 16 years. Thus the sample remains broadly representative of the population of Britain as it has changed through the 1990s.

Six waves of BHPS data were available at the time of writing. For our panel analysis we work with the sub-sample of 6,824 individuals (5,036 adults and 1,788 children) present in each of the six waves and who belong to complete respondent households. The first restriction on the sample arose from the desire to examine income sequences over all six waves. The second restriction yields the sample for whom we can derive our preferred income measure – net income. In order to account for differential non-response at wave 1, and subsequent differential attrition, all statistics for the panel analysis are based on data weighted using the BHPS wave 6 longitudinal enumerated individual weights.

To describe poverty trends from 1961 to 1996, we combine information from three sources: official 'Households Below Average Income' statistics published by the Department of Social Security for 1979, 1981, 1987–95/6 ('DSS/HBAI' series), plus calculations by the authors using Goodman and Webb's (1994) 'Households Below Average Income' data for 1961–91 ('IFS/HBAI' series), and British Household Panel Survey data for 1991–6 ('BHPS'). The first two series are each based on data from the Family Expenditure Survey, a continuous national household survey. The BHPS data used for documentation of trends are the same as for the BHPS panel analysis described above, except that the full cross-section sample for each wave is used (with cross-section weights) rather than a balanced sample.

The definition of income

In both the cross-section and panel analyses, the income distributions are defined in a similar manner. The unit of analysis is the individual, be it a

---

[1] For a detailed discussion of BHPS methodology, representativeness, and weighting and imputation procedures, see Taylor (1994) and Taylor (1996).

child or an adult, and, following standard practice, each individual is attributed the income of the household to which she or he belongs. Net income is the measure of household income and an individual is classified as poor if net income falls below a poverty line.

Net income is a standard measure of disposable household income. It is used to compile the official income distribution statistics (see, for example, Department of Social Security 1998) and is similar to that used by the Luxembourg Income Study and the other studies in this book. Net money income is the sum across all household members of cash income from all sources minus direct taxes.[2] Income receipt for each income component refers to the month prior to the wave of interview, or most recent relevant period, with the exception of employment earnings which refer to the 'usual' amount.[3] We express all incomes in pounds sterling per week in 1996 prices.

Net money incomes are deflated by a household-specific equivalence scale rate in order to account for differences in household size and composition. The equivalence scale we use in the analysis of long-run trends is the 'McClements before housing costs' equivalence scale (see Department of Social Security 1998, for details). This is the scale used to compile the official low-income statistics and is often used in other British income distribution analysis.

The main equivalence scale we use in our panel analysis is the square root of household size, i.e. we choose a scale with an elasticity with respect to household size equal to 0.5, which is the same as used elsewhere in this volume. Coulter, Cowell and Jenkins (1992) and Jenkins and Cowell (1994) demonstrate that the equivalence-scale relativities incorporated in the McClements equivalence scale correspond to a household size elasticity of between 0.6 and 0.7, i.e. lower economies of scale than incorporated in our 'square-root' scale. To check the robustness of our results, we have re-worked our panel analysis calculations using two other elasticity values: 0.75 (low economies of scale) and 0.25 (high economies of scale). The larger the size elasticity value incorporated in the equivalence scale, the lower the economic standing of larger households relative to smaller households in any given year (and hence children relative to the elderly).

[2] For detailed discussion of variable construction and a demonstration of the validity of the derived distributions relative to a range of relevant HBAI benchmarks for waves 1 and 2, see Jarvis and Jenkins (1995) and Redmond (1997).

[3] Because the income observations for each person refer to income just prior to the time of interview (i.e. some time during the last quarters of 1991, 1992, 1993, 1994, 1995, 1996 for most respondents), we cannot take account of any additional changes in income occurring outside those times; hence, our estimates may miss some movements into or out of poverty.

The poverty line

There is no official poverty line in the UK so we looked to several sources for poverty-line definitions. We use two different poverty lines for calculating long-range poverty trends: half contemporary mean income and half 1991 mean income. These are similar to those employed in the official British low-income statistics (for example, Department of Social Security 1998), which each year indicate the proportion of the population with an income below cut-offs equal to fractions (from 0.4 to 1.0 including 0.5) of mean 1979 income, and fractions of contemporary mean income.

For our panel analysis we focus instead on a different poverty line, one which is fixed in real terms. This line is equal to half of the median income in wave 1 (1991).[4] To check robustness of results, we also investigated another fixed poverty line (half wave 1 mean income) and a relative poverty line (half contemporary median income). Use of a contemporary median line provides a link to the cross-national analysis of child poverty dynamics in chapter 4. The other poverty lines provide links with some other British poverty research and our own calculations of long-range trends.

Age groups

We are especially interested in the extent to which poverty experiences differ for children at different stages of childhood and for children relative to adults. Although differentiation of children by age is not possible in the DSS/HBAI and IFS/HBAI sources, it is possible with the BHPS. Hence, in our panel analysis we classify individuals into six groups according to their ages at the time of the wave 1 interview (autumn 1991): 0–5, 6–11, 12–17, 18–29, 30–59, and 60+ years. The age categories for children roughly correspond to major divisions for schooling (pre-school, primary school, and secondary school). The oldest group of children begin the observation period as children (ages 12–17) but end it in wave 6 in the lower range of the adult category (they are aged 18–25 in 1996). Throughout our panel analysis, we report the results for the entire population and for the various age groups separately, paying special attention to the three age groups of children.

---

[4] A poverty line at half wave-1 median income is in the neighbourhood of social assistance benefit (Income Support) eligibility levels, although it is hard to be precise about this because eligibility for Income Support depends in part on housing costs and these differ between persons.

7.4 Trends in child poverty in Britain

Official statistics for 1996/7 (Department of Social Security 1998) show British children over-represented at the bottom of the income distribution, with over a quarter in the bottom fifth of the distribution, and individuals in families with children having a higher risk of low income than those in families with no children. According to the same source, 19 per cent of all persons had below half the average income, but the proportion for children was almost 50 per cent higher, 26 per cent.[5] How have child poverty rates changed over time and have children always fared so badly relative to others?

Long-term trends in poverty

Figures 7.1 and 7.2 help provide some answers. These show poverty rates for all children and for all persons (adults plus children), for each year between 1961 and 1996 using two different poverty lines.[6] Figure 7.1 shows, for each year, the proportions with incomes below half contemporary mean income; figure 7.2 shows, for each year, the proportions with below half mean income in 1991.

The graphs provide strikingly different pictures about long-term trends in child poverty. If one uses a poverty line that is constant in real income terms (figure 7.2), then the story is one of a clear decline in child poverty rates over the last three and a half decades, including the first half of the 1990s. By contrast, according to figure 7.1, child poverty rates more than doubled during the 1980s, to reach a peak in 1992/3 before levelling off at

---

[5] Any concern that income-based measures of poverty may exaggerate levels of child poverty is diminished by recent research using lack of children's necessities as indicators of poverty trends: see, for example, Bradshaw (1997a, 1997b), and Middleton, Ashworth and Walker (1994).

[5] The 'BHPS' series are not contiguous with the HBAI-based ones for several reasons. Most importantly, (a) the HBAI data include some high-income imputations, especially in order to derive better estimates of mean income. Thus mean income estimated from the BHPS for the corresponding year, and the level of any half mean poverty line, is lower than its HBAI counterpart, and hence so too are poverty rates. Less important reasons are: (b) the BHPS covers Britain rather than the UK as a whole; (c) most interviews occur during the autumn of each year rather than through the year as for the Family Expenditure Survey; and (d) the definition of 'child' used here is someone aged less than 18 years. In the HBAI series, a child is someone less than 16 years or less than 19 and in full-time secondary education.

Figure 7.1. *The proportion poor 1961–1996 (poverty line = half contemporary mean income; McClements equivalence scale)*

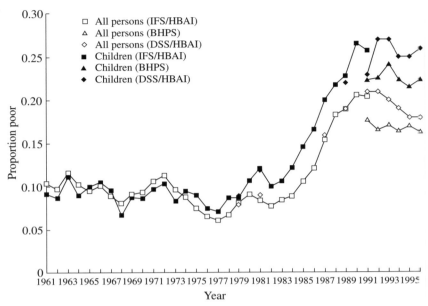

about 25 per cent. Even with the levelling off, according to the figure 7.1 poverty definition, child poverty in 1995/6 is more than double that in 1979 (or 1969). The differences between the pictures can be explained by secular growth in average income, combined with the unparalleled rise during the 1980s in income inequality (Jenkins 1996, 1997) which then levelled off during the 1990s. For a more detailed analysis of child poverty trends focusing on the period 1968–96, see Gregg *et al.* (1999).

Clearly, conclusions about the direction of trends in child poverty over the full three and a half decades are not robust to the choice of poverty-line definition. A finding that is robust to the choice of poverty line, though, is evidence of the child poverty rate being higher than the all-persons poverty rate at least since the mid-1970s. In this sense, there remains a child poverty problem, even if one were to argue that the rates themselves had recently fallen.

This conclusion that there is a child poverty problem in the UK is bolstered by chapter 3's cross-national comparisons.

The nature of trends in childhood poverty is further illuminated by detailed breakdowns of poverty rates for children and adults of different

Figure 7.2. *The proportion poor 1961–1996 (poverty line = half 1991 mean income; McClements equivalence scale)*

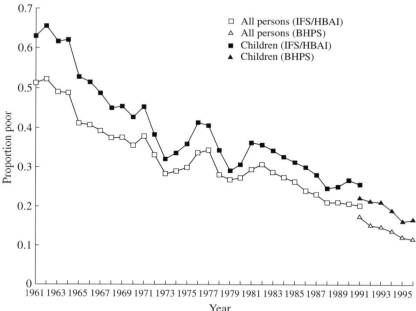

ages: see Hill and Jenkins (1999) for details.[7] This analysis shows distinctly that, during the period 1991–6, poverty was more pronounced – both more widespread and more severe – among younger children than older children. Vulnerability to poverty peaked at each end of the life cycle. It was the elderly (individuals initially age 60 or older) whose patterns of poverty approximated most closely to those of the youngest children. The poverty ranking of young children relative to the elderly was, however, sensitive to the choice of equivalence scale and somewhat sensitive to the choice of poverty line. However, across all variations in equivalence scales and poverty lines, the very young and the elderly ranked highest in poverty of all the age groups.

---

[7] The analysis was based on the panel sample containing the same persons in each year rather than a set of cross-section samples. Although the latter samples provide better estimates in principle, we found that aggregate trends estimated using both types of sample were similar.

7.5 Repeated, chronic and transitory poverty: results

A major limitation of the repeated single-year cross-section estimates is that they cannot tell us the extent to which poverty is concentrated among the same individuals year after year, and this aspect of poverty has important implications for the design and implementation of public policies aimed at eliminating poverty or ameliorating its ill effects. To look at these issues, we turn to assessments of poverty from a panel perspective, and also make a distinction between current and smoothed incomes.

Repeated poverty

The simplest way of summarising poverty experience over time is to count the number of times people are poor over the six-year period. Table 7.1 reports the results of such calculations using current incomes and also assuming people were to receive their six-wave smoothed incomes in each year. Observe that the percentage of persons who have a smoothed income below the poverty line is exactly the same as our measure of chronic poverty based on the headcount index.

During the period 1991–6, only a very small percentage (1.7 per cent) of the population was current-income poor for all six years, but about one-tenth (10.6 per cent) were poor at least half of the time. Young children, pre-schoolers in particular, were more likely than most others in the population to be repeatedly poor. Of the pre-schoolers 20.9 per cent were poor at least three times, with 2.4 per cent poor all six years. This compares with 12.2 per cent and 1.5 per cent, respectively, for primary-school-age children, and 7.2 per cent and zero, respectively, for secondary-school-age children. The youngest children were surpassed by only one age group in terms of susceptibility to poverty in each and every one of the six years: the elderly show 4.4 per cent poor all six years.

The proportion of persons never having smoothed income below the poverty line (and hence not chronically poor) is substantially larger than the proportion who are never poor according to current incomes. For example, among all children the relevant percentages are 62 per cent and 91 per cent. This difference is a manifestation of inter-temporal income variation and hence transitory poverty (which we shall study in more detail shortly).

Among the population as a whole, 6.7 per cent were always poor if incomes were smoothed. The earlier finding that the very young, as well as the very old, have the greatest vulnerability to persistent poverty appears as

Table 7.1. *Number of times poor out of six, by age group (row percentages)*

Age in years (at wave 1 interview)	Number of times poor (current incomes)				Number of times poor (smoothed incomes)		
	0	1–2	3–5	6	0	1–5	6
0–5	54.3	24.8	18.5	2.4	86.0	0	14.0
6–11	64.7	23.1	10.7	1.5	91.8	0	8.2
12–17	67.7	25.1	7.2	0.0	97.2	0	2.9
18–29	71.5	18.3	9.1	1.1	93.5	0	6.5
30–59	79.0	15.3	5.2	0.5	97.7	0	2.3
60+	58.5	26.0	11.3	4.4	88.2	0	11.8
All 0–17	61.7	24.3	12.6	1.4	91.2	0	8.8
All 18+	71.1	19.2	7.9	1.8	93.9	0	6.1
All persons	69.0	20.4	8.9	1.7	93.3	0	6.7

Notes: $N = 6,824$ persons. Poverty line = half wave 1 sample median income (£81.47 per week, in 1996 prices).

well when calculations are made using smoothed incomes. Approximately one tenth of young children were chronically poor: 14 per cent of pre-schoolers and 8.2 per cent of primary-school-age children. And the elderly fell in between these two groups of young children in terms of the percentage chronically poor (11.8 per cent). Hence, chronic poverty appears to be non-trivial in its incidence in Britain, especially among individuals at either end of the life cycle.

We now examine chronic poverty in more detail, relating it to total poverty and transitory poverty and also using an additional alternative poverty index.

Total, chronic and transitory poverty

Estimates of the total poverty experienced by our sample over the six-year period appear in the first column of table 7.2: total poverty is measured using the headcount index in the top panel and the normalised poverty-gap index in the bottom panel. These figures show the average poverty for each age group in a 'typical' year (see section 7.2), and the same age-related patterns appear here as were reported earlier for each year separately: higher total poverty among very young children and the elderly, and the lowest total poverty among prime-aged individuals.

Estimates for our decomposition of total poverty into its chronic and

Table 7.2. *Total, chronic and transitory poverty, by age and poverty index*

Age in years (at wave 1 interview)	Total poverty	Chronic poverty	(as % of total)	Transitory poverty	(as % of total)
Poverty index = percentage of persons poor					
0–5	19.8	14.0	(71)	5.8	(29)
6–11	13.4	8.2	(61)	5.2	(39)
12–17	9.9	2.9	(29)	7.1	(71)
18–29	11.0	6.5	(59)	4.5	(41)
30–59	7.0	2.3	(33)	4.7	(67)
60+	17.5	11.8	(68)	5.7	(32)
All 0–17	14.7	8.8	(60)	6.0	(40)
All 18+	11.1	6.1	(55)	5.0	(45)
All persons	11.9	6.7	(56)	5.1	(44)
Poverty index = average normalised poverty gap × 100					
0–5	4.9	1.8	(37)	3.1	(63)
6–11	3.2	1.0	(30)	2.2	(70)
12–17	2.9	0.2	(8)	2.7	(92)
18–29	2.9	0.9	(30)	2.1	(70)
30–59	2.0	0.4	(18)	1.7	(82)
60+	3.7	1.8	(48)	1.9	(52)
All 0–17	3.7	1.1	(29)	2.7	(71)
All 18+	2.7	0.9	(33)	1.8	(67)
All persons	3.0	0.9	(32)	2.0	(68)

Notes: Total poverty calculated using current incomes for all six waves pooled. Chronic poverty calculated using six-wave smoothed incomes. Transitory poverty = total poverty – chronic poverty. $N = 6,824$ persons. Poverty line = half wave 1 sample median income (£81.47 per week, in 1996 prices).

transitory components appear in the remaining columns of table 7.2. With only two age groups as exceptions, chronic poverty measured using the headcount index comprises more than half of total poverty. It constitutes nearly three quarters of total poverty for the very youngest children. The exceptional age groups are those aged 12–17 and 30–59. The corollary of this result is, of course, that transitory poverty forms less than one half of total poverty for all but these two groups.

This finding about the relative importance of transitory poverty in total poverty is sensitive to the choice of poverty index. When we take account of the depth of poverty using the normalised poverty-gap index (table 7.2, bottom panel), then for every age group the majority of total poverty is made up of transitory poverty, and for those aged 12–17 in 1991 transitory poverty comprises virtually all (92 per cent) of their total poverty (this figure is most likely the consequence of the transition from youth to adult for this group over the period – see the earlier discussion).

Put another way, if incomes could have been (perfectly and costlessly) smoothed, most people's income shortfall from the poverty line would have been relatively small. This finding is consistent with the results of Jarvis and Jenkins (1998) based on data from BHPS waves 1–4. They reported that there was much inter-temporal income mobility throughout the income scale (including the lowest ranges), but that it was mostly short-distance rather than long-distance mobility. Short-distance mobility is likely to have more of an impact on our inter-temporal headcount poverty index than its income gap counterpart because a relatively large proportion of the population are to be found in the income ranges in the neighbourhood of the poverty line. There is substantial clumping of people around the poverty line even if alternative (and commonly used) poverty lines such as half contemporary median or mean income are used (these are higher in real terms than the line here). This helps explain why the patterns we have reported in this section are relatively robust if a differently defined poverty line is used.

Although conclusions about the proportion of total poverty which is accounted for by transitory poverty are sensitive to the choice of poverty index, some findings are not. For example, the rankings of the age groups are the same whether one looks at levels of chronic poverty or the percentage of total poverty which is chronic – those in the very youngest age group have the highest degree of chronic poverty (along with the elderly), and the prime-aged have the lowest chronic poverty. If a different equivalence scale from the square-root one is used, impressions about rankings change somewhat. This sensitivity is most pronounced for the relative rankings of young children and the elderly (as expected). Assumptions of higher economies of household size show chronic poverty as a smaller share of total poverty among young children, but a larger share of total poverty among the elderly.

7.6 Chronic poverty and income transfers to poor children

Reduction of transitory poverty is important, but reduction of chronic poverty probably deserves more attention, especially given the evidence about its long-term effects.[8]

---

[8] The contrary argument – in favour of retaining a focus on current incomes – is that people, especially low-income people, cannot smooth incomes inter-temporally very well. There is little evidence for Britain about this, and it would be useful to have more. Our research could be extended to consider more sophisticated definitions of smoothed incomes, taking into account saving and borrowing along the lines of Rodgers and Rodgers (1993).

Poverty reduction programmes

The main poverty reduction policies in the UK at the time of our analysis were the cash transfer programmes in the social security benefit system. Some pro-active policies aimed at increasing labour-market participation – the so-called 'New Deal' schemes – have recently been introduced but their impact is not yet known. The new Working Families Tax Credit (WFTC), in place since October 1999 (after our analysis), aims to use the tax system to channel more resources to low-income working families with children.

The programmes of principal relevance to families with children prior to October 1999 were: Income Support, providing means-tested social assistance to low-income non-working families; Family Credit, providing means-tested assistance to low-income families with a full-time worker (now replaced by the WFTC); Housing Benefit and Council Tax Benefit, providing means-tested assistance with high housing rents for low-income families; and the Job Seeker's Allowance, which provides unemployment insurance for unemployed workers with satisfactory contribution records and unemployment spells less than six months, with means-tested assistance thereafter. Each of these benefits includes age-related allowances for children. Another important and distinctive programme is Child Benefit, which is a flat-rate payment per child to all mothers with children (i.e. it is not means-tested). In 1996 Child Benefit was paid at the weekly rate of £10.80 for the eldest child and £8.80 per each additional child in the family. There is also One-Parent Benefit paying a weekly addition to Child Benefit for the eldest child, though it is now being phased out (it paid £6.30 per week in 1996). Receipts from all the cash benefits cited in this paragraph (and all others) are included in the definition of net income used in all the calculations reported in this paper: poverty is post-tax and post-transfer poverty.

The overlap between current and chronic poverty

Eligibility for means-tested benefits and amounts paid depend on a family's current income rather than its smoothed income, which is unobserved. But of course it is smoothed income which determines chronic poverty status. Thus if we focus on chronic poverty reduction, then there is an inevitable policy targeting mismatch. The social security benefit system could reduce chronic poverty more if benefits could be targeted at smoothed incomes rather than current incomes.

The less the overlap between current poverty in any year and chronic poverty, the larger the targeting mismatch. Table 7.3 provides information about the degree of overlap for three age groups of children, for all children and for all adults. Rows 1 and 2 in each panel provide reference points: they show the current and chronic poverty rates for each year. The overlap of current and chronic poverty is shown in row 3 and the mismatch – the consequence of transitory poverty – is shown in rows 4 and 5.

Among all children, the percentage both currently poor and chronically poor ranges from 7.0 per cent in 1991 to 4.6 per cent in 1996 ('all children', row 3). This overlapping segment tends to constitute less than half those currently poor. The proportions chronically poor among all children currently poor are 39 per cent in 1991 and 30 per cent in 1996 (row 3 relative to row 1). For all adults the corresponding proportions chronically poor among the currently poor are 34 per cent and 48 per cent. For children aged 0–5 the corresponding proportions are 41 per cent and 57 per cent, and for children aged 6–11 they are 39 per cent and 37 per cent.

Looking to the proportions of the chronically poor not represented among the currently poor, we find among all children the proportion ranges from 20 per cent in 1991 to 47 per cent in 1996 (row 5 relative to row 2). Corresponding proportions for adults are 23 per cent and 30 per cent. The comparable figures for children aged 0–5 are 25 per cent and 41 per cent, and for children aged 6–11 they are 13 per cent and 63 per cent.

Between 1991 and 1996, and for each group, the fraction of the chronically poor who were not also current-income poor rose. By contrast the fraction of those who were currently poor but not chronically poor (row 4) declined over the period in tandem with the secular decrease in current-income poverty. This trend is a consequence of using a fixed poverty line during a period of secular income growth.

Targeting chronic poverty: a numerical illustration

We now illustrate the extent to which benefits targeted on current incomes rather than smoothed incomes are effective in reducing chronic poverty. The hypothetical programme for this illustration is assumed to pay (in addition to existing programmes) a uniform flat-rate weekly payment for each child aged 0–11 in a household that is counted as poor according to current income.

For various levels of flat-rate payment per current-income-poor child (and assuming no behavioural effects), we can calculate the impact on chronic poverty. Given the number of current-income-poor children whose households would receive payments, we also know the total cost of the

Table 7.3. *The overlap between current-income poverty and chronic poverty (per cent)*

	Wave					
	1 (1991)	2 (1992)	3 (1993)	4 (1994)	5 (1995)	6 (1996)
Children aged 0–5						
1. Currently poor	25.5	25.6	20.2	18.3	14.3	14.8
2. Chronically poor	14.0	14.0	14.0	14.0	14.0	14.0
3. Currently poor and chronically poor	10.5	10.4	9.4	10.6	9.1	8.4
4. Currently poor and not chronically poor	14.9	15.2	10.8	7.7	5.2	6.5
5. Not currently poor but chronically poor	3.5	3.6	4.6	3.4	4.9	5.7
Children aged 6–11						
1. Currently poor	18.1	17.9	12.7	13.3	10.0	8.2
2. Chronically poor	8.2	8.2	8.2	8.2	8.2	8.2
3. Currently poor and chronically poor	7.1	5.9	5.8	5.6	4.6	3.0
4. Currently poor and not chronically poor	11.1	12.1	6.9	7.7	5.4	5.2
5. Not currently poor but chronically poor	1.1	2.4	2.4	2.6	3.6	5.2
Children aged 12–17						
1. Currently poor	8.8	9.2	7.7	9.4	13.3	11.1
2. Chronically poor	2.9	2.9	2.9	2.9	2.9	2.9
3. Currently poor and chronically poor	2.3	2.3	1.8	2.3	1.9	1.9
4. Currently poor and not chronically poor	6.6	6.9	5.9	7.1	11.4	9.2
5. Not currently poor but chronically poor	0.6	0.6	1.1	0.6	0.9	1.0
All children						
1. Currently poor	18.1	18.2	14.0	14.0	12.5	11.5
2. Chronically poor	8.8	8.8	8.8	8.8	8.8	8.8
3. Currently poor and chronically poor	7.0	6.5	6.0	6.5	5.5	4.6
4. Currently poor and not chronically poor	11.2	11.7	8.1	7.5	7.1	6.8
5. Not currently poor but chronically poor	1.8	2.3	2.8	2.3	3.3	4.1
All adults						
1. Currently poor	13.8	12.3	10.7	11.0	9.6	9.0
2. Chronically poor	6.1	6.1	6.1	6.1	6.1	6.1
3. Currently poor and chronically poor	4.7	4.7	4.6	4.9	4.6	4.3
4. Currently poor and not chronically poor	9.2	7.6	6.1	6.1	5.0	4.7
5. Not currently poor but chronically poor	1.4	1.4	1.5	1.2	1.5	1.8

Notes: Chronic poverty calculated using six-wave smoothed incomes. $N = 6,824$ persons.
Poverty line = half wave 1 sample median income (£81.47 per week, in 1996 prices).

programme. We can then calculate the impact on chronic poverty of this same budget had it instead been targeted at smoothed incomes and thence directly at chronic poverty. Since current-income poverty includes both chronic and transitory poverty, targeting on current income disperses benefits to alleviate both types of poverty, perforce eliminating less chronic poverty than if targeting were on smoothed incomes. The questions at issue are: how much less, and in what ways does the picture change as the size of the per-child benefit is varied?

Before addressing these questions, we should stress that our example is intended as an illustrative quantification of the impact of transitory poverty rather than a true-to-life simulation of the effects of alternative anti-poverty programmes. Indeed the likelihood of an additional benefit such as this being introduced is small. Nonetheless the formulation of the example does reflect two British realities. First, as described earlier, there is a UK precedent for flat-rate transfers per child, namely Child Benefit and One-Parent Benefit. And there have been on-going debates about whether Child Benefit should become means-tested. Our example considering benefit supplements to poor children is an example of a means-tested programme. Second, our analysis has shown that the level of chronic poverty is greater for younger children than for older children. We therefore focus on children aged 0–11 in 1991.

Our results are summarised in figure 7.3. We consider uniform flat-rate benefits ranging from £5 to £25 per week per current-income-poor child aged 0–11, and compare current-income and smoothed-income targeting strategies. The results are summarised in terms of the impacts on chronic poverty rates of all children aged 0–11 and all persons: hence there are two pairs of lines drawn in the figure. The current 'no change' situation is the case with the uniform flat-rate transfer set equal to zero.

Smoothed-income targeting is clearly much more effective than current-income targeting in reducing chronic poverty. Even a flat-rate £5 payment targeted on smoothed incomes would reduce the chronic poverty rate among children aged 0–11 to exactly the same rate as for all persons. The chronic poverty rate for these children is cut in half (from 11.2 per cent to 5.2 per cent). By contrast, targeting on current income with a £5 payment would reduce the chronic poverty rate for these children by one third, with 7.7 per cent remaining chronically poor. To reduce chronic child poverty to the level achieved with a £5 payment with smoothed-income targeting (5.2 per cent), current-income targeting requires a flat-rate transfer of between £10 and £15, which represents a more than doubling of the programme budget. Transitory poverty thus has expensive consequences in terms of effective targeting of chronic poverty reduction programmes.

As the size of the uniform payment is increased, chronic poverty rates for children fall and fall quite sharply initially. The relative advantage of smoothed-income targeting over current-income targeting remains sizeable until the uniform flat-rate benefit is very large and virtually all chronic poverty among children aged 0–11 has been eliminated.

The chronic poverty impact of both current- and smoothed-income targeting strategies is more muted among the population as a whole. Chronic

Figure 7.3. *The impact on chronic poverty of a uniform flat-rate transfer to each poor child*

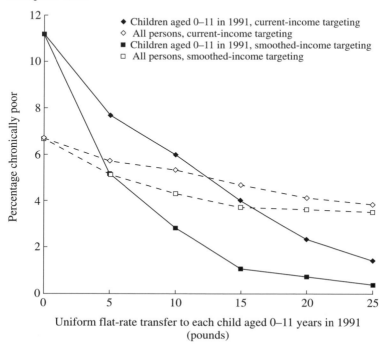

poverty rates for children aged 0–11 are higher than for other groups, but these children comprise only about one sixth of the population. Thus totally eliminating children's chronic poverty would reduce the overall chronic poverty rate significantly, but non-negligible chronic poverty would still remain.

7.7 Concluding remarks

Our focus has been on the incidence and depth of childhood poverty in Britain, with special attention given to differences by stage of childhood and for children relative to adults. We have supplemented the standard cross-sectional perspective on trends with information about longitudinal dimensions of child poverty, highlighting a distinction between chronic and transitory poverty.

We have found that both total and chronic poverty are of sizeable magnitude among British children, especially very young children. Only the poverty of the elderly approaches that of the very young. If income were able to be perfectly and costlessly smoothed inter-temporally, the poverty rate among children would be almost halved, but a significant level of chronic poverty would remain.

If the reduction of chronic poverty is the goal of policy, then programme designers have a problem: it is current incomes that are observed rather than smoothed incomes. Income variability from one year to the next, and thence transitory poverty, compromises the effectiveness of cash benefit programmes. Our numerical illustration considering supplementary flat-rate benefits to current-income-poor children shows that this unobservability problem is important to consider: it can significantly reduce the effectiveness of cash benefits in reducing chronic poverty.

We should stress once again that our example is a quantitative illustration of the impact of transitory poverty. As a guide to practical policymaking it is less relevant, since the counterfactual reference point (the smoothed-income distribution) is not observed. How might benefit agencies derive better information about claimants' longer-term standards of living and hence chronic poverty status? On the one hand, one might consider collecting information about claimants' past income as well as current income, though a distinct problem with this is the possible instability across time in the unit used for assessing economic status. Household membership can change over time in ways that make it difficult to retrospectively measure household income. On the other hand, and more optimistically, many of the household characteristics associated with a child's current-income poverty are also associated with his or her chronic poverty status. For example, the presence of a working spouse markedly reduces the probability of having a low smoothed income and the probability of having a low current income. (We are drawing on the results of regression analyses not reported here.) Moreover, even though current-income targeting does not reduce chronic poverty by as much as smoothed-income targeting would, observe that in our illustration there is a marked reduction in chronic poverty among children with even a current-income-targeted £5 payment.

Acknowledgements
Hill acknowledges with appreciation funding support from the Institute for Social and Economic Research at the University of Essex during her visit in spring 1998. The authors thank the other contributors to this book for their helpful comments and suggestions.

References

Blair, T., 1999, The Beveridge lecture. Speech given at the Toynbee Hall, London, 18 March 1999. http://www.number-10.gov.uk/public/info/index.html

Bradbury, B. and Jäntti, M., 1999, 'Child poverty across industrialised nations', Innocenti Occasional Papers, Economic and Social Policy Series 71, UNICEF International Child Development Centre, Florence. http://www.unicef-icdc.org

Bradshaw, J., 1997a, 'Children in poverty', unpublished paper, University of York. Presented at launch of 'Breadline Britain in the 1990s' at the House of Commons, London, 22 July 1997.

Bradshaw, J., 1997b, 'Child welfare in the United Kingdom: rising poverty, falling priorities for children', in Cornia, G. A. and Danziger, S. (eds.), *Child Poverty and Deprivation in Industrialized Countries, 1945–1995*, Clarendon Press, Oxford.

Brown, G., 1999, Speech by the Chancellor of the Exchequer at the Sure Start Conference, 7 July 1999. http://hm-treasury.gov.uk/speech/cx70799.html

Buhmann, B., Rainwater, L., Schmaus, G. and Smeeding, T., 1988, 'Equivalence scales, well-being, inequality and poverty: sensitivity estimates across ten countries using the Luxembourg Income Study (LIS) database', *Review of Income and Wealth*, 34: 115–42.

Chaudhuri, S. and Ravallion, M., 1994, 'How well do static indicators identify the chronically poor?', *Journal of Public Economics*, 53: 367–94.

Coulter, F. A., Cowell, F. A. and Jenkins, S. P., 1992, 'Equivalence scale relativities and the extent of inequality and poverty', *Economic Journal*, 102: 1067–82.

Department of Social Security, 1998, *Households Below Average Income 1979–1996/97*, Corporate Document Services, London.

Department of Social Security, 1999, *Households Below Average Income 1994/95–1997/98*, Corporate Document Services, London.

Goodman, A. and Webb, S., 1994, 'For richer, for poorer. The changing distribution of income in the United Kingdom, 1961–91', Commentary 42, Institute for Fiscal Studies, London. Abridged version in *Fiscal Studies*, 15: 29–62.

Gregg, P., Harkness, S. and Machin, S., 1999, 'Poor kids: trends in child poverty in Britain, 1968–1996', *Fiscal Studies*, 20: 163–87.

Hill, M. S. and Jenkins, S. P., 1999, 'Poverty among British children: chronic or transitory?', ESRC Research Centre on Micro-Social Change Working Paper 99–23, University of Essex, Colchester. http://www.iser.essex.ac.uk/pubs/workpaps/wp99–23.htm

Jalan, J. and Ravallion, M., 1997, 'Consumption variability and rural poverty in post-reform China', unpublished paper, World Bank Research Department, Washington DC.

Jarvis, S. and Jenkins, S. P., 1995, 'Do the poor stay poor? New evidence about income dynamics from the British Household Panel Survey', ESRC Research Centre on Micro-Social Change Occasional Paper 95–2, University of Essex, Colchester.

Jarvis, S. and Jenkins, S. P., 1998, 'How much income mobility is there in Britain?', *Economic Journal*, 108: 428–43.

Jenkins, S. P., 1996, 'Recent trends in the UK income distribution: what happened and why', *Oxford Review of Economic Policy*, 12: 29–46.

Jenkins, S. P., 1997, 'Trends in real income in Britain: a microeconomic analysis', *Empirical Economics*, 22: 483–500.

Jenkins, S. P. and Cowell, F. A., 1994, 'Parametric equivalence scales and scale relativities', *Economic Journal*, 104: 891–900.

Middleton, S., Ashworth, K. and Walker, R., 1994, *Family Fortunes: Pressures on Parents and Children in the 1990s*, Child Poverty Action Group, London.

Redmond, G., 1997, 'Imputing council tax bands for households in the British Household Panel Study', ESRC Research Centre on Micro-Social Change Working Paper 97–17, University of Essex, Colchester.

Rodgers, J. R. and Rodgers, J. L., 1993, 'Chronic poverty in the United States', *Journal of Human Resources*, 28: 25–54.

Taylor, A., 1994, 'Appendix: sample characteristics, attrition and weighting', in Buck, N., Gershuny, J., Rose, D. and Scott, J. (eds.), *Changing Households: The British Household Panel Survey 1990–1992*, ESRC Research Centre on Micro-Social Change, University of Essex, Colchester.

Taylor, M. F. (ed.), 1996, *British Household Panel Survey User Manual*, 'Introduction, Technical Reports and Appendices', ESRC Research Centre on Micro-Social Change, University of Essex, Colchester.

HM Treasury, 1999, *Supporting Children Through the Tax and Benefit System*, HM Treasury, London. http://hm-treasury.gov.uk

UK, 1999, *Opportunity for All: Tackling Poverty and Social Exclusion*, Cm 4445, The Stationery Office, London. http://www.dss.gov.uk

8 Child income poverty and deprivation dynamics in Ireland

BRIAN NOLAN, BERTRAND MAÎTRE AND
DOROTHY WATSON

8.1 Poverty, deprivation and the Irish context

Research on poverty and on poverty dynamics generally focuses on income. Thus in part I of this book, the dynamics of child poverty have been measured in terms of the extent to which households with children move above or below income poverty lines over time. Such a focus involves measuring the income of a set of households with children at various points in time, using different waves of a longitudinal household survey, and looking at the extent to which they move across income poverty lines from one wave to another. This provides a basis for not only assessing how much movement there is into and out of poverty, but also for identifying the characteristics of those affected and what triggers poverty entries or escapes.

This chapter aims to show how that picture of income poverty dynamics can be usefully complemented by analysis of information on an extensive set of non-monetary indicators of lifestyle or deprivation. It uses two waves of an Irish panel survey to examine how deprivation changed from one year to the next for households with children. This allows us to examine the extent of stability versus change in deprivation levels, compared with the income poverty transitions for the same set of Irish households as described as part of the comparative analysis of income dynamics presented in chapter 4. This exercise helps in assessing and understanding the implications of income poverty dynamics for living standards. It also helps to bring out the importance of going beyond income at a point in time, and the need to identify children in households most affected by persistent low income and resources and make targeting them a priority for anti-poverty policies.

These topics have particular relevance for Ireland, given the scale of child poverty and current debates about how best to tackle it. In Ireland, relative income poverty for households with children has grown rapidly over the past twenty-five years and now affects a particularly high proportion of children. Figures produced by Eurostat from the first wave of the European

196

Community Household Panel show that Ireland has the second-highest percentage of children living in poor households of all the participating countries (when half average income in each country is used as the poverty line). National studies have shown a marked divergence in poverty trends between Irish households with and without children (Nolan and Farrell 1990, Callan, O'Donoghue and O'Neill 1995). Relative income poverty rates have been rising markedly for children since the early 1970s, with a widening gap between the rates for children and adults. In 1973 about 15 per cent of Irish adults and children lived in households with an income below half the national average. By 1994, the poverty rate for adults was 18 per cent, but for children it had risen to almost 30 per cent.

This deterioration in the position of children reflects both the impact of unemployment on families, and the tax and welfare policies followed over the period. Unemployment rose very rapidly during the 1980s, reaching 18 per cent of the labour force at one point, and its effects on household income had a direct and substantial impact on the number of children in households below relative income poverty lines. In addition, tax and social security policies during the 1980s tended to disadvantage families with children. From a social welfare perspective, increases in social welfare pensions were seen as providing a way of targeting resources to a needy group without distorting financial incentives to work. As a result, at one point, rates of payment for many of the unemployed were close to 40 per cent of average household income (adjusted for household size), while those on social insurance pensions received close to 60 per cent of that average. On the tax side, erosion of the real value of allowances and bands pulled an ever-increasing proportion of the population into the tax net, and from the mid-1980s no account was taken of the presence of children in determining tax liabilities.

Unemployment has been falling rapidly since 1994, as Ireland experiences quite exceptionally high rates of economic growth – among the highest in the OECD. Nonetheless, a stubborn core of long-term unemployment remains, and child poverty has come to be recognised as a major challenge facing Irish policymakers. Options for improving the situation for families with children are being intensively canvassed. In particular, there has been on-going debate about the potential of substantial increases in universal Child Benefit to improve the situation of children without adversely affecting work incentives (see, for example, Callan *et al.* 1995). The best way of assisting families with the costs of childcare have also been the focus of debate, not least in the recent report by the expert Commission on the Family (1998) set up to advise the government. This makes it all the more timely to be able to explore here how Irish children move into and out of poverty, from the perspective of not only income but also other indicators of household welfare and living standards.

8.2 Using non-monetary indicators to measure child poverty

A relative standard for measuring poverty in developed countries is now widely, though not universally, accepted. The definition of poverty employed in the National Anti-Poverty Strategy recently adopted by the Irish government is typical:

> People are living in poverty if their income and resources (material, cultural and social) are so inadequate as to preclude them from having a standard of living which is regarded as acceptable by Irish society generally. As a result of inadequate income and resources people may be excluded and marginalised from participating in activities which are considered the norm for other people in society (National Anti-Poverty Strategy 1997: 3).

In implementing such a definition to measure the extent of poverty, the most common approach has been to define a poverty line in terms of income, and to regard as poor those individuals with incomes below the line. One way to set that income poverty line is then to take it as a proportion of average income, adjusted for the greater needs of larger families, and this is the general approach widely adopted in comparative studies of poverty across industrialised countries.

However, low income on its own may not be an entirely satisfactory measure of *exclusion* arising from lack of resources. It assumes that those falling below the specified income poverty line are not able to participate fully in the life of the community. This cannot be simply taken for granted; it requires validation. Indeed, Ringen's (1987, 1988) stringent critique of the use of income poverty lines is based precisely on the argument that low income is unreliable as an indicator of poverty, because it often fails to distinguish households experiencing deprivation and exclusion. This is not primarily because of the (real) difficulties in measuring income accurately, but more because a household's command over resources is affected by much more than its current income. Long-term factors, relating most importantly to the way resources have been accumulated or eroded over time, as well as current income, play a crucial role in influencing the likelihood of current deprivation and exclusion.

Two complementary routes can be pursued in moving away from reliance on income at a particular point in time. The first is of course to measure income as it evolves over time by means of longitudinal surveys (or administrative data), and the analysis of income dynamics measured in this way is the central focus of this volume. At the same time, seeking to measure various aspects of living standards and deprivation directly through non-monetary indicators also has considerable potential, as we seek to show in this chapter. The use of such indicators was pioneered by Townsend (1979), and they have been used in studying poverty from a cross-section perspective in, for example, Mack and Lansley (1985), Mayer and Jencks (1988), Mayer (1993), Muffels (1993), Callan, Nolan and Whelan (1993), Hallerod (1995) and Nolan and Whelan (1996a, b). These studies have sought to use non-monetary indicators in rather different ways. They all face hard questions such as how the most satisfactory indicators for the purpose are to be selected, whether they are to be combined into a summary deprivation measure, and if so how, and how they are then to be employed in exploring poverty.

It may be particularly important to know the extent to which distinct dimensions of deprivation can be identified, since some may be better than others as measures of generalised deprivation and exclusion. In earlier research with data for Ireland, three such dimensions were identified (Nolan and Whelan 1996a):

1 *basic lifestyle deprivation* – enforced absence of basic items such as food or clothing, considered by most people to be necessities;
2 *secondary lifestyle deprivation* – enforced absence of items such as cars, telephones and holidays commonly possessed but not considered by a majority of people to be necessities.
3 *housing deprivation* – enforced absence of items relating to housing such as having an indoor toilet, hot and cold running water, or a bath/shower, generally considered to be necessities but absence of which bore a weak relationship to other types of deprivation.

The key finding emerging from in-depth analysis of these deprivation indicators is that current income is only one of the factors influencing deprivation levels. Other variables which were significant in predicting deprivation levels included the household's level of financial savings, whether it rented or owned its accommodation, the value of the house, the extent of unemployment experienced by the main earner over his or her career, and his or her social class origin and educational qualifications. This brings out the fact that current living standards will be influenced by the accumulation or erosion of resources over a long period, and highlights the importance of a dynamic perspective. The housing indicators were also seen to be quite distinctive, with single people and farm households particularly likely to experience this but not the other forms of deprivation. Such indicators are thus less likely to be suitable as indicators of generalised deprivation, but in many surveys they are the only ones included.

Focusing on households that are both at relatively low income levels and experiencing basic deprivation should give a better indication of the scale of generalised deprivation or exclusion due to lack of resources than those below income lines alone. In the Irish case, about 10 per cent of households were below half average income and experiencing enforced basic deprivation in 1994, and about 15 per cent were below 60 per cent of mean income and experiencing such deprivation. Compared with income poverty lines alone, this suggests that poverty affects fewer self-employed people and farmers and more households headed by someone working full-time in the home. It also produces a higher poverty rate for children. This way of identifying those most in need has already proved important from a policy perspective. It has recently been incorporated in the global poverty reduction target adopted in the Irish National Anti-Poverty Strategy, which will form the benchmark against which progress in combating poverty is assessed (National Anti-Poverty Strategy 1997).

To date only cross-section data have been available on such non-monetary indicators. Here we are able for the first time to use panel data to explore deprivation dynamics using non-monetary deprivation indicators, which provides a new perspective on the implications of income dynamics for the living standards of households with children. In doing so, we will be employing both a summary index of overall deprivation and sub-indices reflecting different dimensions. We focus on Ireland, but employing the set of non-monetary indicators obtained in the European Community Household Panel survey. This means that, in the future, the same analysis could be undertaken for all the EU countries participating in that survey.

A detailed description of these indicators is given in the next section. Before doing so, it is important to emphasise that they were designed to measure the extent and nature of deprivation at the level of the household rather than the individual. While here we will be concentrating on households containing children, we still do not have direct measures of living standards or deprivation for the children themselves. Exactly as in using household income to measure poverty, the assumption is made that pooling of resources within the household equalises living standards and poverty risks for all household members. The situation where children are in poverty because of insufficient sharing of resources within the household will not be captured, either with conventional income measures or with the deprivation indicators we have available. Poverty research has found it very difficult to look within the household 'black box', as brought out in, for example, Jenkins (1991). Non-monetary deprivation indicators do indeed have some potential for capturing differences in individual living standards within the household, as explored in Cantillon and Nolan (1998), and specially designed indicators for children would be enormously valuable. We hope to include such indicators in a forthcoming Irish survey, but for the present are restricted to measuring deprivation at the level of the household.

8.3 The Living in Ireland Survey and the definitions of poverty and deprivation

The data set on which we rely is the first two waves of the Living in Ireland Survey, the Irish element of the European Community Household Panel (ECHP). Wave 1 was carried out in the second half of 1994; wave 2 in the same period in 1995. The achieved sample size in 1994 was 4,048 households. In the second wave 3,430 of these plus 154 'generated' households were successfully interviewed.[1] This obtained *inter alia* detailed data on income from various sources accruing to each household member in the previous calendar year. Those income data provided the base for the results for Ireland on the dynamics of low income and income poverty among children included in the cross-country analysis in chapter 4.

The ECHP also contains information on the seventeen non-monetary indicators shown in table 8.1. As we have noted, none of these indicators relate specifically to children. They are intended to reflect the situation of the household – for example, whether resources allow adequate heating or meals. The questions asked in most cases specifically seek to distinguish where the household head or manager says that she or he cannot afford the item, rather than does not want it. Distinguishing the effects of resource constraints from tastes is of course problematic, but the format of the questions does allow one to go beyond simply whether the household has or has not got the item. In our analysis we will be concentrating on where the household appears to be experiencing enforced lack, that is doing without because the item cannot be afforded.

Application of factor analysis to these deprivation indicators in the wave 1 sample for Ireland confirms the results of earlier work that the indicators cluster into distinct dimensions. Thus, in addition to employing a summary index based on all seventeen items, we will also make use of sub-indices for basic, secondary and housing deprivation. Table 8.1 shows the way the items are divided into these three dimensions. The table also shows for each item how many households in the wave 1 Irish sample experienced enforced lack, and the percentage of households with children in that position. We see first that the housing items are rarely lacked – almost all households have an indoor toilet, bath and hot running water, and most have a colour television. For households containing children, having to go without these items is even

---

[1] The following rule is that in principle all members of the household in wave 1 are followed in the second and subsequent waves, whether the household has 'split' or not and whether such splits are due to divorce or any other factor. Those who turn out to have emigrated or moved into a non-household institution are not, however, retained within the panel. In practice, some types of split may of course make follow-up more difficult than others.

Table 8.1. *Seventeen non-monetary indicators in the 1994 Living in Ireland Survey*

Non-monetary indicator	Percentage of households doing without	Percentage of households with children doing without
Housing		
Bath or shower	4.8	0.8
Indoor flushing toilet	3.7	0.6
Hot running water	5.5	1.6
Colour TV[a]	1.9	0.9
Secondary		
Car (available for private use)[a]	17.8	20.6
Microwave[a]	16.7	19.8
Video[a]	10.4	10.0
Dishwasher[a]	20.2	30.6
Telephone[a]	13.9	17.0
Second home[a]	39.4	53.1
Replacing worn-out furniture[b]	29.5	36.6
Paying for a week's holiday away from home[b]	40.7	50.1
Basic		
Buying new rather than second-hand clothes[b]	7.9	10.8
Keeping your home adequately warm[b]	9.9	10.6
In arrears in the past 12 months on rent, mortgage, utility bills or loans	13.5	22.0
Eating meat, chicken or fish every second day, if you wanted to[b]	4.5	5.0
Having friends or family for a drink or meal at least once a month[b]	17.9	25.7

Notes: [a] Question asks whether household does/does not have; if the response is does not, then asks whether 'would like but cannot afford' or 'don't want/don't have for other reasons'.   [b] Question asks 'whether your household can afford [the items] if you want them'.

rarer: this reflects the fact that such very poor-quality housing is now virtually confined to a small number of mostly elderly people living in rural areas.

The secondary items are much more widely lacked, with about 10–20 per cent of all households saying that they want the item in question but are doing without because they cannot afford it. Interestingly, the percentage of households with children doing without is generally higher for these items.[2] Turning to the basic items, only about 8 per cent to 18 per cent of

---

[2] One of these items, having a second home, was included in the ECHP, but we regard this as problematic. Only 5 per cent of households in Ireland actually have a second home, but 55 per cent said they did not want one, leaving 40 per cent who said that they wanted one but could not afford it. For such a rarely possessed item, distinguishing those who are 'deprived' of it by means of a simple question seems particularly difficult.

households say they have to do without these items, though for households with children the percentages are again generally substantially higher.

Before going on to analyse deprivation levels and dynamics using these data, an important point must be made about timing. As already mentioned, the accounting period employed for income in the ECHP is the previous calendar year, which means 1993 in the case of wave 1 and 1994 in the case of wave 2. The information about non-monetary indicators, on the other hand, relates to the position at the time of the interview. Given the timing of the survey, this would have mostly been in the third quarter of 1994 and 1995 respectively. Thus the deprivation measures relate to a period significantly after the end of the period to which the income data for that wave refer. Indeed, it is well into the period to which the income data for the *subsequent* wave refer, though some of that income would accrue after the survey date. This clearly poses serious problems for direct analysis of the relationship between changes in deprivation and changes in income. If one had annual income data from wave 3 of the survey, covering 1995, one could then relate changes in deprivation between the wave 1 and wave 2 survey dates to changes in income between 1994 and 1995. Since this information is not yet available, we do not attempt to directly link deprivation dynamics to contemporaneous income dynamics. Instead, we concentrate on assessing the extent of deprivation for households with children, examining how it is related to income in each wave, and measuring how it changed from one wave to another. This serves to establish the overall patterns of deprivation and deprivation dynamics, and bring out the importance of the dynamic perspective in assessing poverty and living standards.

8.4 Deprivation patterns

Our first step in using the non-monetary indicators is to describe the overall pattern of deprivation revealed by households' scores on the various non-monetary indicators and indices in waves 1 and 2 of the ECHP survey for Ireland. We then look at the situation of children in terms of the deprivation levels of the households in which they live. Table 8.2 shows the mean score on the seventeen-item summary index for the entire sample wave 1 and wave 2. As in the part I chapters, we are in effect attaching a measure of the household's welfare level to each person, and then counting the person as the unit of analysis: here, though, instead of household income, we are using the household's deprivation score as that welfare indicator. We see that the mean score on the seventeen-item index over the sample as a whole fell from 2.8 to 2.5. This is quite a marked fall, but is not surprising

Table 8.2. *Scores on seventeen-item summary deprivation index, all persons, 1994 and 1995*

Seventeen-item deprivation score	Wave 1 (%)	Wave 2 (%)
0	21.5	24.1
1–2	34.3	36.5
3–4	20.6	18.4
5–6	11.3	12.2
7–9	9.1	7.2
10–12	2.9	1.4
13+	0.2	0.2
All persons	100.0	100.0
All persons: mean score	2.79	2.52

given the exceptionally rapid increase in average income over the period in the Irish case.

We now turn to the situation of children. Once again, the deprivation score of the household is being attached to each child in it, and the child now becomes the unit of analysis. Table 8.3 shows the pattern of scores on the seventeen-item summary index in wave 1 and wave 2 for those children present in both waves. Comparison with table 8.2 shows that mean deprivation scores are a good deal higher for children than for all persons. In wave 1, for example, the mean score across all persons was 2.8, whereas the mean score across children was 3.4. However, the generalised decline in scores between wave 1 and wave 2 also applies to children, with their mean score falling from 3.4 to 3.0. The percentage scoring zero rose from 15 per cent in wave 1 to 18 per cent in wave 2, and the percentage scoring 7 or above fell from 17 per cent to 12 per cent. The scale of this decline in measured deprivation occurring over such a short period must be emphasised – it is nearly as great as over the preceding seven-year period from 1987 to 1994.

8.5 Deprivation compared to income

How does the level of deprivation being experienced by a household with children relate to its level of income? As we have already noted, the timing of the annual income information obtained in the ECHP poses problems. Wave 1 income, for calendar year 1993, is significantly before the survey

Table 8.3. *Scores on seventeen-item summary
deprivation index, children, 1994 and 1995*

Seventeen-item deprivation score	Wave 1 (%)	Wave 2 (%)
0	14.8	18.0
1–2	32.5	35.1
3–4	22.1	19.6
5–6	13.3	14.9
7–9	12.8	10.2
10–12	4.3	2.0
13+	0.2	0.2
All children	100.0	100.0
All children: mean score	3.43	3.01

Notes: Calculations based on children present at both wave 1
and wave 2.

date at which deprivation was measured in 1994, whereas wave 2 income for
calendar year 1994 covers that date but goes beyond it. On the other hand,
one might in any case expect levels of deprivation to be influenced not only
by income in the recent past, but by income over a long period – and this is
certainly what previous research has led us to expect. It is therefore interesting to look first at the correlation between the individual deprivation
indicators and income in wave 1 versus wave 2.

Table 8.4 shows that there is in fact very little to choose between the two
income measures in these terms: the correlations with each of the items are
very similar indeed for the two income measures. Where there is a
difference, the correlations with wave 1 income are marginally higher more
often than wave 2. The fact that the correlations are so similar suggests that
income over the two years is relevant, so the table goes on to show the correlation between each item and income averaged over the two years. This is
indeed almost always higher than the correlation with either year individ-
ually, though the difference is not great. It is worth noting how much lower
the correlations with income are for the housing items than any of the
others, bringing out the idiosyncratic nature of these items and their limitations – certainly in the Irish case – as indicators of generalised deprivation due to lack of resources.

We can then move from the individual deprivation items to carry out the
same comparison for the scores on the overall seventeen-item deprivation
index, and the scores on the sub-indices for the three dimensions of deprivation described in section 8.2. Table 8.5 shows that this reveals very much
the same pattern. The correlation between index scores and wave 1 income

Table 8.4. *Correlation between non-monetary indicators in waves 1 and 2,
households with children*

	Correlation with income at		
	wave 1	wave 2	wave 1 + wave 2
Housing			
Bath or shower	−0.05	−0.06	−0.06
Indoor flushing toilet	−0.04	−0.05	−0.05
Hot running water	−0.08	−0.07	−0.08
Colour TV	−0.06	−0.06	−0.07
Secondary			
Car	−0.28	−0.26	−0.29
Microwave	−0.24	−0.22	−0.25
Video	−0.19	−0.19	−0.20
Dishwasher	−0.17	−0.15	−0.17
Telephone	−0.26	−0.26	−0.28
Second home	−0.09	−0.10	−0.10
Replacing worn-out furniture	−0.32	−0.29	−0.33
Paying for a week's holiday away from home	−0.38	−0.36	−0.40
Basic			
Buying new rather than second-hand clothes	−0.21	−0.20	−0.22
Eating meat, chicken or fish every second day, if you wanted to	−0.15	−0.15	−0.16
Having friends or family for a drink or meal at least once a month	−0.30	−0.29	−0.32
In arrears in the past 12 months on rent, mortgage, utility bills or loans	−0.26	−0.25	−0.28
Keeping your home adequately warm	−0.21	−0.20	−0.22

is very similar to the correlation with wave 2 income, though slightly higher
for wave 1 except for the housing index. Averaging over the two years produces a slightly higher level of correlation than either year on its own. This
brings out the importance, in trying to understand current deprivation
levels for households with children, of measuring income over a longer
period than, for example, the current week, month or even year. The longitudinal perspective on income is crucial not just to understanding how
households arrived at their current income levels, but also the implications
for their experience of hardship and deprivation.

Analysis of the income–deprivation relationship also highlights the fact
that very low income at a point in time may mislead as to the longer-term
income level and living standards of the household. This is highly relevant
since policymakers seeking to focus on children who are in most need could
be directed towards the wrong group. To bring this out, we categorise chil-

Table 8.5. *Correlation between summary deprivation indices in 1994 and income in wave 1 and wave 2, households with children*

	Correlation with income in		
	wave 1	wave 2	wave 1 + wave 2
Housing	−0.09	−0.09	−0.10
Secondary	−0.43	−0.41	−0.45
Basic	−0.34	−0.33	−0.36
Summary index	−0.43	−0.42	−0.46

dren in terms of whether the equivalised income of their households in wave 1 was below 40 per cent of the median, 40–50 per cent, 50–60 per cent, or above 60 per cent of the median. (Income is equivalised using the 'square-root' equivalence scale, namely the square root of the number of persons in the household.) Table 8.6 then shows mean deprivation scores for the different income groups.

This shows that children in households with very low incomes – below 40 per cent of the median – in wave 1 were certainly not those with the highest deprivation scores. Indeed their mean score was only half that of the children on slightly higher incomes, between 40 per cent and 50 per cent of the median. It is also noteworthy that there was virtually no difference in mean deprivation score between the latter, just below the half median poverty line, and those just above that line between 50 per cent and 60 per cent of median income. The sharp contrast is between those with incomes between 40 and 60 per cent of the median, who have mean scores of about 6, and those either below 40 per cent or above 60 per cent, each with scores of about 3. This is not simply produced by a mismatch between the timing of the income and deprivation measures, since one gets a similar picture if wave 2 income is substituted.

Measuring income and deprivation in combination may thus be more effective than income alone in distinguishing those most in need from cross-section data, as recognised in the recently adopted Irish National Anti-Poverty Strategy. This once again reflects the role of income dynamics, and in particular the high probability that households on very low incomes in a cross-section will not be in that position in the longer term. We therefore now focus on income dynamics, and the contribution that a dynamic perspective on income can make to understanding why deprivation levels vary across children's households.

Table 8.6. *Mean score on seventeen-item deprivation index in wave 1 for children, by income category*

Income in wave 1 as fraction of median	Mean deprivation score in wave 1
< 40%	3.1
≥40%, <50%	6.0
≥50%, <60%	5.9
≥60%	2.7
All	3.4

8.6 Deprivation and income dynamics

To bring out the role of income dynamics, we now look at deprivation scores when children are categorised in terms of the income poverty status of their household in both wave 1 and wave 2. Table 8.7 first shows deprivation scores on the seventeen-item index in wave 1, for children categorised by income poverty status in each wave. We see that children in poverty in both 1993 and in 1994 had an average deprivation score of 5.5. Those below the relative income line in wave 1 but not wave 2 had a significantly lower score of 4.8, not very different to those in poverty in wave 2 but not wave 1 who had a mean score of 4.6. Those above the income poverty line in both waves had the much lower average deprivation score of 3.0. So there is an extremely pronounced difference between those who were income poor in both versus neither waves, but there is also a marked difference between either of these and the intermediate group who were income poor in one but not the other wave.

Indeed, it is striking that very much the same pattern is seen when we focus on deprivation scores in wave 2. The table also shows that, even though we are then looking at deprivation levels 6–9 months after the end of 1994, knowing poverty status in both 1993 and 1994 helps to predict deprivation levels. Those who were income poor in both 1993 and 1994 turn out to have much higher deprivation scores in mid to late 1995 than those who were poor in only one of those years, and very much higher than those who were poor in neither. Income in 1993 and 1994 does nearly as good a job in capturing the divergence in deprivation scores in 1995 as in 1994: again, testimony to the role of income over a prolonged period in influencing current deprivation levels.

Income dynamics also help to explain the relatively low levels of deprivation we saw earlier for those who are right at the bottom of the income

Table 8.7. *Mean score on seventeen-item deprivation index for children, by income poverty status at each wave*

	Income poverty status			
	Poor at both waves	Poor at wave 1, not poor at wave 2	Poor at wave 2, not poor at wave 1	Poor in neither wave
Wave 1	5.5	4.8	4.6	3.0
Wave 2	5.4	4.5	4.2	2.4

distribution, below 40 per cent of median income. The pattern of income dynamics for Irish children from wave 1 to wave 2 was included in the comparative cross-country results discussed in detail in chapter 4 of this volume. It may, however, be helpful to recall here the extent of mobility in terms of the income categories below 40 per cent of the median, between 40–50 per cent, 50–60 per cent, or above 60 per cent of the median. Table 8.8 shows the location in wave 2 of children categorised by their income in wave 1. The finding we wish to focus on here is the extent of mobility for those on very low incomes in wave 1.

The table shows that 46 per cent of those below 40 per cent of the median in wave 1 were still in that position in wave 2. However, fully 37 per cent of that group had seen their household incomes rise to over 60 per cent of the median by wave 2. By contrast, of those between 40 per cent and 50 per cent of the median in wave 1, only 17 per cent had risen to above 60 per cent by wave 2. So the group on very low incomes includes a disproportionate number experiencing relatively substantial income increases. This is consistent with the notion that very low income in a cross-section may not always be a good indicator of permanent income, as reflected in the relatively low average deprivation scores for this group. The pattern of income dynamics also serves to reveal, though, that a substantial sub-set do stay on very low incomes for at least two waves. The relatively low deprivation score for the group as a whole therefore needs careful interpretation, an illustration of the complementary nature of what one learns from longitudinal income and from non-monetary indicators.

8.7 Deprivation dynamics

We now consider the transition matrix for children in terms of their household's deprivation score in waves 1 and 2, grouping deprivation scores into

Table 8.8. *Income mobility of children between wave 1 and wave 2 (row percentages)*

Income at wave 1 as fraction of median	Income at wave 2 as fraction of median					
	<40%	≥40%, <50%	≥50%, <60%	≥60%	All children	(column percentage)
<40%	46	12	4	37	100	(4)
≥40%, <50%	5	52	27	17	100	(11)
≥50%, <60%	4	15	42	39	100	(12)
≥60%	3	3	5	89	100	(73)
All children	5	10	12	73	100	(100)

five categories which contain similar numbers of children. About 42 per cent of children were in households in the same deprivation category in each wave. About 22 per cent were in a higher category in wave 2 than wave 1, while a greater number, about 35 per cent, were in a lower category in wave 2 – reflecting the overall decline in the mean level of deprivation.

Table 8.9 shows that for those with a score of zero in wave 1, over half had the same score in wave 2. Similarly, for those at the other extreme, with a score in wave 1 of six or more, half remained at this relatively high level of deprivation in wave 2. The percentage with a score unchanged from wave 1 to wave 2 was somewhat less – about 30–40 per cent – at intermediate levels of deprivation. This reflects the common pattern, whereby measured mobility is least in the top and bottom categories because movement can only occur in one direction.

It is difficult to directly compare the extent of stability versus change in deprivation with that displayed by income in terms of, for example, a quintile group transition matrix. Using income one can define categories (such as quintile or decile groups) containing an identical number of cases both at a given point in time and in each wave. With the deprivation index, on the other hand, the discrete nature of the measure does not allow exactly equally sized groups to be distinguished, and the overall numbers in the categories differ across the two years because deprivation is declining. More than half of all Irish children remained in the same fifth of the distribution of annual equivalised income in wave 1 and wave 2, but this statistic is not directly comparable with the 42 per cent who remained in the same deprivation category.

Breaking down changes in deprivation into the three dimensions outlined earlier, we find that housing deprivation scores were quite stable between the two surveys. As one would expect, basic and more particularly secondary deprivation scores showed greater variability, with significant

Table 8.9. *Deprivation score mobility of children between wave 1 and wave 2 (row percentages)*

Deprivation score at wave 1	Deprivation score at wave 2						
	0	1	2–3	4–5	6+	All children	(column percentage)
0	53	30	14	2	1	100	(17)
1	32	39	22	7	1	100	(21)
2–3	16	24	41	14	5	100	(25)
4–5	4	12	35	30	19	100	(18)
6 or more	2	4	17	28	50	100	(19)
All children	20	22	27	16	15	100	(100)

numbers experiencing either increases or declines in respect of those sub-indices.

The differences in timing between the income and deprivation measures in the ECHP, already outlined, severely limit our ability at this stage to analyse the relationship between income dynamics and deprivation dynamics. As one might expect, knowing income poverty status in terms of 1994 and 1995 annual income does help to predict whether deprivation scores rise between late 1994 and late 1995 (i.e. from wave 1 to wave 2). Indeed, the group remaining on very low incomes – below 40 per cent of the median – in both those years then saw particularly pronounced increases in deprivation between the two survey dates. Until wave 3 data for income in 1995 becomes available, however, we cannot look at how deprivation changes as annual income changes contemporaneously.

In the meantime we looked at the summary information, also obtained in the ECHP, about current monthly household income at the time of the survey. This was elicited by means of a single question posed to one household member, and cannot be expected to provide a measure of household income as reliable as the detailed series of questions about annual incomes from different sources that were put to each adult in the household. When we compared changes in monthly income from the time of the wave 1 to the wave 2 surveys with changes in deprivation scores, there was little consistency in the pattern of results. Apart altogether from the fact that current income is measured using a single question, income in the most recent month covers a very short period in this context, since the whole emphasis of our discussion has been on the importance of resources over a long period in influencing deprivation levels. Progress on the precise relationship between income dynamics and deprivation dynamics affecting Irish children will thus have to await the availability of new data.

The other, related, priority for future research will be to assess in depth precisely what one learns from the pattern of deprivation dynamics over time about the households most in need. Table 8.9 shows that about 10 per cent of Irish children were in households which had persistently high deprivation levels – scores of 6 or more on the seventeen-item index – in the two waves of the ECHP. About the same number were in households below the half median income poverty line in 1993 and 1994. There is a very substantial overlap between these two groups: about 85 per cent of those with very high deprivation scores were also below the income poverty line, and this figure would probably be slightly higher if one had exactly contemporaneous information on these two measures of welfare. Between them they must contain a very high proportion of the children most vulnerable to poverty. Deciding how best to use such complementary information about both income and deprivation dynamics to identify priority groups for policy and understand the processes at work is perhaps the most important issue now facing researchers in this area.

8.8 The implications for understanding and combating child poverty

In this chapter, we have described and analysed information on a range of non-monetary indicators, to see what they reveal about the living standards of the households in which Irish children live. Looking at both income and non-monetary indicators of household deprivation levels has been instructive in a number of important respects. It suggests that resource accumulation and life experiences over a long period affect current living standards and extent of deprivation. This highlights the importance of a dynamic perspective on income, the central theme of this volume.

The results demonstrate that cross-section income measures alone will not tell us all we need to know about which children are in poverty. For example, the results of our analysis for Irish children suggest that some of those living in households on *very* low incomes at a particular point are not amongst those facing the greatest deprivation. From a policy perspective, the children most in need at a point in time, at whom social protection and other interventions should be targeted, are mostly to be found just below or just above an income poverty line such as half median income, rather than well below it. However, sustained low income, as indicated by careful analysis of longitudinal data on income dynamics, is more likely to be a good indicator of need. Even at this early stage, our findings suggest that information on both income dynamics and non-monetary indicators of household welfare and deprivation levels can substantially complement one another in helping policymakers to identify and target poor children.

In conclusion, it is worth setting out what we see as priorities for developing this research in the future. One is using longitudinal data to directly link income and deprivation dynamics, in a way which we have not been able to do here. As further waves of the European Community Household Panel become available this will be possible not only for Ireland but for other participating European Union countries. This will also open up exciting avenues of comparative research on deprivation as well as income dynamics. Finally, a key priority in terms of monitoring and tackling child poverty has to be the incorporation of measures of deprivation relating directly to children themselves into the data sets which serve as the basis for analysis and poverty formulation.

Acknowledgements
We have benefited from very helpful comments and advice from Bruce Bradbury, Markus Jäntti, Stephen Jenkins, John Micklewright and participants in a workshop at UNICEF Innocenti Research Centre, Florence, October 1998.

References
Callan, T., Nolan, B. and Whelan, C. T., 1993, 'Resources, deprivation and the measurement of poverty', *Journal of Social Policy*, 22: 141–72.

Callan, T., O'Donoghue, C. and O'Neill, C., 1995, 'Supplementing family income', Policy Research Series Paper 23, Economic and Social Research Institute, Dublin.

Callan, T., Nolan, B., Whelan, B. J., Whelan, C. T. and Williams, J., 1996, 'Poverty in the 1990s: evidence from the Living in Ireland Survey', General Research Series Paper 170, Oak Tree Press, Dublin.

Cantillon, S. and Nolan, B., 1998, 'Are married women more deprived than their husbands?' *Journal of Social Policy*, 27: 151–71.

Commission on the Family, 1998, *Strengthening Families for Life*, Final Report, Stationery Office, Dublin.

Hallerod, B., 1995, 'The truly poor: direct and indirect measurement of consensual poverty in Sweden', *European Journal of Social Policy*, 5: 111–29.

Jenkins, S. P., 1991, 'Poverty measurement and the within-household distribution: agenda for action', *Journal of Social Policy*, 20: 457–83.

Mack, J. and Lansley, S., 1985, *Poor Britain*, Allen and Unwin, London.

Mayer, S., 1993, 'Living conditions among the poor in four rich countries', *Journal of Population Economics*, 6: 261–86.

Mayer, S. and Jencks, C., 1988, 'Poverty and the distribution of material hardship', *Journal of Human Resources*, 24: 88–114.

Muffels, R., 1993, 'Deprivation standards and style of living indices', in Berghman, J. and Cantillon, B., 1993, *The European Face of Social Security*, Avebury, Aldershot.

National Anti-Poverty Strategy, 1997, *Sharing in Progress: National Anti-Poverty Strategy*, Government Publications Office, Dublin.

Nolan, B. and Farrell, B., 1990, *Child Poverty in Ireland*, Combat Poverty Agency, Dublin.

Nolan, B. and Whelan, C., 1996a, *Resources, Deprivation and Poverty*, Clarendon Press, Oxford.

Nolan, B. and Whelan, C., 1996b, 'The relationship between income and deprivation: a dynamic perspective', *Revue Economique*, 3: 1–9.

Ringen, S., 1987, *The Possibility of Politics*, Clarendon Press, Oxford.

Ringen, S., 1988, 'Direct and indirect measures of poverty', *Journal of Social Policy*, 17: 351–66.

Townsend, P., 1979, *Poverty in the United Kingdom*, Penguin, Harmondsworth.

9 Young people leaving home: the impact on poverty in Spain

OLGA CANTÓ AND MAGDA MERCADER-PRATS

9.1 Why focus on young people?

One of the features of Spanish society that puzzles foreign observers is how Spain can have an unemployment rate and an incidence of temporary jobs that are well above those of other European Union countries (especially for young people) while, at the same time, keeping a fairly high degree of social cohesion. And all this without spending more on social protection than neighbouring countries. The answer to the puzzle may be found in the predominant role played by the family in Spanish society (see, for example, Robinson 1998). Family ties are critical in Spain in ensuring financial protection against adverse labour-market conditions. Indeed, despite its high unemployment rate, Spain has an incidence of jobless households – households in which no one is employed – which is no higher than the average for the European Union. Against this background, this chapter explores the relationship between poverty, living arrangements and the labour market, focusing on young people.

The sharp rise in unemployment in Spain since the early 1980s and the increasing flexibility in the labour market have especially affected young people – those persons who have just left childhood – who are the focus of this chapter. In parallel with the increases in unemployment and temporary employment among the young, there has been a growing proportion of young people, particularly of those aged 25–29, still living with their parents. (Nearly 90 per cent of 20–24-year-olds and more than half of 25–29-year-olds are still in the parental home.) Public policy has tended to reinforce this trend. A reliance on social insurance within the Spanish system of social protection, with benefit entitlements linked to employment history, has meant that cash benefits for the young unemployed are often not available. Where a young person does manage to qualify for unemployment insurance he or she may receive benefit for only a short period of time. A residual means-tested social assistance scheme (paying a low level of benefit) is also unlikely to provide support. The lack of financial support from the state for young unemployed people (and some other groups in need) has left family arrangements to play a key role in providing a basic safety net for all household members.

On the one hand, the presence of young people in the household might indeed be seen as a burden – the great majority of Spanish children who attain the age of 18 do not immediately leave home and may thus be considered as still being 'dependent' on their families, just like children aged less than 18. In this sense, parents cover the lack of other economic support for the students, young first-time job seekers and other young unemployed at the cost of a reduction in their own economic well-being. This phenomenon has been repeatedly suggested for Spain: see, for example, Robinson (1998) or Toharia *et al.* (1998). According to this view, the notion of 'childhood' needs to be considered in a broad sense when discussing child poverty in the Spanish context and in other countries where many young people in their twenties still live in the parental home.

On the other hand, youth employment may contribute to prevent overall household poverty. If young people still living with their parents have jobs, then total household income will be higher as a result. Other things being equal, children aged less than 18 who live in households in which their elder sibling works will be better off than those children with unemployed siblings still at home. This may be particularly important for their well-being (and for that of others in the household, including the elderly) if the head of the household is out of work. According to this view, it is the employed youths who are providing the safety net for low-income households with younger dependants, at the cost of delaying their departure from the parental home.

This chapter addresses the following related questions. First, how does poverty among children and young people in Spain relate to the household arrangements and employment status of both young people themselves and of their parents? Second, are young people always an economic burden for households or does their labour-market activity help prevent child poverty? Third, what are the implications of a young person leaving the household for the poverty status of the household left behind? In tackling these questions we analyse both cross-section and longitudinal survey data from the 1990s. The last of the questions just posed can only be addressed in a direct way with information drawn from a panel survey. It is only this type of source that allows one to observe young people leaving the parental home, rather than drawing inferences by comparing households with and without young people at a single point in time.

In section 9.2 we describe in more detail the Spanish context, including recent trends in youth unemployment and temporary employment as well as changes in the proportion of young people in their twenties who live with their parents. We underline the important differences between Spain and other European Union countries. Section 9.3 describes our data – both the cross-section and the panel data – and methodological issues such as the definition of the poverty line that we adopt. Section 9.4 provides an analysis of child and youth poverty in Spain in 1990–1 with the cross-section data, focusing on the apparent differences due to the employment status of young people still in the household. Section 9.5 turns to the panel data. We first show which young people leave the parental home over the course of a year and then consider the effect that this has on the poverty status of the household they leave behind. Section 9.6 concludes.

9.2 Is Spain different?

Spain is one of the European countries with the highest proportion of individuals in the working-age population not at work because of either unemployment or inactivity. It is also the country with the highest rate of 'precarious' employment, in the sense of jobs with temporary contracts.[1] Key to the analysis of this chapter is the fact that unemployment and temporary employment are found among young people in particular. In 1994, the unemployment rate among 15–29-year-olds was as high as 39 per cent and temporary contracts were held by more than 60 per cent of all people of this age with jobs.

Table 9.1 shows youth unemployment rates in Spain compared to those in one other Southern European country, Italy, two countries from Northern Europe, France and the UK, and the European Union as a whole. (We use the words 'youth' and 'young people' interchangeably in this chapter, in both cases including people in the 25–29 age bracket as well as those of younger ages.) Spain is clearly an outlier, with the highest unemployment rates for all three age groups considered, and levels that are at least double the European Union average. Unemployment rates in all countries are highest for the youngest age group, 15–19-year-olds, and lowest for the oldest group, 25–29-year-olds.[2] It is, however, particularly worrying to see that the unemployment rate for 25–29-year-olds in Spain was over 30 per

---

[1] Temporary contracts are temporary in the sense of their duration being fixed in advance. Also particularly important is that workers are not eligible for redundancy payments at the end of the contracts, whereas the termination of a 'permanent' contract implies very large redundancy payments.

[2] It should be borne in mind that the figures relate to the incidence of unemployment among those young people who are in the labour force. It is far from the case that half of all 16–19-year-olds are unemployed since many persons of this age are still in full-time education – and are thus excluded from the denominator of the unemployment rate.

Table 9.1. *Youth unemployment rates, 1986 and 1994 (per cent)*

	15–19-year-olds		20–24-year-olds		25–29-year-olds	
	1986	1994	1986	1994	1986	1994
Spain	51.1	52.3	44.2	42.5	25.8	31.3
Italy	41.8	36.7	29.8	30.0	14.4	16.8
France	33.6	36.6	21.1	27.6	11.9	15.7
UK	20.8	18.8	17.0	15.1	13.8	10.4
European Union	25.6	23.2	21.2	21.6	13.2	14.1

Source: Eurostat (1988, 1996: table 08). Results are based on the ILO definition of unemployment. The youngest age group includes 14-year-olds in 1986. European Union figures refer to the weighted average for all member states.

cent in 1994, a clear increase from the level in 1986. And the difference between the rate in Spain and that in the other countries is higher for this age group (in relative terms) than for other age groups.

Spain is again an outlier regarding the type of jobs held by young people who do find work after finishing full-time education. Table 9.2 shows the importance of temporary employment contracts among the jobs held by 16–29-year-olds one year after leaving secondary or tertiary education. In Spain the contract is a temporary one in 85 per cent of cases and in the great majority of these it is because the person could not find a permanent job. The contrast with the UK is particularly striking but the Spanish figures are also well above the EU average (and are easily the highest in the Union). Toharia *et al.* (1998) report that access to permanent employment over 1992–7 was lower for young people who were below 30 years of age at the beginning of the period than it had been for earlier cohorts.

The weakness of the youth labour market is clearly one issue that young people in Spain confront when considering their departure from the parental home. A further difficulty is restricted access to housing. In Southern European countries like Italy or Spain, the incidence of home ownership is high and the market for rental housing is not a large one (Castles and Ferrera 1996). Moreover, rents in Spain in the 1990s increased much faster than wages. Average rents increased by 49 per cent over 1992–7 compared to rises in the average and minimum wages of 26 per cent and 18 per cent respectively. Average house prices rose by 38 per cent. Young people's relatively low wages and high labour instability militate against their access to both the rental and owner-occupied sectors.[3]

---

[3] Housing policy in Spain since the 1980s is evaluated in Valenzuela Rubio (1994: chapter 10.6).

Table 9.2. *Share of temporary jobs out of all jobs held by young persons aged 16–29 one year after leaving full-time education, 1996 (per cent)*

	Men		Women	
	Total	(Involuntary)	Total	(Involuntary)
Spain	85.8	(59.5)	87.4	(62.1)
Italy	32.8	(5.8)	51.9	(13.1)
France	68.3	n.a.	66.3	n.a.
UK	27.3	(7.1)	25.7	(6.5)
European Union	50.3	(15.7)	50.2	(16.7)

Source: OECD (1998: table 3.5). European Union figures are unweighted averages of figures for fourteen member states. n.a.: not available. Involuntary means the person could not find a permanent job.

Unsurprisingly, the majority of the Spanish youth therefore live with their parents. Table 9.3 shows the situation for those aged 20–29. More than 90 per cent of young Spanish men aged 20–24 and two thirds of those aged 25–29 still lived with their parents in 1994. The figures are slightly lower for young women, but it is still the case that almost half of 25–29-year-old females were still in the parental home. Italy (and other Southern European countries not shown in the table) displays similar percentages to those in Spain, but far fewer young men and women in their twenties live with their parents in France and the UK. In both these latter countries, less than half of women aged 20–24 lived at home in 1994 and among 25–29-year-olds four out of five men and nine out of ten women had left home. Not only is the percentage of young people living at home relatively high in the Southern European countries but it also increased substantially over 1986–94. This is particularly the case for 25–29-year-olds; taking the sexes together, the figure for Spain rose by twelve percentage points and that for Italy by seventeen points, compared to rises in France and the UK of just three points and one point respectively.

As we have already implied, these patterns in Spain are not independent of labour-market conditions or the context of the social protection system touched on in the introduction to the chapter. Ahn and Mira (1999) conclude that the lack of stable jobs is an important factor forcing many young people in Spain to delay marriage and childbearing. Martínez and Ruiz-Castillo (1999) confirm that age, possession of a job and the cost of housing in the region where an individual lives are clearly related to the decision to leave the parental home. However, household arrangements and the design of Spanish social policy cannot be fully understood without taking into account the predominant role traditionally played by the family in Spanish

Table 9.3. *Young people still living with their parents (per cent)*

| | Men | | | | Women | | | |
| | Aged 20–24 | | Aged 25–29 | | Aged 20–24 | | Aged 25–29 | |
	1986	1994	1986	1994	1986	1994	1986	1994
Spain	88.1	91.5	53.2	64.8	76.1	84.3	35.3	47.6
Italy	87.8	92.2	49.6	66.0	70.4	82.4	25.5	44.1
France	56.9	61.8	19.3	22.5	36.4	41.6	8.4	10.3
UK	57.2	56.8	21.9	20.8	33.8	37.0	8.6	10.8

Source: Fernández Cordón (1996: tables 1 and 2), based on labour-force survey data.
Figures for all European Union countries for 1987 and 1995 can be found in Eurostat (1997) but these do not distinguish by sex.

society. As argued by Sven Reher (1998), in Spain and other Mediterranean countries, the family is seen as the main institution defending its members against adverse economic and labour-market conditions. A stable job, access to adequate housing, leaving the parental household and marriage, all tend to be closely intertwined events and young people receive support from their families until they leave for good.

Worsening labour-market conditions for young people have tended to reinforce rather than weaken family ties in Spain, in one sense a positive development. Despite the huge unemployment rates experienced by young Spaniards, the great majority do live in households where someone works. In 1996, only a quarter of unemployed young people in Spain aged 15–24 lived in a household where no adult worked, compared to an average of nearly a third in all European Union countries (OECD 1998: table 1.5), countries which table 9.1 shows to have lower youth unemployment rates. However, the cost of the increased dependency of young people on their parents is the reduced individual autonomy that they enjoy, a fact likely to be related to the very low fertility levels found in Spain and typically in other Southern European countries.

9.3 Data and poverty lines

Data sources

The data used in this chapter come from two household budget surveys: the 'Encuesta de Presupuestos Familiares' (EPF) and the 'Encuesta Continua de Presupuestos Familiares' (ECPF). The EPF is a large cross-section survey that has been conducted about once every ten years since the mid-1970s. We use data from the survey held in 1990–1. The ECPF is a quarterly rotating panel survey that started in 1985. Data from the surveys are used in the two cross-national chapters in part I of this book, the EPF in chapter 3 and the ECPF in chapter 4. The surveys are both conducted by the Spanish central statistical office, and their interview structures are similar. In both cases the sample excludes the homeless and people living in institutions.[4]

The EPF sample is large. The 1990–1 sample contains 20,934 households and 71,333 individuals, including 17,983 children (persons aged under 18) and 13,573 young people (persons aged 18–29). Households were interviewed once between April 1990 and March 1991, with the interviews equally distributed over the period. The information on income refers to the sources received during the twelve months prior to the interview. Grossing-up factors provided by the statistical office are used to ensure the representativeness of the sample.

The ECPF panel is much smaller, containing data on 3,200 households each quarter. Information is collected on each household's income during the previous three months. (The cross-national analysis in chapter 4 also makes use of the expenditure data in the survey, information that we do not use in the present chapter.) To overcome the small size of the sample, we pool the data from 1985–92. We use information collected from each household at a pair of interviews one year apart, i.e. at each household's first and fifth quarters of participation in the survey. In principle each household is surveyed for eight consecutive quarters before being dropped from the survey and replaced with a freshly selected household. However, many households drop out earlier of their own accord (see Cantó-Sánchez 1998) and we apply longitudinal weights to the data in order to take account of possible bias arising from this unplanned sample attrition.[5] By pooling the data across the years we arrive at a sample of 20,960 households observed at both the first and fifth interviews. These households contain 69,046

[4] See Instituto Nacional de Estadística (1990, 1992) for details. Persons living in the North African enclaves of Ceuta and Melilla are excluded from our analysis (although these settlements are included in the EPF sample frame).

[5] To obtain these weights we estimated a probit regression of the probability that a household stays in the panel for a year (until the fifth interview) using as explanatory variables household characteristics observed at the first interview (age, level of education, civil status, sex and labour status of the household head, together with the number of household members and the township of household residence). Weights were constructed by taking the inverse of the predicted probability of staying in the sample, constraining the sum of the weights to be the total number of households in the sample at first interview.

individuals of whom 19,352 are children and 13,807 are young people – the sizes of the EPF and pooled ECPF samples are thus very similar.

Of these 13,807 young people in the ECPF sample, 2,747 are in households with a youth head and can therefore be considered out of the parental home. Another 832 young people are married to household heads who are not youths – they too can be treated as having left the parental home. This leaves 10,228 young people, of which 1,326 (12.9 per cent) were no longer in the household at the fifth interview, and we assume that they left the parental home over the course of the year.[6] The 'following rule' in the ECPF means that no attempt is made to trace and interview any individual who leaves a sample household (see chapter 2 for discussion of this issue). Unfortunately we are therefore not able to observe the new household circumstances of the young persons who do leave, and hence cannot make comparisons with the household that is left behind (which we do continue to observe).

Table 9.4 summarises the EPF sample for 1990–1, showing amongst other things how many young people live in their own households, how many children live with young people, and the employment status of both household heads and youths. (The distributions are similar in the ECPF data.) Besides children (persons aged under 18) and youths (young people aged 18–29), we identify 'adults' (persons aged 30–59) and the elderly (those aged 60 or more). An individual is classified as employed if he or she receives any income from employment or self-employment during the previous twelve months. (In our analysis of the ECPF we define employment as receipt of such income over a much shorter period – the previous three months; this may be the main reason why the employment rate of youths in the EPF is almost double that found in the ECPF, 49 per cent compared to 25 per cent, the longer period picking up any work done during the year, including occasional work by students.) We distinguish households where the head works and those where he or she does not, and within these whether any young people present are employed.

One in six (17 per cent) of young people are in their own households – in the sense of a household headed by a youth. Not all the other 83 per cent are necessarily living with their parents; the head might be an adult spouse or some other adult or an elderly person. (We noted above the number of youths in our ECPF sample for 1985–92 who are married to non-youth household heads.) This great majority of young people who are not in 'youth households' are most likely to be living with a head who does work – only 23 per cent of all young people (the last two columns of the 'youth'

---

[6] We do not treat as leavers those individuals who are merely not present at the time of fifth interview but who are still members of the household.

Table 9.4. *Young people and household arrangements, 1990–1991 (row percentages)*

	Total	Youth head	Adult or elderly household head					
			Head works			Head does not work		
			No youth in household	Some youth in household		No youth in household	Some youth in household	
				No youth employed	Some youth employed		No youth employed	Some youth employed
Children	100.0	6.0	57.6	14.7	11.5	4.7	2.1	3.4
Youths	100.0	17.1	n.a.	24.8	34.9	n.a.	7.2	16.0
Adults	100.0	1.2	46.5	16.6	18.1	9.1	3.2	5.3
Elderly	100.0	0.9	13.3	4.6	7.0	58.5	5.7	10.0
All persons	100.0	5.3	33.5	15.9	16.8	16.4	4.2	7.9

Source: EPF microdata (71,333 individuals). Children are aged 0–17, youths 18–29, adults 30–59, and the elderly 60 and over. n.a.: not applicable. The entries in the table show the percentage of individuals (children, youths, adults and elderly) living in households of different characteristics (headed by a youth, headed by a working adult or elderly person, etc.).

row in the table) are in households where the head is not a youth and does not have a job. One half of all young people are in households headed by an adult or elderly person where at least one youth present (including themselves) is employed.

Only 6 per cent of all children live in a household that is headed by a young person. But another 32 per cent are in households where a youth is present as another household member, and it is slightly more likely to be the case that the young people in these households do not have jobs. One in ten children live in a household headed by an adult or an elderly person who has no job (the last three columns of the child row) but in a third of this relatively small group of children the household contains at least one employed young person.

A final point to note is that more than a quarter of all the elderly live with young people (28 per cent). And one in six of the elderly live in households in which at least one youth is employed.

The definition of poverty and the poverty line

We use the same poverty line as in the cross-national analysis of chapter 4: half the median household income, adjusted for household needs. (This poverty line is around 40 per cent of average income in Spain.) Income is adjusted for household needs by dividing by the square root of household size (again as in chapter 4). Incomes are aggregated over all persons within each household, and an individual is considered to be poor if the total income of the household to which he or she belongs (adjusted for household size) is less than the poverty line. (Our unit of analysis, as opposed to the income unit, is the individual.) The sources included in household income are employment and self-employment income, income from regular state transfers (including pensions and unemployment benefits), investment income and non-monetary income, that is, wages in kind and the value of home production. From these are deducted 'pay-as-you-earn' income taxes and social insurance contributions (hence where no tax is deducted at source incomes are included gross). The reference period for income is the twelve months prior to the interview in our analysis of the EPF ('annual income'), and the three months prior to the interview in the case of the ECPF ('quarterly income').[7]

---

[7] There is evidence that the Spanish survey income data show some discrepancies with national accounts data (as in other countries: see, for example, Atkinson and Micklewright 1983), particularly among self-employment and capital income (see, for example, Sanz

Underlying our analysis is the assumption of equal income sharing among household members. This of course is the standard assumption in analysis of poverty based on household incomes or expenditures. However, this may be a particularly strong assumption in the case of young people living in the parental home, especially those in relatively well-off households. Unfortunately, little research has been done on income pooling within Spanish households and we lack any measure of the extent to which income is in fact shared in practice with, or by (in the case when a young person is earning), young people still living with their parents.

How does our poverty line relate to an official definition of low income in Spain? There is no official Spanish poverty line and the nearest administrative definition of need is the level of the minimum wage. Minimum wages are set by the government as the minimum salary a full-time worker should be paid. In 1990 our poverty line per equivalent adult calculated from the EPF was 73 per cent of the statutory minimum wage, or just below half of the average wage for that year. The poverty line that emerges from the ECPF panel survey in 1991 is about 5 per cent higher.

9.4 Young people and their households: employment and poverty

The evidence on the evolution of poverty in Spain among the population as a whole is clear: EPF data show a reduction in the overall poverty rate over 1980–90 (see Ruiz-Huerta and Martínez 1994, INE 1996, Del Río and Ruiz-Castillo 1997, and Cantó-Sánchez and Mercader-Prats 1998). The decline in poverty was only slight if household resources were measured in terms of expenditure, but clearer if measured in terms of income. Regarding poverty among children, Cantó-Sánchez and Mercader-Prats (1998) found a very slight increase over the same period but the broad conclusion is that the overall rate of child poverty shows little change from the mid-1970s (the end of the Franco era). The incidence of poverty among children relative to that among the elderly rose much more notably over 1980–90, a fact that can be attributed in part to the development of the old age pension system. Over the 1980s child poverty increased for large households, particularly for couples with more than two children. It also rose for children in single- and, in particular, lone-parent families. (The presence of other adults appears to be effective in limiting poverty in households headed by single

1996). In Cantó-Sánchez and Mercader-Prats (1999) we show that the results presented in this chapter are robust to a wide range of methodological choices, including the switch to expenditure as the measure of well-being.

parents.) There was also an increase in the poverty rate for children living in households headed by an unemployed person.

What about poverty among young people – and the effect of the presence of young people on the poverty of others? Table 9.5 summarises the situation derived from the 1990–1 EPF data, using the same population groups as in table 9.4. Young people benefit from the lowest poverty rate of any of the four age groups, while children have the highest rate. However, the differences between age groups are not nearly as large as those between children or youths living in different types of household.

Poverty is notably higher for the (small) group of children living in a household headed by a young person: 19 per cent of children in these households are poor. These are mainly young children with mothers who are particularly unlikely to work.[8] Hence the high poverty rate here in part represents a life cycle effect found in all countries, albeit with conditions worsened by the weak labour market for young people in Spain and the relatively weak system of public assistance.

How effective is youth employment in reducing poverty? In all age groups, poverty risk is lower when the head of household works and, not surprisingly, if any young people present in the household are employed. People living with a young person who does *not* have a job are more likely to be in poverty than people in households with no young person present at all: in this case young people add to the household's needs but not to household income. For example, 9 per cent of children living in households headed by someone other than a youth are in poverty if the head works and no youth is present, but 13 per cent are poor in those households in which there are one or more young people present but none of them at work. The lowest child poverty rate of all (6 per cent) is found where both the head and youth in the household work. Other things being equal, a child's risk of poverty is thus much lower than average if his or her elder sibling is still in the household and works but is somewhat higher than average if the sibling remains at home but has no job.

The presence of an employed youth is particularly important in preventing poverty (among all age groups) in households in which the head is not employed. Child poverty in this situation is even slightly lower than the average for all children – 10 per cent versus 12 per cent – and is far lower than the figure of about 40 per cent that is found in the two other household types where the (adult or elderly) head has no job. Indeed, youth employment appears as effective as head's employment in preventing child

---

[8] In our sample 75 per cent of the households headed by a youth contain couples (with 70 per cent of these couples having children). In 58 per cent of them the spouse does not work.

Table 9.5. *Poverty rates by household arrangements, 1990–1991 (percentages)*

	All household types	Youth head	Adult or elderly household head					
			Head works			Head does not work		
			No youth in household	Some youth in household		No youth in household	Some youth in household	
				No youth employed	Some youth employed		No youth employed	Some youth employed
Children	11.8	19.2	9.0	12.8	5.7	36.3	45.6	9.9
Youths	7.6	9.7	n.a.	8.3	2.4	n.a.	33.3	4.7
Adults	8.2	10.4	6.8	7.7	2.2	21.4	32.6	4.9
Elderly	10.8	3.3	4.7	4.4	1.9	14.0	23.1	2.4
All persons	9.5	12.2	7.5	8.9	2.8	17.2	31.9	4.7

Source: EPF microdata (71,333 individuals). Children are aged 0–17, youths 18–29, adults 30–59 and the elderly 60 and over. n.a.: not applicable.

poverty, although it should be noted that such households with employed youths but no employed head contain only 3 per cent of all children (see table 9.4). Employed young people in the household are associated with notably lower poverty risk for the elderly too. Table 9.4 showed that one in ten old people live in a household where the head does not work but a young person does – only 2 per cent of these old people are poor.

9.5 Young people leaving home – and the effect on the households left behind

Our interest in this section is to see whether the departure of young people from the household raises or lowers the chances of being found in poverty for those who remain behind. The results in the previous section are suggestive but do not provide a firm answer. The comparison of poverty incidence in cross-section data between households with and without young people is hindered by the other differences that may exist between them, which are not held constant in the comparison. In this section we use the ECPF panel data to look directly at the changes that occur in the poverty status of households which young people leave. (Unfortunately, as explained earlier, the ECPF sample design prevents us from looking at the changes in poverty for the young people themselves who leave their parental homes.)

Who leaves home?

We saw in section 9.3 that 13 per cent of young people aged 18–29 still in the parental home leave their households in the ECPF panel over the course of the twelve months between the household's first and fifth quarterly interviews.[9] Table 9.6 shows how this leaving rate differs according to the characteristics of the youth himself or herself that were recorded at the first interview and those of the household he or she leaves behind.

Leaving rates are higher for older youths, in line with the information shown earlier in section 9.2 on the differences by age between young people in Spain still living with their parents. The results relating to youth employment status at the household's first interview are striking. The leaving rate

---

[9] We restrict attention to the 10,228 young people described in section 9.3 as not in households headed by a youth and who are not married to a non-youth head.

Table 9.6. *Probability of a young person leaving the parental home over twelve months*

	Percentage of young people leaving
Characteristics of young persons	
aged 18–24	10.9
aged 25–29	19.6
employed	2.2
not employed	14.6
Characteristics of household heads	
employed	9.6
not employed	6.5
retired	22.8
low education	15.5
medium education	11.9
high education	11.2
Characteristics of the household	
has children	5.2
has no children	20.1
is in poverty	9.3
is not in poverty	13.3
All young people	12.9

Source: ECPF panel, pooled sample 1985–92 of all 10,228 young people in households at the first interview with adult or elderly heads (youths married to the head have been excluded). Table cell entries read, for example, 9.6 per cent of young people in a household with an employed household head leave the parental home over a twelve-month period (between the first and fifth ECPF quarterly interviews).

among young people who were employed is far lower than among those who did not have a job – indeed, the latter make up the vast majority of all leavers. This reflects findings of other authors who have considered the leaving decision. For example, Jurado Guerrero (1997) shows that unemployed and inactive young women tend to leave their parental home earlier than their employed peers, exchanging 'parental dependency' for 'husband dependency'. Other leavers of course may enter employment – the acquisition of a job providing them with the financial independence that allows them to leave home. Again, we can only lament that the ECPF sample design does not permit us to follow those who leave.

We do not observe the educational attainment of the young people themselves, another characteristic found by Jurado Guerrero to be linked to departure from the parental home, with less-educated persons leaving sooner. (Amongst other things, financial support from parents is clearly important to continuing in higher education.) But we do have information on the education of the head of household. Table 9.6 shows leaving rates to be much higher where the head of household has less education. Young people are also more likely to leave households in which the head is retired. In contrast to the situation with their own employment status, young people are *less* likely to leave households in which the head is not employed (but not retired). Where there are children present (typically younger siblings) leaving rates are also notably lower.

Finally, the table shows the probability of leaving by the poverty status of the household. Young people are somewhat *less* likely to leave poor households – 9 per cent of poor youths leave the parental home compared to 13 per cent of the non-poor. It should be noted that poverty status is assessed on the basis of quarterly income rather than annual income as in the case of the analysis of the cross-section EPF data in section 9.4.

The impact of leaving home

We now turn to the impact of the young person's departure, considering separately the effect on the flow out from poverty and on the inflow to poverty over a twelve-month period. In doing so we have to confront the fact that a young person's departure from the household may be correlated with other factors that influence the household's probability of remaining in poverty or of becoming poor. For example, we have already seen that young people are less likely to leave households where the head does not have a job. But these are households that are less likely to exit poverty and, unless we control for this, the measured 'impact' of the young person leaving will in part reflect the correlated factor. Or the youth leaving may be correlated with some other change in the household's demographic composition or its income.

In order to try and isolate the effect of a young person leaving the household, we have therefore estimated multivariate statistical models (probit regressions) to explain the flows into and out of poverty of remaining members of the household, taking other socio-economic and demographic characteristics of the household into account. Table 9.7 reports the results of three models. First, we include no 'control variables' at all – this represents the 'impact' of leaving without holding constant any factors that would be correlated. It thus represents a base-line for the other models. Then we obtain the estimated impact of the young person leaving while holding constant characteristics of the household that are observed at the first interview, for example the head of household's educational status. We do not, however, report the estimated impact of these other control vari-

Table 9.7. *The impact of youth departure on movements out of and into poverty over twelve months*

	Difference in predicted probability of leaving poverty	Difference in predicted probability of entering poverty
Model with no controls		
youth leaves	insignificant effect	$+0.007^{b}$
Model controlling for characteristics at first interview		
youth leaves	insignificant effect	insignificant effect
Model controlling for other changes between interviews		
youth leaves	insignificant effect	$+0.008^{b}$
non-youth leaves	insignificant effect	insignificant effect
head gets a job	$+0.212^{a}$	insignificant effect
head loses job	-0.448^{a}	insignificant effect
more children	-0.500^{a}	$+0.025^{b}$
divorce or separation	insignificant effect	$+0.036^{a}$

Source: ECPF panel, pooled sample 1985–92 of all individuals in households with youth. The results show the marginal effects from probit regressions of the probability of exit from and entry to poverty over a twelve-month period, evaluating these effects at the average probabilities (0.573 for leaving poverty and 0.026 for entry). ^{a} Significant at 5 per cent level. ^{b} Significant at 10 per cent level. The model with controls for characteristics at first interview contains variables measuring the age of the young person, the age, sex, marital status, education and labour status of the household head, the type of municipality in which the household resides, a dependency index (number of dependants per income receiver) and a youth dependency index (number of youth dependants per income receiver).

ables. Finally, the last part of the table shows the effect, instead, of holding constant several other changes in the household that may occur over the course of the year. In this case we do report the impact of the other variables. In all three cases the impact of the youth leaving is reported in terms of the *difference* in the predicted probability from the value that applies in the case where the youth stays.[10] We only report this difference if it is statistically significant.

The impact on the probability of the household leaving poverty is clear – we find *no* significant effect of the young person leaving, whether we control for households' characteristics (or changes to them) or not. On

---

[10] We evaluate the size of the difference assuming that the person in question has an average probability of exiting or entering poverty. Readers familiar with the probit regression technique will recognise that we are presenting the marginal effects, evaluated at the mean probability.

average, a young person leaving a poor household neither increases the chance that the household will remain poor nor aids it to escape poverty. On the other hand, there is some indication that the entry rate into poverty *is* higher when a young person leaves. In the absence of controls for other factors, the probability of becoming poor is estimated to rise from 2.6 per cent (see the notes to the table) to 3.3 per cent. This is in line with our earlier finding from the EPF data that young people are quite often contributing to household well-being. With the controls introduced in the second model this impact disappears but it returns again in the last model that controls for other changes in the household's circumstances over the course of the twelve months.

By contrast, the arrival of more children in the household has a much larger and better-defined impact. An addition to the number of children sharply reduces the chances of leaving poverty and sharply increases the chances of becoming poor. For example, another child increases the probability of entry to 5.1 per cent. The arrival of a child increases household size and hence reduces equivalised household income (income adjusted for size), and in addition total household income will also fall if the mother gives up work. On the other hand, a young person leaving may have two opposite effects: equivalised income rises as the household becomes smaller, but if, as noted above, the youth was bringing money into the household its total income will fall. As this illustrates, the dynamics of family composition may have a variety of impacts on the dynamics of family income, depending on what type of compositional changes take place.

9.6 Conclusions

Despite young people facing a very weak labour market in Spain, the incidence of youth poverty in 1990–1 was somewhat lower than for other age groups – children, adults and the elderly. Our analysis shows that this is explained by two main factors. First, the great majority of young Spanish people aged 18–29 still live with their family. And in line with higher levels of youth unemployment and of temporary employment, the percentage of young people living with their parents has risen still further over recent years, particularly among those aged 25–29. Poverty is substantially higher among those young people who have left their parental home.

Second, around 50 per cent of young people who are still living with their parents are employed (at least for part of the year), thus contributing to total income in their households. This group of youths living with their parents are more a relief than a burden: they notably reduce the risk of poverty for other household members – including children. Furthermore, when the head of the household is out of work, youth employment appears as effective in preventing poverty as employment of heads in those households where heads do work. And we saw that, on average, the departure of young people from the parental home over the course of a twelve-month period is associated with an increase in the probability that remaining household members will enter poverty (although there seems no association with exits from poverty).

The role of the traditional Spanish family of providing help to its members when in need has without doubt been reinforced over recent decades. Parents have played a key role in supporting their adult children. But some employed youths too are acting as a safety net for low-income families, particularly when the head is out of work. It would be tempting to conclude that the Spanish family model has therefore been successful in combating the increased threat of poverty for the young. In part this is true – we believe that in Southern European societies, in which family ties are strong, the solidarity and protection available at the family level is a good thing. However, the costs are also important to bear in mind. First, many families must bear an increased economic burden. Second, many young people live in a situation of semi-dependency for too long. Third, employed youth in low-income families bear the responsibility of supporting their relatives at a time when they might be starting their own families. (We cannot talk about a 'crisis' of the Spanish family but we can certainly talk about its 'strangling'.) The direction policy could take to confront this situation is twofold. First, there could be an increase in support for families in need and, second, there could be more help to young people to set up their own households.

Acknowledgements

We are grateful to the editors for their advice and for comments on earlier drafts. We also benefited greatly from comments by other chapter authors, in particular Peter Gottschalk. We would also like to thank Lluís Flaquer for helpful discussions.

References

Ahn, N. and Mira, P., 1999, 'Job bust, baby bust: the Spanish case', Documento de trabajo 99–06, Fundación de Estudios de Economía Aplicada (FEDEA), Madrid.

Atkinson, A. B. and Micklewright, J., 1983, 'On the reliability of income data in the Family Expenditure Survey, 1970–77', *Journal of the Royal Statistical Society,* Series A, 146: 33–61.

Cantó-Sánchez, O., 1998, 'The dynamics of poverty in Spain: the permanent and transitory poor', unpublished Ph.D. thesis, European University Institute, Florence.

Cantó-Sánchez, O. and Mercader-Prats, M., 1998, 'Child poverty in Spain: what can be said?', Innocenti Occasional Papers, Economics and Social Policy Series 66, UNICEF International Child Development Centre, Florence.

Cantó-Sánchez, O. and Mercader-Prats, M., 1999, 'Poverty among children and youth in Spain: the role of parents and youth employment status', Documento de trabajo 99.07, Universitat Autònoma de Barcelona, Barcelona.

Castles, F. G. and Ferrera, M., 1996, 'Home ownership and the welfare state: is southern Europe different?', *South European Society and Politics*, 1: 163–85.

Del Río, C. and Ruiz-Castillo, J., 1997, 'TIPs for poverty analysis. The case of Spain, 1980–81 to 1990–91', Universidad Carlos III Working Paper 97–58, Madrid.

Eurostat, 1988, *Labour Force Survey. Results 1986*, Eurostat, Luxembourg.

Eurostat, 1996, *Labour Force Survey. Results 1994*, Eurostat, Luxembourg.

Eurostat, 1997, *Youth in the European Union: From Education to Working Life*, Office for Official Publications of the European Communities, Luxembourg.

Fernández Cordón, J. A., 1996, *Youth Residential Independence and Autonomy. A Comparative Study*, Instituto de Economía y Geografía, Consejo Superior de Investigaciones Científicas, Madrid.

Instituto Nacional de Estadística, 1990, *Encuesta de Presupuestos Familiares, metodología*. Instituto Nacional de Estadística, Madrid.

Instituto Nacional de Estadística, 1992, *Encuesta Continua de Presupuestos Familiares*, Instituto Nacional de Estadística Metodología, Madrid.

Instituto Nacional de Estadística, 1996, *Encuesta de Presupuestos Familiares. Desigualdad y pobreza en España. Estudio basado en las Encuestas de Presupuestos Familiares de 1973–74, 1980–81 y 1990–91*, Universidad Autónoma de Madrid and INE, Madrid.

Jurado Guerrero, T., 1997, 'Un análisis regional de los modelos de convivencia de los jóvenes españoles', Las cuatro Españas de la emancipación familiar, *Estudios de Juventud*, 39: 17–35.

Martínez, M. and Ruiz-Castillo, J., 1999, 'The decisions of Spanish youth: A cross-section study', Estudios sobre la economía española, EEE–14, Fundación de Estudios de Economía Aplicada, Madrid.

OECD, 1998, *Employment Outlook,* OECD, Paris.

Robinson, A., 1998, 'Spanish family values: Spain's welfare system is let off the hook by the family', *New Economy*, 4: 188–92.

Ruiz-Huerta, J. and Martínez, R., 1994, 'La pobreza en España: ¿Qué nos dicen las Encuestas de Presupuestos Familiares?', Documentación Social ('La Pobreza en España, Hoy') 96, Cáritas, Madrid.

Sanz, B., 1996, 'La articulación micro-macro en el sector hogares: de la Encuesta de Presupuestos Familiares a la contabilidad nacional', in *La Desigualdad de los Recursos, II Simposio sobre Igualdad y Distribución de la Renta y la Riqueza*, vol. VI, Fundación Argentaria, Madrid.

Sven Reher, D., 1998, 'Family ties in Western Europe: persistent contrasts', *Population and Development Review*, 24: 203–34.

Toharia, L., Albert, C., Cebrián, I., García Serrano, C., García Mainar, I., Malo, M. A., Moreno, G. and Villagómez, E., 1998, *El mercado de trabajo en España*, Serie McGraw-Hill de Management, Madrid.
Valenzuela Rubio, M., 1994, 'La vivenda', in Juárez, M. (ed.), *V informe sociológico sobre la situación social en España*, Fundación Fomento de Estudios y de Sociología Aplicada, Madrid.

10 Are children being left behind in the transition in Hungary?

PÉTER GALASI AND GYULA NAGY

10.1 Hungary during the transition

Before the economic and social transition of the 1990s, children in Hungary, as in other Central and Eastern European countries, benefited both from an absence of open unemployment and from generous family policies that included various child-related cash transfers (see Atkinson and Micklewright 1992 and Jarvis and Micklewright 1995). This is not to say that child poverty was entirely absent in the socialist period (see, for example, Szalai 1989), but it is reasonably true to say that the socialist regime in Hungary, as elsewhere, placed a higher premium on support to families than governments in most Western countries (Ferge 1991).

How have children fared since 1989? In the early years of the transition, between 1989 and 1993, Hungary faced serious economic hardship affecting the well-being of children as well as other groups in the population; GDP fell by nearly a fifth, employment and real wages declined, and registered unemployment increased from almost zero in 1989 to 14 per cent in 1993 – see figure 10.1. Although unemployment has fallen back somewhat during the recovery in output since 1994, employment has continued to decline as have real wages (in 1995–6).

These processes have been coupled with the weakening of the social safety net. From 1992 the unemployment benefit system turned less and less generous both in terms of the coverage of the unemployed and the amounts of benefit paid (Micklewright and Nagy 1996, 1999). (Hungary was the first country in the region to introduce explicit support for the unemployed.) Family allowance rates were frozen in nominal terms from 1992 to 1997. From 1996 levels of family benefits were reformed in two ways: the earnings-related childcare allowance paid until the second birthday of the child was replaced by a fixed-rate scheme paying lower benefits, and means-testing was introduced for the formerly universal family allowance. The real value of overall expenditures both on unemployment-related benefits and

236

Figure 10.1. *Changes in macro-economic indicators in Hungary, 1989–1997*

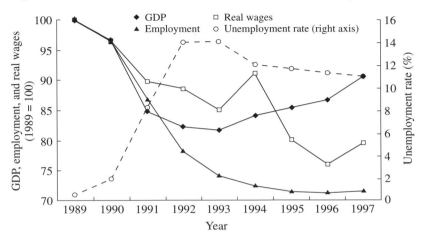

Source: Central Statistical Office.

family allowance was more than 50 per cent lower in 1996 compared to 1992 and the share of both components in the income of households also halved on average (Förster *et al.* 1998). When coupled with the substantially greater inequality in the labour market, the net result of all these changes was that overall income inequality increased (Milanovic 1996).[1]

So far no research has focused directly on child poverty in Hungary during the transition, but there is some evidence that children have been at greater risk. Analysis of income inequality based on the Hungarian Household Panel Survey (Andorka and Spéder 1994, 1996, 1997a, 1997b) and an investigation by the World Bank of poverty in Hungary using the official budget survey (World Bank 1996) shows the incidence of poverty rising with the number of children in a household; these studies also draw attention to the situation of children in lone-parent families. Results from Galasi (1998) confirm that the position of children has worsened during the transition due to income losses resulting from joblessness, low pay, or less generous child-related and other benefits.

---

[1] Flemming and Micklewright (2000) report a rather modest rise in the Gini coefficient of per capita income of three percentage points over 1988–97, as recorded by the Central Statistical Office's household budget survey, to a value of 0.25 at the end of the period. They show that the source used in this chapter, the Hungarian Household Panel Survey, shows a notably greater dispersion of per capita income, the Gini coefficient exceeding 0.30 by 1993. Inequality of earnings of full-time workers (measured by the ratio of ninetieth to tenth percentiles) rose much more sharply – by a third over 1988–97.

In this chapter we investigate how household characteristics are associated with the incidence, persistence and dynamics of poverty among children in Hungary. The data we use are restricted to 1992–6 and unfortunately do not cover the early transition shock of 1989–91, which, as we have seen, was a period of considerable decline in GDP and employment and rapidly emerging unemployment. From 1993, the second year of our observation window, figure 10.1 shows that GDP ceased to fall, the unemployment rate stopped rising, and the decline in employment slowed down. Our analysis is one of the period of 'emergence from the trough' and it is of considerable interest to see how child poverty has changed as a result of this macro-economic turnaround. Our results give grounds for some pessimism and the answer to the title we have taken for the chapter is unfortunately in the affirmative.

In section 10.2 we describe our data source, the Hungarian Household Panel Survey, together with the definitions of income and poverty used in the chapter. Section 10.3 presents results on changes in child poverty over time, and on its relationship with household characteristics, treating each year's wave of the panel as a separate cross-section. Here we are examining each frame from the ciné film provided by panel data, treating them as a series of snapshots of the situation. Ensuing sections then exploit the panel nature of the data, following the experience of individual children over time. Section 10.4 is concerned with the persistence of child poverty. Following children in five consecutive waves of the panel survey, we examine the frequency of being poor and analyse how persistence of child poverty is related to various household characteristics. Section 10.5 deals with the dynamics of poverty by analysing changes in inflows and outflows over time; it also investigates the association between changes in households' position in the labour market – a key feature of transition – and the movements by children into and out of poverty.

All our results refer to the years immediately prior to the reforms mentioned above that reduced the generosity of family benefits, reforms that are characteristic of the trend throughout the former communist countries of Eastern Europe in that they saw an increase in means-testing in the social safety net. What do our findings suggest about how these reforms should be viewed in terms of their impact on child poverty? In concluding, section 10.6 both highlights our key results and comments on this key policy issue.

10.2 Data source and definitions of income and poverty

Our analysis uses the first five waves of the Hungarian Household Panel Survey, conducted by the Tárki research institute. The survey started in

Table 10.1. *Households and children in the Hungarian panel*

	1992	1993	1994	1995	1996
Unweighted number of households	2,049	1,922	1,814	1,888	1,642
Weighted number of households	2,049	2,147	2,156	2,154	1,884
Unweighted number of children	1,377	1,227	1,130	1,250	1,080
Weighted number of children	1,377	1,357	1,355	1,399	1,242
Weighted number of children with zero income	7	0	6	14	8

1992 with a nationally representative sample of Hungarian households.[2] All persons living in first-wave households were followed and re-interviewed at one-year intervals, even if they quit the original households and found or formed new ones (in this event all members of the new households were interviewed as well).[3]

While the ability to track children over more than just two to three years is a distinct advantage, the relatively small sample size of the panel imposes a limitation on the analysis, reducing what can be said with precision for particular sub-groups. As can be seen from table 10.1, the number of households is about 2,000 in each wave and the number of children ranges from 1,100 to 1,400. We define children as persons aged less than 18 years.

We use several different samples of children. Section 10.3 is based on *cross-section* samples for 1992–6, including all children present in the panel in each year irrespective of whether they were present in other years. Section 10.4 examines persistence of poverty using the balanced sample of *children present in all five waves* (i.e. children that were aged 0–13 in the first wave). Finally, the analysis in sections 10.5 and 10.6 is based on samples of children present in *consecutive pairs* of waves (1992/93, 1993/94, 1994/95, 1995/96).

The panel survey collects detailed information on individual and household incomes (expenditures are not recorded). Each household member aged over 15 is interviewed about his or her personal income, while household-level incomes are recorded using a household questionnaire. The questionnaires include information on net and after-tax earnings and incomes. (In order to obtain more precise information on income, interviewing is conducted in spring and early summer soon after the late-March deadline for personal income tax declarations.)

Our results are based on figures for net annual equivalised household

[2] Household response rates have fluctuated between 85 and 91 per cent. More information on the panel is given in Tóth (1995).
[3] In order to account for sample attrition, cross-section statistics for waves 2–5 presented in the chapter are based on weighted data using the individual weights supplied by Tárki.

Table 10.2. *Child poverty rates with different poverty lines*

Year	Bottom quintile	Half median	Subsistence minimum
1992	17.7	7.2	36.0
1993	19.2	7.4	40.7
1994	19.3	6.3	44.7
1995	19.6	7.4	–
1996	22.8	10.1	–

Notes: Figures are based on cross-section samples (all children aged 0–17 in the wave concerned). The data for 1993–6 are weighted to allow for panel attrition. Poverty rates for bottom quintile and half median lines are based on annual incomes equivalised by the square-root scale. The poverty rate based on the Central Statistical Office (CSO) subsistence minimum is based on monthly incomes equivalised with the CSO scale (1 for the first adult, 0.75 for any other adult, 0.65 for the first child, 0.5 for the second and 0.4 for any other child). Calculations of the subsistence minimum by the CSO were discontinued in 1995.

income (amounts are converted to 1996 prices using March to March consumer price indices).[4] The reference period covers April of the previous year to March of the year of interview. The last twelve-month period covered by the data therefore ends in March 1996, just before the reforms to family benefits referred to in section 10.1.

The equivalence scale used is the square root of household size (the income concept is thus the same as for the annual figures for Hungary in the cross-national analysis of chapter 4). Children living in households with zero reported income are excluded from the analysis – the last row of table 10.1 shows that their numbers are very small.

We experimented with three different poverty lines: (i) the bottom quintile (the twentieth percentile) of the distribution of equivalised income (of all individuals and not just children), (ii) 50 per cent of the median of the same distribution, and (iii) the official subsistence minimum published by the Hungarian Central Statistical Office (CSO), available only until 1994. Table 10.2 shows poverty rates for children over 1992–6 using these three lines.

Based on the half median line, the child poverty rate is less than half that obtained when using the bottom quintile cut-off: 6 per cent in 1994 on the former basis, for example, compared to 19 per cent on the latter. The patterns of the year-to-year changes in poverty rates based on these two relative lines do differ, but in both cases the rate is significantly higher in 1996 than that in 1992. The poverty rate applying the subsistence minimum in 1992–4 is very much higher than those based on the two relative lines. In

[4] For detailed information on the income types included and the method of calculation of annual household income, see Förster and Tóth (1997: annexe 4).

Figure 10.2. *Poverty rates for children, adults and pensioners*

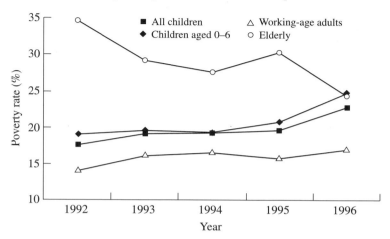

Figures are based on cross-sectional samples and on weighted data (except for 1992).

the remainder of the chapter we use the *bottom quintile* as our poverty line. Our main motivation for this is technical: the lower cut-off of the half median would provide many fewer observations for the analysis of the poor, which is a consideration given the small sample sizes in the Hungarian panel. The child poverty rates given by the bottom quintile cut-off are still far lower than the incidence of child poverty implied by the CSO subsistence minimum, which, unlike the two relative lines, was specifically calculated for Hungarian conditions.

10.3 Poor children and the characteristics of their households

Figure 10.2 shows for 1992–6 the poverty rate for all children, children aged 0–6, working-age adults, and the elderly (defined as 60 years or over for men, and 55 years or over for women, the normal pension ages in Hungary). The all-child rates are those shown in the first column of table 10.2. In 1992 children were slightly under-represented in the poorest fifth of the income distribution; just under 18 per cent of children were poor in this year whereas by 1996 the figure had risen to nearly 23 per cent (the rise is statistically significant). The poverty rate of working-age adults also increases over the period, but to a smaller extent than that of children, while young children have slightly higher poverty rates than children as a whole.

It is wrong to see the defence of child well-being as a 'battle for resources' against the elderly – another traditionally vulnerable group, which figure 10.2 shows to have had a notably high poverty rate at the start of the period (and a rate still above average in 1996). Nevertheless, the contrasting fortunes of the two groups is striking. While the child poverty rate rose by five percentage points over 1992–6, that for the elderly fell by ten points; children have become more concentrated over time in the bottom fifth of the income distribution and the elderly markedly less so, with the result that the gap between the poverty rates in the two groups had almost disappeared by 1996. The poverty rate among young children exactly equalled the rate for the elderly by 1996, the gap having been fifteen percentage points in 1992.

What household characteristics are associated with child poverty and has the worsening of children's position been accompanied by changes in household characteristics? We chose three demographic indicators and one of labour-market status to describe household characteristics that might affect child poverty. The demographic indicators are: the age of the child, the number of children in the household and whether the child lives in a household with a single-parent head, all characteristics typically associated with a higher risk of a child being poor (Duncan *et al.* 1993).

The labour-market indicator relates to the status of the household head and his or her spouse. (In most cases these are the parents of the children in the sample.) We distinguish between those heads and spouses in work (including self-employment) and those not in work. The latter includes pensioners, the unemployed, persons on childcare allowance and others not active in the labour market (for example, housewives). In general, children living in families with more workers can be expected to have much better chances of avoiding poverty, although of course the impact depends on the level of wages paid and the marked rise in earnings inequality in Hungary during the 1990s needs to be borne in mind.[5] The impact of the lack of work on poverty may well have become stronger during the period under investigation due in part to cuts in unemployment-related benefits and the rise of long-term unemployment uncovered by insurance benefit (Micklewright and Nagy 1996, 1999).

Table 10.3 shows child poverty rates broken down by these household characteristics for 1992 and 1996. The figures by age of child confirm that it is young children that are most at risk (see figure 10.2). The number of children in the household has a much greater association with child poverty at the beginning than at the end of the period. Indeed, the rise in child

---

[5] See footnote 1.

Table 10.3. *Children's household characteristics, 1992 and 1996*

Characteristic	1992		1996	
	Poverty rate (%)	Distribution of the sample (%)	Poverty rate (%)	Distribution of the sample (%)
Age of child:				
0–6	19.2	32.3	24.8	38.9
7–13	17.0	41.8	22.7	36.1
14–17	16.9	25.9	19.7	25.0
Number of children:				
1	17.5	27.1	21.5	17.1
2	13.4	49.1	22.7	33.3
3+	26.6	23.8	23.3	49.6
Lone-parent household	35.4	14.0	32.0	14.2
Labour-market status: couple with adults				
both working	4.7	39.3	5.6	44.9
both not working	51.3	11.6	74.2	11.6
1 working/1 not	14.0	35.7	24.4	29.4
lone parent				
working	21.4	8.2	18.4	9.5
not working	60.0	5.1	60.8	4.6
All children	17.7	100.0	22.9	100.0

Notes: Cross-sectional samples ($N = 1,360$ in 1992 and $N = 1,237$ in 1996). For 1996, the percentages are based on weighted data.

poverty appears concentrated among the one- and two-child families. Children in lone-parent households are clearly at a higher risk of poverty: about one third are poor in both years but their position did not worsen over time.[6]

Clear results emerge relating to the labour-market status of the household head and his or her spouse. It comes as no surprise that children from households where neither the head nor spouse is working have a very high probability of being poor – a half are poor in 1992 and three quarters in 1996. (Similarly, child poverty rates are very high in households with a single parent not in work.) Children in these types of households represent a small but not insignificant proportion of the total – some 12 per cent in both waves. (Despite the small numbers, the rise in the poverty rate over the period is sufficiently large to be statistically significant.)

[6] Our definition of a lone-parent household in this chapter is the same as that used in chapter 4, namely a household with one or more children, one adult (not necessarily the parent of any of the children) and with no other adults present.

There is also a notable increase in the poverty rate for children in households where either the head or the spouse – but not both of them – works: from 14 per cent to 24 per cent. The latter figure means that children in such households are over-represented among the poorest fifth of the income distribution, a result that is worth underlining; despite having one parent in work, children in these households have a greater than average risk of being poor.[7] The need for a second earner in the household in order to reduce the risk of poverty for children to below the average stands in contrast to any argument that a reduction in employment among mothers during the transition is a desirable social goal to further 'family values'. Only the children in two-parent households where both parents work have a poverty rate which is well below that for all children.

10.4 Which children are in persistent poverty?

The analysis of the previous section did not exploit the fact that the survey concerned is a panel, tracking the same children over time. In this section we use the sample of children present in all five waves of the panel (aged 0–13 years at wave 1) to examine the relationship between household characteristics and the persistence of poverty. Table 10.4 shows how many times a child was poor over the five years, breaking down the results by the same demographic and labour-market status indicators as were used in the previous section.

A high proportion of Hungarian children experienced poverty (i.e. income in the poorest fifth of the overall distribution) at least once over 1992–6: 44 per cent. For many of them, however, poverty is transitory; one in five of all children experienced poverty only once and 13 per cent were poor in two or three years. About one tenth of all children were poor in four years or more.[8]

There are no differences between younger and older children in the proportion ever found in poverty. However, some intriguing differences can be seen in the number of times children are in the poorest fifth of the income distribution given that they are found there at least once. Children aged 0–6 in wave 1 are more likely to be poor for one to three years, while those aged

---

[7] Strictly speaking, the results refer to the head of household and his or her spouse who in a few cases are not the child's parents.

[8] The percentages for ever poor and poor in all five years are very close to the figures for Hungary for ever in the poorest fifth and always in the poorest fifth over five years given in the cross-national analysis of table 4.4 (annual net income). However, table 4.4 refers to persistence in the poorest fifth of the distribution of all children while table 10.4 refers to the poorest fifth of the distribution of individuals of all ages.

Table 10.4. *Persistence of child poverty, 1992–1996 (row percentages)*

| Characteristics at wave 1 | Number of times poor | | | | | |
	0	1	2–3	4	5	All
Age of child:						
0–6	56.1	18.2	16.8	3.3	5.6	100.0
7–13	56.2	21.8	9.0	5.2	7.8	100.0
Number of children:						
1	47.0	23.4	12.8	7.4	9.5	100.0
2	67.1	15.5	10.5	4.0	2.9	100.0
3+	39.8	27.8	16.2	2.9	13.3	100.0
Lone-parent household	35.8	30.5	12.1	8.6	13.0	100.0
Labour-market status: couple with adults						
both working	72.7	21.7	5.4	0.2	–	100.0
both not working	15.2	19.1	6.9	8.4	50.4	100.0
1 working/1 not lone parent	57.6	14.6	20.7	5.8	1.3	100.0
working	49.1	44.5	6.4	–	–	
not working	13.4	15.9	20.3	20.1	30.4	100.0
All children	56.0	19.5	12.8	4.4	7.3	100.0

Notes: Sample: children in all waves, $N = 716$. All inter-group differences are statistically significant at the 5 per cent level.

7–13 are more likely to be poor for four or five years. The reasons for these differences are unclear.

The number of children in the household has a strong association with poverty persistence, although some aspects of the results are a little puzzling. A child from a household with three or more children was almost twice as likely as the average child to be in the poorest fifth of the distribution in all five waves, and over four times as likely as a child from a household with two children. However, children living in a household where there was no other child at wave 1 were also three times more likely to be in poverty in all five years than the children from two-child households; and if one defines persistent poverty as being found poor four or five times, there is no difference in its incidence between the children in one and three or more child households. It may be that the one-child households at wave 1 are those where it is most likely that other children are born during the ensuing waves, leading to continued withdrawal from the labour market by mothers (we have not investigated this further).

More than one fifth of children from lone-parent households experience poverty four or five times and two thirds are poor at least once, reinforcing the picture of disadvantage obtained from the cross-section analysis in table 10.3. Almost one third are poor just once. Thus children in lone-parent households have relatively high probabilities both of moving into and out of poverty *and* of remaining poor over the period.

The bottom part of the table shows the breakdown by households' labour-market characteristics. Over a quarter of children living in households with both head *and* spouse working in wave 1 do experience poverty at least once over the five years. A minority are in poverty at the time of the first wave – see table 10.4 (although note that the samples differ). Others fall into poverty in later waves, due, for example, to one or other parent losing their job – a good illustration of how the dynamic perspective differs from the snapshot shown in table 10.3. However, no children in this group are found to be persistently in poverty. The contrast is stark with children in households where neither head nor spouse worked in wave 1 and those from households with a lone parent not in work; more than 50 per cent of these children are poor four or five times.

These results can be easily summarised. Almost half of the children experience poverty at least once over a five-year period, and about one tenth can be considered as persistently poor. The risk of persistent poverty is notably high in lone-parent households and in households where both the head and the spouse were workless at the start of the period.

10.5 Poverty dynamics and labour-market changes

In this section we focus on the moves into and out of poverty from one year to the next. We first examine these movements for each consecutive pair of waves in the panel in order to see whether the deterioration of children's position over the period is due to low exit or high entry rates. We then investigate how *changes* in households' labour-market status are associated with entry and exit. This contrasts with the analysis of persistence in the previous section that provided a classification according to the characteristics of households measured at the time of the first wave, without considering whether labour-market status changed subsequently.

Figure 10.3 reports the movements to and from poverty by children for each of the wave pairs. These rates are computed using the total number of all children in the sample as the denominator. This contrasts with the conventional calculation of entry and exit rates, which take as the denominator the number of children 'at risk' – that is, rates calculated as the number entering poverty as a percentage of all those who are not poor and the number leaving poverty as a percentage of all those who are poor. Our

Figure 10.3. *Children flowing into and out of poverty*

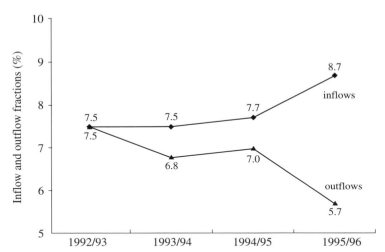

The figures are percentages of all children (poor and not poor) present in each pair of waves.

figures are therefore the inflow and outflow 'fractions' analysed in the cross-national context in chapter 4 (the difference between the two methods of calculation is discussed in section 4.4).

The higher rate of inflow than outflow reflects the rising poverty rate over the period shown earlier in the chapter – poverty rises if more children become poor than manage to escape being poor. The marked rise in poverty in 1996 (see table 10.2 and figure 10.2) is shown to result from *both* an increase in inflows *and* a fall in outflows (of broadly similar magnitudes).[9]

The relationship between inflows and outflows and changes in labour-market characteristics is given in table 10.5, distinguishing between children in households where the numbers of persons in work and the number unemployed stayed the same, rose or fell between the two years in question. The rates are calculated in the same way as described above, that is with denominators of all children, so they are again the inflow and outflow fractions. We restrict attention to the first and last wave pairs, 1992–3 and 1995–6.

The third column for each pair of waves shows how often there is a

[9] The inflow fraction for 1995–6 is significantly different from those for 1992–3 and 1993–4 while the 1995–6 outflow fraction is significantly lower than that for 1992–3 (only).

Table 10.5. *Poverty dynamics of children and changes in the labour market characteristics of households*

	1992–3			1995–6		
Changes in employment status of the child's household	Inflow fraction (%)	Outflow fraction (%)	Distribution of the sample (%)	Inflow fraction (%)	Outflow fraction (%)	Distribution of the sample (%)
Number of persons working:						
same	4.8[a]	5.3[b]	67.3	8.4	6.1	74.7
greater	8.5	15.4[a]	17.5	7.4[b]	9.3[a]	14.5
fewer	16.5[a]	9.6	15.2	14.0[a]	1.4[a,b]	10.8
Number of persons unemployed:						
same	6.0	8.5	78.8	8.4	6.3[b]	81.1
greater	17.2[a]	3.0[a]	10.8	20.9[a,b]	4.4	9.3
fewer	8.5	5.4	10.4	4.3[a]	3.2	9.6
All children	7.5	7.5	100.0	9.2	5.7	100.0

Notes: [a] Significantly different from the average at the 5 per cent level. [b] Significantly different from the 1992–3 value at the 5 per cent level. Figures are based on weighted data. The inflow and outflow fractions show the percentages of all children (poor and not poor) who enter or leave poverty. Samples include children in both waves (*N* = 1,241 in 1992–3 and *N* = 984 in 1995–6).

change in labour-market status. Some explanation of exactly what the figures imply is required. For example, for one third of children, the number of persons working in their household changed between 1992 and 1993, and for nearly one fifth the number of persons unemployed changed. These are big numbers and they underline the extent of the changes over time in employment that occur in children's households. By 1995–6, the changes were smaller, especially the numbers for whom employment in the household had fallen (this is consistent with the time-path of aggregate employment shown in figure 10.1).

Number working. Children living in households with an increase in the number of persons working are about twice as likely as the average child to flow out from poverty (somewhat more than this in 1992–3 and somewhat less in 1995–6). Where there was a fall in the number working, the inflow fraction was also about twice the average in the earlier period and again slightly less than twice in the later period. The outflow fraction was notably lower in 1995–6 where the number working fell (but not in 1992–3).

Number unemployed. There is a sharply higher inflow fraction for children in households in which the number of unemployed persons rises, something true of both periods (this increase in the number unemployed could be from zero to one). And there was also a notably lower outflow fraction in 1992–3. In the later period, inflows were less than half the average if the number of unemployed fell. The outflow fraction shows no statistically significant variation with any changes in the number unemployed in 1995–6, while in the earlier period children were only half as likely to leave poverty as the average child if the number of unemployed rose.

Of course, most of these results are not surprising in one sense. Loss of work leads to falls in income, and increases in work lead to gains in income – both with consequences for the probability of moving across the poverty line. Nevertheless, table 10.5 quantifies the differences in the probabilities associated with these labour-market events, helping make clear one important factor pushing children into or out of poverty.

Table 10.6 presents some of these findings in a different way, showing the percentage of all entries and exits that are accounted for by increases or reductions in the number of persons working in the household. We have seen, for example, that the inflow fraction was double the average in 1992–3 when the number of workers in the household fell. But what percentage of all entries into poverty is explained by this phenomenon?

Starting with this example, we can see that when the data are viewed in this way job loss does not appear paramount as an explanation for entry into poverty. Little more than a third of children entering poverty between 1992 and 1993 are in households where the number of workers fell and the figure is only half this for 1995–6. Most entries to poverty take place where

Table 10.6. *Percentage of child poverty entries and exits accounted for by changes in the number of workers in the household*

Number of workers	Entries		Exits	
	1992–3	1995–6	1992–3	1995–6
Same	44.5	70.0	46.8	77.9
Greater	20.4	12.9	34.9	20.5
Fewer	35.1	17.1	18.3	1.5
Total	100.0	100.0	100.0	100.0

the number of workers in the household stays the same (or rises). The same is true when one looks at exits. Over 1995–6, nearly four out of every five exits from poverty were in households where the number of workers stayed the same. This underlines the importance of explanations *other than* job loss or gain. These include those variations in earnings and other incomes, especially state benefits, that take place with no change in the overall number of persons working (for example a change of job or the expiry of limited-duration unemployment insurance benefit).

10.6 Conclusions

The impact of transition on children is a natural cause for concern. In this chapter we have considered how the incomes of children have fared in a country at the forefront of the transition process, looking at the years 1992–6 that were mostly a period of (weak) economic recovery. A number of clear findings emerge.

- Taken as a group, children have moved down the income distribution, moving from a situation of being under-represented in the poorest fifth of the population in 1992 to being over-represented in 1996. This movement contrasts with that made by the elderly, whose representation in the poorest fifth of the distribution fell markedly over the period.
- The importance of work to avoid being poor (defined as being in the poorest fifth of the population) rose over the period. This is summarised by the fact that, in 1996, a child with only one parent in work had a greater than average probability of being poor.
- Poverty is a persistent phenomenon for some children but is experienced occasionally by many. On the one hand, one in ten children were in the

bottom fifth of the income distribution in every year from 1992 to 1996 while, on the other, 44 per cent of children were found there at least once.

• Changes in the number of workers (or unemployed persons) in a household are often associated with a marked shift in the probability of entering or leaving poverty, but the majority of entries and exits take place with no such changes occurring, emphasising the importance of other explanations.

These results refer to the period before major reforms to family benefits were introduced in April 1996, reforms that saw the introduction of income-testing of family allowance and a reduction for most families in the generosity of benefits paid to mothers with infant children on leave from their employment. Redmond (1999) shows that these reforms had only a modest impact on the incomes of families with children. In particular, income testing removed family allowance entitlement from only about 10 per cent of families (those at the top of the income distribution) while the poorest tenth of households with children actually gained slightly – their average income is estimated to have risen by 0.6 per cent (due to a consolidation of several maternity-related benefits).

Despite this picture of little apparent change, Redmond argues that the reforms represented 'an important psychological shift in the orientation of social policy in Hungary, away from universalist and contingent policies and towards means-testing' (1999: 87). This shift can be thought of as opening the way to much greater means-testing of family benefits. Redmond illustrates what could be the result of going down this road by simulating the impact on family incomes in Hungary of the introduction of a family benefit system of the type found in the UK. Although there is a universal family allowance in the UK, a much greater proportion of total support for families with children is income-tested than in Hungary. (The universal UK allowance is worth much less as a proportion of average income than the Hungarian family allowance.)

The impact of the introduction of a UK-style scheme into Hungary was found to be substantial. The incomes of the poorest tenth of households with children were estimated to rise substantially, by 16 per cent. This was despite the overall cost of family benefits falling by a tenth in the particular simulation that is implemented. In short, state transfers would become much more firmly targeted on lower-income families with UK-style benefits. At first sight this would represent a significant alleviation of child poverty in Hungary.

But the price of achieving better targeting of family benefits is much higher implicit marginal rates of tax at the bottom of the distribution. These 'tax rates' measure the proportion of any additional earnings that a family would gain from more work that would be lost in the form of income tax, social insurance contributions, and reduced receipt of means-tested state transfers. High marginal rates of tax at the bottom of the distribution are one of the disadvantages of increased income-testing. Redmond estimates that the marginal tax rate faced by working households with children in the bottom three decile groups would be about 70 per cent, compared to only 35 per cent with the benefit system after the 1996 reforms. These much higher marginal tax rates at the bottom of the income distribution clearly raise the issue of incentives to work.

The dynamic perspective we have taken of child poverty in Hungary in this chapter underlines just how important it is to take this issue seriously. Our evidence shows that there was already substantial persistence in child poverty before the 1996 reforms. A move to a family benefit system that substantially reduced incentives to work for low-income families would threaten to reinforce this picture.

References
Andorka, R. and Spéder, Zs., 1994, 'A szegénység alakulása 1992 és 1994 között' ('Poverty between 1992 and 1994'), in Tóth, I. Gy. (ed.), *Társadalmi átalakulás 1992–4, Jelentés a Magyar Háztartás Panel 3. hullámának eredményeiről (Social Changes 1992–4. Report on the Third Wave of the Hungarian Household Panel Survey)*, Department of Sociology, Budapest University of Economics, Tárki and Central Statistical Office, Budapest.
Andorka, R. and Spéder, Zs., 1996, 'Szegénység' ('Poverty'), in Sik, E. and Tóth, I. Gy. (eds.), *Társadalmi páternoszter 1992–5, Jelentés a Magyar Háztartás Panel 4. hullámának eredményeiről (Social Paternoster 1992–5. Report on the Fourth Wave of the Hungarian Household Panel Survey)*, Department of Sociology, Budapest University of Economics, Tárki and Central Statistical Office, Budapest.
Andorka, R. and Spéder, Zs., 1997a, 'Szegénység' ('Poverty'), in Sik, E. and Tóth, I. Gy. (eds.), *Az ajtók záródnak, Jelentés a Magyar Háztartás Panel 5. hullámának eredményeiről (Mind the Doors. Report on the Fifth Wave of the Hungarian Household Panel Survey)*, Department of Sociology, Budapest University of Economics and Tárki, Budapest.
Andorka, R. and Spéder, Zs., 1997b, 'Poverty in Hungary in 1992–1995', paper delivered at the conference 'Inequality and Poverty in Transition Economies' held at the European Bank for Reconstruction and Development, 23–4 May, London.
Atkinson, A. B. and Micklewright, J., 1992, *Economic Transformation in Eastern Europe and the Distribution of Income*, Cambridge University Press, Cambridge.
Duncan, G. J., Gustafsson, B., Hauser, R., Schmaus, G., Messinger, H., Muffels, R., Nolan, B., and Ray, J.-C., 1993, 'Poverty dynamics in eight countries', *Journal of Population Economics*, 6: 295–334.

Ferge, Z., 1991, 'Social security systems in the new democracies of central and eastern Europe: past legacies and possible futures', in Cornia, G. A. and Sipos, S. (eds.), *Children and the Transition to the Market Economy*, Avebury, Aldershot.

Flemming, J. and Micklewright, J., 2000, 'Income distribution, economic systems and transition', in Atkinson, A. B. and Bourguignon, F. (eds.), *Handbook of Income Distribution*, North-Holland, Amsterdam.

Förster, M. and Tóth, I. Gy., 1997, 'Poverty and inequalities: Hungary and the Visegrad countries compared', paper delivered at the conference 'Inequality and Poverty in Transition Economies' at the European Bank for Reconstruction and Development, 23–4 May, London.

Förster, M., Szivós, P. and Tóth, I. Gy., 1998, 'A jóléti támogatások és a szegénység: Magyarország és a visegrádi országok tapasztalatai' ('Welfare benefits and poverty. The experiences of Hungary and other Visegrad countries'), in Kolosi T., Tóth, I. Gy. and Vukovich, Gy. (eds.), *Társadalmi riport*, Tárki, Budapest.

Galasi, P., 1998, 'Income inequality and mobility in Hungary 1992–1996', Innocenti Occasional Papers, Economic and Social Policy Series 64, UNICEF International Child Development Centre, Florence.

Jarvis, S. and Micklewright, J., 1995, 'The targeting of family allowances in Hungary', in van de Walle, D. and Nead, K. (eds.), *Public Spending and the Poor: Theory and Evidence*, Johns Hopkins University Press, Baltimore ML.

Micklewright, J. and Nagy, Gy., 1996, 'Labour market policy and the unemployed in Hungary', *European Economic Review*, 40: 819–28.

Micklewright, J. and Nagy, Gy., 1999, 'Living standards and incentives in transition: the implications of UI exhaustion in Hungary', *Journal of Public Economics*, 73: 297–319.

Milanovic, B., 1996, 'Income, inequality and poverty during the transition: a survey of the evidence', *Most*, 6: 131–47.

Redmond, G., 1999, 'Incomes, incentives and the growth of means-testing in Hungary', *Fiscal Studies*, 20: 77–99.

Szalai, J., 1989, 'Poverty in Hungary during the period of economic crisis', background paper prepared for the 1990 Human Development Report, UNDP, New York.

Tóth, I. Gy., 1995, 'The Hungarian household panel: aims and methods', *Innovation*, 8: 106–22.

World Bank, 1996, *Hungary: Poverty and Social Transfers*, Washington DC.

11 Mobility and poverty dynamics among Russian children

JENI KLUGMAN AND ALEXANDRE KOLEV

11.1 Introduction

In creating a free economy, we consciously departed from the rigid regimentation and regulation of all aspects of life, and failed to notice how the state was increasingly becoming indifferent to the fate of its children . . . It cannot continue like this, we urgently need to change the situation. This has to start from the state. (Boris Yeltsin 1997)

It is now abundantly clear that the tremendous economic and social changes associated with the Russian transition have led to a serious deterioration in living standards. Dramatic increases in poverty have been well documented (Doyle 1996, Klugman and Braithwaite 1998, Kolev 1996, Milanovic 1998, World Bank 1995). This trend at the aggregate level has occurred alongside substantial and increasing differences in poverty across family types. Families with children have been particularly affected, especially single-parent families and those in rural areas (Klugman and Kolev 1999).

Rising poverty generally, and especially among children, is obviously worrying. For policymakers, an understanding of the flows of children into and out of poverty is important for the choice and design of government (or non-government) interventions that might seek to influence those flows. Against this background, this chapter is the first study of mobility and poverty dynamics among children in Russia.

In the next section we put the situation of children in Russia in the mid-1990s into the context of the economic and social changes associated with the transition. We then discuss our data and definitions before turning to look at three issues. First, we examine the overall picture of how the consumption levels of children and their families varied between 1994 and 1996. How large was mobility, and which types of children were more likely to remain persistently at the bottom (or the top) of the distribution of consumption? Second, flows into and out of poverty are investigated. Rural children, children in lone-parent families and younger children are all found to have high flows into poverty.

Finally, we begin to identify the characteristics of those children who are most vulnerable to persistent poverty. We find that children are more likely than working-age adults and pensioners to experience poverty, both in the short and longer term (over three years). We find significant regional variation in persistent poverty. And we find that those children who were poor three years out of three were less likely to be in households receiving child benefit. This points to substantial problems in the targeting of this form of social assistance.

11.2 The Russian context

The transition from the former planned economy has been characterised by a deep and prolonged period of economic crisis.[1] In this section we provide a brief summary and the economic backdrop to our analysis of children's living standards, before going on to review trends in poverty and public income support.

The early years of transition were associated with rapidly rising prices and, following price stabilisation, there has been on-going and widespread stagnation of economic activity and sharp falls in the value of real earnings and social transfers. Figure 11.1 shows that GDP fell more than 40 per cent between 1991 and 1996. In the latter year, GNP per capita was only $4,190, compared to $24,680 for the USA and $17,230 for the UK, for example (UNDP, 1996, annex table 26, incomes adjusted according to purchasing power parity). Alongside declines in output, real wage levels have fallen substantially. By 1998, the real wage was still only half of the 1990 level. Moreover, the official wage figures understate the actual extent of decline, in so far as a substantial portion of wages go unpaid, often for months, and are not indexed for inflation if and when payment is made (Standing 1997).

Declines in wages and output, reduced administrative capacity of the state and the growing importance of informal sector activity have translated into lower government revenues. This has created significant downward pressure on public spending, given the government's inflation targets and the commensurate need to limit budget deficits (UNICEF 1998). Government social expenditure has dropped, as a share of GDP, from about 10 per cent in 1989 to around 8 per cent in 1998. Another important characteristic which has shaped social policy is the decentralisation of social expenditure. This has been associated with increasing regional

---

[1] The nature of this crisis and the underlying causal factors are far beyond the scope of this chapter, and the interested reader is referred to Popov (1996), Desai (1997) and references cited therein.

Figure 11.1. *Trends in GDP and average real wages*

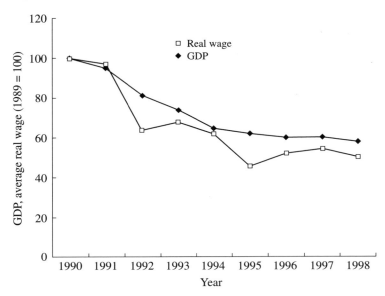

Source: UNICEF Innocenti Research Centre TransMONEE database.

disparities, in part because the system of redistribution from richer to poorer regions within the Federation is notably weak (Stewart 2000).

It is clear that Russia has experienced very adverse macro-economic and labour-market developments over the 1990s. Measuring the social impact of these trends is difficult, however, not least because of the unreliability of many official statistics (Koen 1996). For example, the extent of the decline in national output has been subject to some dispute, in part because the reliability of statistical systems based on enterprise reporting has clearly weakened over time. This increases the usefulness of detailed empirical investigation based on representative household surveys.

Poverty during the transition: an overview

Household surveys have shown that the scale and depth of poverty in Russia have increased during the transition. This point is generally accepted, though again there is debate as to the extent of the changes. The best estimates of the scale of poverty in the late 1980s suggest that about one in ten Russians fell below what was then regarded as subsistence levels

(Atkinson and Micklewright 1992, Braithwaite 1997). Estimates based on the Russian Longitudinal Monitoring Survey (RLMS), the nationally representative survey that is used in the analysis in this chapter, suggest that the poverty headcount (share of households living under the poverty line), rose from about 25 per cent in 1992, following the liberalisation of many consumer prices, to 35 per cent in 1995 (Klugman and Braithwaite 1998). Figures derived from the official household survey show somewhat less deterioration in poverty, although that data source is highly problematic (Atkinson and Micklewright 1992) and is not relied upon here.[2]

Despite divergent views about the scale of the increases in poverty during the 1990s, analysts using official and alternative data sources have drawn very similar profiles of poverty. There is agreement that, as during the Soviet period, the majority of the poor are in families with working-age members and that families with children have a greater probability of being poor, with the risk rising with the number of children. Other vulnerable categories include households headed by single parents and the unemployed, and households which rely solely on income from pensions, particularly pensioners living alone (World Bank 1995, Kolev 1996).

The contemporary profile of poverty differs from the picture prior to reform mainly in the significantly higher incidence of poverty among the working-age population and the emergence of open unemployment as an important risk factor. Research has also been undertaken to identify the separate impacts during the transition of the risk factors described above (since people can belong to more than one 'at risk' group at the same time).[3] This research confirms that family size and in particular the presence of children under 18 has a significant effect on the likelihood of the family being poor, and that, whereas the presence of additional adults increases the probability of being poor, the presence of additional pensioners does not. The presence of an unemployed working-age member also has a clear impact on the probability of the household being poor.

Trends in the incidence of poverty for some of these important population groups are shown in figure 11.2. The figure covers the years 1994 to 1996, the period on which the empirical analysis in this chapter focuses. The poverty rates here are lower than in the Klugman and Braithwaite (1998) study

[2] See Klugman and Marnie (forthcoming) for a comparison of trends in poverty in the official data against the RLMS and other survey estimates. It is worth noting that even the official household survey shows a substantial increase in per capita income inequality – from a Gini coefficient of about 0.24 in 1987–8 to 0.39 by 1993–5, compared to a rise from 0.21 to 0.23 in Hungary over the same period (Flemming and Micklewright 2000, Milanovic 1998).

[3] Examples are the World Bank's poverty assessment for Russia for 1992–3 (World Bank 1995) and Foley (1997) and Kolev (1996) for 1995.

Figure 11.2. *Poverty rates, 1994–1996*

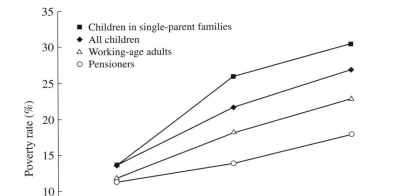

Source: authors' estimates based on the RLMS.

referred to above because these, and subsequent calculations in this chapter, take into account price variations across the different regions of Russia. Nonetheless, the trends are the same. Poverty has risen generally, but most sharply for children, and especially for children in single-parent families.

These high and increasing rates of poverty among Russia's children raise obvious concerns. Poverty has a strong negative impact on child welfare, both in terms of educational achievements, health status and, later, social inclusion. As former President Yeltsin's statement reported at the start of the chapter makes clear, there have been some indications of increased official concern about the situation of children in Russia. Yet public income support for poor families with children remains seriously limited.

Public income support for children in poor families

The government's social policy response to the economic crisis has failed to stem the rise in poverty. The formal system of social protection that was inherited from the Soviet period has become increasingly inadequate for many vulnerable population groups, including children. Problems of coverage have been compounded by the fiscal pressures and large real cuts in social spending noted above.

During the Soviet period, family allowances were paid to single mothers and to large families (see Klugman and McAuley 2000 for a discussion of the ideological and other concerns which underpinned the approach). A new approach to child benefits evolved in the wake of price liberalisation; there was a complicated system with some eighteen different benefits for families with children, but payments, set as a share of the (infrequently indexed) minimum wage, were very low (World Bank 1994). In 1994 the system was simplified with the introduction of a unified benefit, but the real value remained at only about one fifth of the pre-transition level. The overall level of public spending on social assistance amounts to only a small proportion of the poverty gap, and would therefore be inadequate even if perfectly targeted (Milanovic 1998).

Social transfers were nonetheless an important component of average household income in Russia in the mid-1990s. In 1995 about 68 per cent of poor families received some public income support, and for recipients this represented about 40 per cent of their total income (Klugman and Braithwaite 1998: table 7). The poverty impact of such benefits is, however, limited by extensive errors of exclusion. A large number of poor families do not receive benefits at all (Foley and Klugman 1997). In 1995 more than one out of four households classified as poor, and one in five of the very poor, did not report receipt of any transfers. At that same time the majority – about 60 per cent – of non-poor families did receive public transfers. The shortcomings of the system of social protection result in eligible households in need often being left without any state income support. The high rates of exclusion from support among poor households suggest that inadequate information about eligibility and lack of physical access to allow claims to benefit may be important contributory factors. Errors of inclusion (receipt of benefit by those who are not entitled) appear to be relatively limited, to around 5 per cent of households. The RLMS data suggest that these overall patterns have persisted throughout the transition.

We can summarise the background to this chapter as follows. At the macro-economic level large declines in output have taken place alongside substantial real wage cuts and declining levels of employment. Poverty has risen sharply and remains high among some socio-economic groups. Government responses in terms of income support have been quite inadequate, and many poor families with children have been left without state benefits.

11.3 Data and definitions

The Russian Longitudinal Monitoring Survey

The source used in this chapter is the Russian Longitudinal Monitoring Survey (RLMS). We analyse data from three interviews which form a panel over a two-year period, late 1994 to late 1996.[4] As in the other chapters of this book, the unit of analysis here is the child, unless otherwise indicated. (As chapter 2 noted, because family composition can change over time, it is preferable to focus on individuals rather than households in a dynamic analysis.) Unfortunately, the RLMS only re-interviews those individuals who do not change address (movers are not followed). The implications of this 'following rule' are discussed below. Our sample is restricted to children aged 15 or less at the time of the first wave of interviews in 1994 (i.e. aged 17 or less two years later in 1996) for whom there is information at the household level on the main variables of interest. We excluded households with zero expenditure on food.[5]

There are several problems with the RMLS for the purposes of the present chapter. First, the short length of the RLMS panel inevitably limits the investigation of dynamics. Second, the reported income and expenditure refer only to the month preceding the interview. Hence, we can observe the poverty state of a particular family at three points in time, but are unable to observe the *length* of any poverty spells. (See chapter 2 for discussion of this issue.) Third, the following rule in the panel is unfortunate. It implies that in the case of divorce or separation, if one of the partners leaves the household, he or she is lost from the survey. Our final problem, a frequent one in panel analyses, is that some individuals who do not move are also lost between waves due, for example, to non-response.

Sample attrition (whether due to moves out of the household, to non-response or to some other reason) may bias our estimates of poverty rates and transitions into and out of poverty if poor children, or children more likely to become or stay poor, are more likely to be 'lost' between the waves than other children. The extent of child attrition after one and two years is shown in table 11.1. The table shows that 23 per cent of all children who were present in the sample in 1994 were lost after one year. The figure rises

---

[4] The number of households sampled in this survey is 3,973 in round V (November 1994 to January 1995), 3,781 in round VI (October to December 1995), and 3,750 in round VII (October to December 1996). (Earlier rounds of the RLMS were based on a different panel.) For further details on the survey see Klugman and Braithwaite (1998).

[5] These households are included in the Russian data used in the cross-national analysis of chapter 4.

Table 11.1. *Sample attrition in the RLMS*

Poverty status in 1994	Number of children in 1994	Number of children remaining in 1995	(As percentage of 1994 sample)	Number of children remaining in 1996	(As percentage of 1994 sample)
Not poor	2,339	1,799	(76.9)	1,608	(68.7)
Poor	368	291	(79.1)	279	(75.8)
All	2,707	2,090	(77.2)	1,887	(69.7)

to over 30 per cent after two years. If anything, there is a tendency for poor children to be *less* likely to leave the survey – only 24 per cent of children poor in 1994 were lost from the survey by 1996. Overall, however, attrition does not appear seriously to distort the relative distribution of children by poverty status. In subsequent results in this chapter we use weights to reduce the impact of any bias.[6]

The definition of expenditure

Our analysis of mobility and poverty dynamics uses household expenditure as the indicator of well-being. The reference period is the month preceding the interview. Total household expenditure is constructed by aggregating the total consumption expenditure of the household, plus the imputed expenditure represented by the consumption of home-produced goods (such as food), minus expenditure on consumer durable goods. We do not impute consumption for subsidised social services or for owner-occupied housing.[7]

The nature of the RLMS obliges us to restrict the accounting period to one month. As noted in chapter 2, a longer accounting period would likely reduce the extent of mobility, especially for those families able to smooth

---

[6] These weights adjusting for non-response were constructed by the Population and Nutrition Center, University of North Carolina, Chapel Hill.

[7] Our sample selection on the basis of positive food expenditure includes allowance for the imputed value from the consumption of home-produced food. The failure to impute housing costs should not have a dramatic impact, since housing expenditure was relatively low in the mid-1990s: in late 1995, spending on rent and utilities combined averaged only 4.5 per cent of household expenditure. The treatment of social services (healthcare and education) is possibly more problematic. However, since subsidised services were still fairly universally available at the time of the survey, welfare comparisons between households should not be too much affected.

transitory fluctuations in income and expenditure by borrowing or lending. And a longer accounting period might have reduced the impact of arrears in the payments of salaries, pensions or social benefits which, as noted above, was a pervasive problem in Russia in the mid-1990s.

Reliance on expenditure rather than income data has a number of advantages in Russia, given the widespread incidence of wage arrears and unpaid leave, the residual stigma associated with the informal sector and the desire to avoid tax. Moreover, income is subject to larger variation than consumption, and households naturally may try to smooth the latter over time.[8] There are nonetheless some disadvantages. First, people may choose a low level of consumption and, in contrast to income, total expenditure (and our picture of household welfare) is thereby influenced. Second, expenditure patterns may be lumpy (though we minimise this problem by excluding the purchase of durable goods). Third, it may be more difficult for households to recall their past expenditure than their income. On balance, however, expenditure is preferable to reported income as a measure of well-being in Russia in transition.[9]

The poverty line

There is an official national poverty line in Russia, referred to as the Minimum Subsistence Income (MSI), which has been in use since 1992. However, we use regional MSIs as our poverty line. These are based on a similar methodology to the national threshold but allow for variation across regions in prices and consumption patterns.[10] The equivalence scale is that embodied in the national MSI. This takes into account both a household's size and its composition (see Foley 1997).[11] As far as size is concerned, the need of a household with two members is treated as 1.88 times that of a one-person household (ignoring the differences in composition), a three-person household as 2.43 times and a four-person household as 3.0

[8] This is, however, more the case in countries where capital markets are well developed, so that families are easily able to dissave or to borrow to finance current consumption, which is not the case in Russia in the mid-1990s. According to official data from the Russian statistical office, Goskomstat, only 2 per cent of households had access to credit from banks in 1998.

[9] See chapter 4 for a comparison of movements into and out of poverty in Russia using both income and expenditure measures.

[10] See Popkin *et al.* (1995) for an elaboration of the approach used.

[11] Note that chapter 4 uses a different equivalence scale (the square root of household size). It also uses a different poverty line (half median income or expenditure) and uses only two years of data.

times (with similar adjustments for larger household sizes). The adjustment for composition treats the needs of a child and a pensioner as about 90 per cent and 65 per cent respectively of those of a working-age adult (the adjustment factors have varied slightly over the period). The much lower needs accorded to pensioners in the equivalence scale should be borne in mind when assessing the relative poverty rates of children and the elderly. (If the needs of pensioners were in fact greater than have been allowed for, their real poverty rate would be higher than that assessed using the MSI line.)

Our poverty estimates are based on comparison of each household's nominal monthly expenditure with the corresponding monthly regional MSI specific to the household type in question. (The MSI is indexed monthly for price inflation.) Our analysis of expenditure mobility in the next section also makes use of the regional MSIs: we calculate an expenditure-to-needs ratio for each household by simply dividing total expenditure by the household-specific poverty line.

11.4 Expenditure mobility among children

We begin with an examination of patterns of mobility across the whole distribution of living standards. We examine both overall mobility and mobility among children of different ages, in lone-parent families and in urban and rural locations. A number of studies have indicated that poverty is relatively worse in rural areas (Braithwaite 1997, Milanovic 1998). Is this associated with different patterns of mobility across the whole distribution?

Overall mobility

In this section we examine mobility in terms of movements into and out of different expenditure quintile groups for urban and rural children between 1994 and 1996. In each year, all children are ranked in increasing order by their expenditure-to-needs ratio and divided into five groups of equal size, where the first group is the poorest. Mobility is then described by the extent to which children change between these groups over the two-year period.

The extent of mobility between 1994 and 1996 is shown separately for rural and urban children in tables 11.2 and 11.3. Note that the quintile groups are defined for all children, with equal numbers of children in each fifth. Since rural children tend to be poorer, they are concentrated in the

Table 11.2. *Expenditure mobility among urban children between 1994 and 1996 (row percentages)*

1994 expenditure group	1996 expenditure group					
	Poorest fifth	Second fifth	Third fifth	Fourth fifth	Richest fifth	All
Poorest fifth	30.3	28.5	16.5	14.3	10.1	100.0
Second fifth	23.0	24.5	22.5	21.8	8.2	100.0
Third fifth	17.0	17.3	27.8	23.9	14.0	100.0
Fourth fifth	13.9	14.6	20.6	28.6	22.3	100.0
Richest fifth	4.8	6.1	13.9	25.6	49.6	100.0
All	17.2	17.6	20.1	23.1	22.0	100.0

Notes: $N = 1,298$ urban children included in the 1994 and 1996 samples. Expenditure is equivalalised household expenditure.

bottom quintile group, as shown by the 'all' row in table 11.3. The opposite pattern applies to urban children. Table 11.2 shows that fewer than one third of urban children who were in the poorest fifth in 1994 were still situated in this quintile group in 1996. One quarter had moved up to the top two fifths of the distribution. Rural children had generally lower incomes, and so about 50 per cent remained in the poorest fifth in 1996 and fewer than 15 per cent moved into the top two fifths (table 11.3).[12]

In general, there is substantial mobility over the two-year period at all levels of expenditure. Among children at the top end of the distribution in 1994 only a half (49 per cent) of urban children and just over a third (36 per cent) of rural children remained in the highest quintile group in 1996. Mobility in the middle three quintile groups is even greater: over the two-year period under investigation, only 25 to 30 per cent of urban children and 17 to 35 per cent of rural children in this part of the distribution remained there. However, while children often experience movements in expenditure group, the extent of change tends to be limited. This is especially evident in the middle ranges of the distribution. Between 1994 and 1996, 70 per cent of urban children and 65–80 per cent of rural children in the middle three quintile groups remained in the same or a neighbouring group (one higher or one lower). This is not unexpected given the brevity of the period under review.

[12] See chapter 4 for further discussion of the relationship between poverty levels and transition rates.

Table 11.3. *Expenditure mobility among rural children between 1994 and 1996 (row percentages)*

1994 expenditure group	Poorest fifth	Second fifth	Third fifth	Fourth fifth	Richest fifth	All
	1996 expenditure group					
Poorest fifth	48.9	21.9	13.9	9.3	6.0	100.0
Second fifth	29.2	34.6	15.4	11.2	9.6	100.0
Third fifth	22.5	30.6	22.3	12.8	11.8	100.0
Fourth fifth	12.6	20.1	25.0	17.5	24.8	100.0
Richest fifth	7.1	15.5	27.4	13.6	36.4	100.0
All	26.6	25.4	20.0	12.5	15.5	100.0

Notes: $N = 589$ rural children included in the 1994 and 1996 samples. Expenditure is equivalised household expenditure.

Transition and immobility rates

Table 11.4 focuses on selected aspects of mobility. For those children in the poorest fifth of the distribution in 1994, we estimate the proportion that had moved up the ranking by 1996. Similarly, we estimate the proportion moving down from the richest fifth. We also construct immobility rates, defined as the proportion of children who were in the same fifth in both 1994 and 1996. These estimates are shown for all children, children in lone-parent families, young and old children, and urban and rural children. As before, the quintile groups are defined across all children (rather than separately for each sub-group).

Only about one third of all children stayed in the same fifth between the two periods. This confirms the significant mobility reported above, and is consistent with the scale of the economic and income changes that were described in section 11.2. Children living in lone-parent households in both 1994 and 1996 are less mobile than those in other households. This would be expected if, for example, single parents are less able to take advantage of any new market opportunities and thereby to move out of the poorest fifth.

A focus on movements into and out of the poorest and richest groups suggests that greater disadvantage is associated with lone parenthood and rural residence. The share of children escaping from the bottom fifth is the highest among urban children, and lowest among rural children and children in lone-parent families. We consider reasons for this pattern of disadvantage below. Among the different groups considered here, the share of

Table 11.4. *Expenditure mobility from poorest and richest fifth and the immobility rate between 1994 and 1996*

	Moving up from lowest fifth[a]	Moving down from richest fifth[b]	Immobility rate[c]
All children	63.0	53.2	32.7
Children in lone-parent households in both waves	59.8	48.0	36.2
Children aged 0–6 in 1994	63.8	48.3	32.7
Children aged 7–15 in 1994	62.4	55.5	32.6
Rural children	51.1	63.6	32.6
Urban children	69.7	50.4	32.7

Notes: [a] Percentage of the poorest 1994 fifth in a richer 1996 fifth.   [b] Percentage of the richest 1994 fifth in a poorer 1996 fifth.   [c] The immobility rate is the percentage of all children who were in the same fifth in both 1994 and 1996. $N = 1,887$ children included in the 1994 and 1996 sample. Lone-parent households are defined as a one-adult household containing children.

children falling out of the top fifth is the highest for children living in a rural household. This is consistent with the overall mobility patterns reported earlier in the section.

There are two caveats to bear in mind, however. First, the data at each panel wave provide a snapshot of a single month, and we do not know whether any observed deterioration or improvements in welfare between waves are permanent. The instability in expenditure may partly arise from the monthly frame of expenditure collected, given limited savings and lack of access to borrowing in the financial market. Section 11.6 tries to cast some light on this question by looking in addition at the intervening data from 1995 rather than only the first and last observations from 1994 and 1996. The second caveat is that the duration of the panel is rather short. We are not looking in this chapter at changes over periods of, for example, five years or more.

Of special concern is the widespread problem of arrears in the payment of salaries and public benefits, noted earlier. This has a crucial effect on income observed on a monthly basis, and it has a non-negligible impact on the household expenditure that we use here (see Klugman and Kolev 1999). If expenditure was measured over a longer period, and if arrears were eventually repaid, this source of expenditure instability could be less important and measured mobility reduced. Evidence about the patterns of wage arrears is presented by Lehmann *et al.* (1999). In October 1996, 54 per cent of employees were experiencing wage arrears, of whom 26 per cent had been owed for less than one month, another 26 per cent for between one and two months, 18 per cent for two to three months and 30 per cent over three months. The longer the repayment period, the smaller the real value of payments when they are eventually made, since inflation was high during this period, and indexation to allow for inflation is very rare.

11.5 Flows into and out of poverty

The large falls in real incomes in Russia mean that some of the children who moved up the distribution may nonetheless have experienced a fall in living standards. In the remainder of the chapter, we therefore focus on movements into and out of poverty using a poverty line fixed in real terms.

As figure 11.2 showed, there were very large increases in rates of child poverty between 1994 and 1996. But this does not necessarily mean that the poor remained poor and were simply joined by additional children. Previous research suggested that there was substantial mobility among the poor in Russia. Foley (1997) using the earlier waves of the RLMS shows that, at least in 1992–3, there was considerable movement into and out of poverty. For example, nearly half of those households that were very poor in the summer of 1992 had risen above the poverty line a year later, while a quarter of non-poor households fell into poverty over the same period. More than half of all households were found in poverty at least once between 1992 and 1994, but there was a much smaller group of chronically poor. (It has been estimated that the core of chronically poor households who have remained below the MSI since 1992 represents around 8–12 per cent of all households – see Commander *et al.* 1999.) This section examines the extent of flows into and out of poverty for a later period, and of course focuses on children. As discussed in section 11.3, poverty is defined by comparing household expenditure to household specific poverty lines, which take both family size and regional price variation into account.[13]

Figure 11.3 shows that entry rates to child poverty – the proportion of children who were not poor in 1994 who were below the poverty line in 1995 – vary substantially across population sub-groups. The highest entry rate is observed for children that were living in rural areas. Almost a quarter of these children enter poverty, an entry rate that is nearly twice as high as that

---

[13] Using income-based poverty measures, the entry rate into poverty between 1994 and 1995 would be about 26 per cent, compared to 17 per cent on an expenditure basis. The effect on exit rates is not as large: 50 and 48 per cent for the income- and expenditure-based measures respectively. Chapter 4 includes further results for both the expenditure and income measures using a different equivalence scale and poverty line.

Figure 11.3. *Entry rates into child poverty, 1994 to 1995*

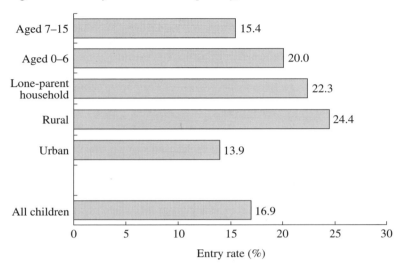

Child's status is that in 1994. N = 2,090 children included in the 1994 and 1995 sample.

among urban children. The entry rate for children who were in a lone-parent household in both years is also high compared with the rate for all children. Young children (those aged 0–6) also have an above average entry rate – a fifth of these children enter poverty between the two years.[14]

Among the reasons which explain the greater disadvantage in rural regions in Russia are the concentration of the new marketised sectors in cities and the lower levels of education in rural areas. For instance, a recent World Bank report noted that only 3 per cent of Russia's poor live in the major metropolitan areas of Moscow and St Petersburg. Extreme poverty (households living on expenditures estimated to be less than half the MSI level) is very much a rural phenomenon, with rural areas accounting for about 44 per cent of the extreme poor which is much higher than the rural population share of 27 per cent (Goskomstat 1998).

The high rate of poverty entry for single-parent children is consistent with earlier studies showing high cross-sectional poverty rates for these children (see, for example, Klugman and Kolev 2000, Mohzina and

[14] These entry rates to poverty are of course calculated for children who were present in the RLMS in both 1994 and 1995, but it needs to be noted that in addition many children are born into poverty. The World Bank (1999) reports that 62 per cent of families with a newborn child in 1995 were poor.

Figure 11.4. *Exit rates from child poverty, 1994 to 1995*

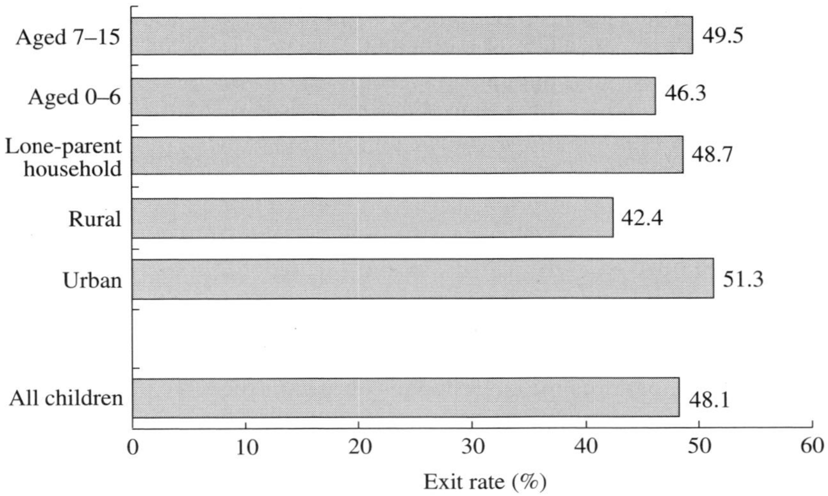

Child's status is that in 1994. $N = 2,090$ children included in the 1994 and 1995 sample.

Prokofieva 1997). The vast majority of single parents are women, and our earlier investigations have suggested that the causes of relatively high rates of poverty in single-parent families lie more in the labour-market disadvantage faced by women than in special features of lone parenthood *per se*. We know that lone-parent participation rates in the labour market are high – and they are therefore apparently less constrained than one might expect by childcare responsibilities (in part because many live with other adults, such as parents or siblings). It is nonetheless true that lone mothers were more likely than married mothers to be affected by unemployment. Rates of payment of child support and alimony are low (Klugman and Kolev 2000).

Although the results in figure 11.3 refer to children who were in lone-parent families before they entered poverty, studies in other countries also show that entry into lone parenthood itself is associated with substantial falls in living standards. For example, Jarvis and Jenkins (1999) show that marital splits are associated with large declines in real income for UK children. The relatively high poverty rates for children in lone-mother families suggest that we might expect to find the same patterns in Russia.

Figure 11.4 shows the corresponding patterns of poverty exits – the proportion of children who were poor in 1994 but who were above the poverty line in 1995. Despite poverty among children rising sharply between these two years, as shown earlier in figure 11.2, the average exit rate was almost 50 per cent. Exit rates are lowest for rural and young children. However, in contrast to what we observe for poverty entry, lone-parent children have exit rates close to the average for all children. The last result is encouraging, although it is quite possible that this is due to sampling error, as the exit rate is based on only twenty-one lone-parent children below the poverty line in 1994.[15]

11.6 Patterns of poverty persistence

We have seen that the extent of poverty has increased substantially between 1994 and 1996. Significant volatility was also evident during these years. What do these patterns mean for longer-term child poverty outcomes? In this section, three rounds of RLMS data are exploited to investigate the frequency and risk of persistent poverty over the period, as well as the characteristics associated with transitory and persistent poverty. We first compare children with other groups in the population and then focus on just the children alone.

Transitory and persistent poverty

The first task is to estimate the frequency of different poverty states. We estimated the share of children who were never found in poverty at the three survey dates in 1994–6, those who were sometimes poor (observed poor once or twice) and those always poor (observed poor at all three interviews). The results are given in table 11.5, together with the same breakdown for working-age adults and the elderly.

Just over 40 per cent of children were found poor at least once over the period, compared with 36 per cent of working-age adults and 30 per cent of the elderly. Of those children that did experience poverty during the period, about three in every ten were poor in two out of the three survey rounds while just over one in ten were poor at all three interviews. Table 11.5 also shows that children are much more likely than adults to be always poor during our observation period. The share of children poor in each of the three rounds is about one and a half times higher than the share of working-

---

[15] Note also that this result is not found in chapter 4 when using a different poverty line and data for a subsequent year.

Table 11.5. *Number of times observed poor, 1994–1996 (row percentages)*

	0	1	2	3	All
All children	59.4	23.7	12.1	4.8	100.0
Children					
Aged 0–6 years	54.6	24.9	14.8	5.7	100.0
Aged 7–15 years	61.6	23.2	10.9	4.3	100.0
Rural	47.4	32.4	12.4	7.8	100.0
Urban	64.7	19.9	11.9	3.5	100.0
With lone parent	57.9	23.4	12.6	6.1	100.0
Working-age adults	63.7	22.9	10.2	3.2	100.0
Elderly	69.5	21.0	8.0	1.5	100.0

Notes: $N = 2,636$ households included in all of the 1994, 1995 and 1996 samples. Working-age adults are women aged 16–54 and men aged 16–59. Elderly are those women aged 60 and above and men aged 65 and above.

age adults, and three times higher than the share of the elderly.[16] The frequency of poverty is particularly high for children living in a rural area, for children of lone parents and for young children. In particular, the share of children poor at all three interviews is twice as high for rural children as for urban children.

Characteristics of the persistently poor

From a policy perspective, it is important to distinguish the characteristics of the families whose children remain poor, as opposed to those whose children experience short-term poverty. We would expect chronic poverty to be more closely associated with setback along other key dimensions of human development, such as nutritional status and schooling.[17] Thus the profile of the persistently poor may point to appropriate indicators for targeted interventions to avert such reversals.

In table 11.6 we compare the socio-demographic and economic characteristics of households with children that were poor at all three interviews – the persistently poor – to those found poor just once – the transitory poor – and those never found in poverty (those found poor twice are not

[16] The difference in the proportion of individuals always poor is significant at the 5 per cent level between children and elderly, but not between children and working-age adults.
[17] The OECD has commented on the increased inequality in opportunities in the Russian educational system, linking this to the increased inequality of income (OECD 1998). See also Micklewright (1999).

Table 11.6. *Selected characteristics of the transitory and persistently poor*

Characteristics of the household in which the child lives in 1994	Never poor	Poor at only one annual interview	Poor at all three annual interviews
Fraction with the specified characteristic			
Single parent	0.17	0.16	0.16
Head graduated from a university[a]	0.25	0.10	0.02
No child benefits at all three interviews	0.21	0.21	0.28
Urban[b]	0.79	0.63	0.48
Mean			
Age of head (years)	37.6	36.5	36.3
Number of unemployed[b]	0.14	0.22	0.52
Number of children aged under 18[b]	1.57	1.69	2.01
Number of children aged 0–6[b]	0.45	0.56	0.82
Number of children aged 7–15	1.11	1.12	1.28
Number of working-age adults	2.00	1.99	1.92
Number of elderly people	0.25	0.23	0.18
Distribution across regions			
Moscow and St Petersburg[b]	0.09	0.03	0.00
North and North West	0.07	0.07	0.06
Central and Central Black Earth	0.18	0.17	0.19
Volga-Vaytski and Volga Basin	0.18	0.19	0.17
North Caucasian[b]	0.14	0.12	0.04
Urals	0.15	0.21	0.23
Western Siberia	0.12	0.10	0.14
East Siberia and Far East	0.07	0.11	0.16
Total	1.00	1.00	1.00

Notes: $N = 1,086$ households interviewed in the 1994, 1995 and 1996 samples with children in all three waves. [a] and [b] indicate that the mean values for those never poor and always poor are significantly different at the 10 and 5 per cent level respectively.

included).[18] (The unit of analysis in this table is therefore the household and not the child.) Each entry in the first part of the table shows the shares of households with the characteristic concerned. The entry in the first row and the first column thus shows that 17 per cent of those households with children who were never poor were lone-parent households in 1994. The next part of the table shows mean values of household characteristics and the last part shows the share living in each region. For example, among the households with children that were never found poor, the mean age of the

[18] These labels for the patterns of poverty recorded in the data must be interpreted as applying within the period of our observation window of three years and not necessarily more generally. A person observed poor at the first of the three interviews only is classified here as in transitory poverty but could have been poor for a long time prior to this – see chapter 2 for discussion of these issues.

household head in 1994 was 37.6 years and 9 per cent of them were in the Moscow and St Petersburg regions.

The age of the head is slightly younger among the persistently poor households. Not surprisingly, the average number of unemployed in the family is much higher for the persistently poor – three times higher than among the transitory poor and almost four times higher than the households never found poor. But it is also worth noting that the average value for persistently poor households is only 0.5, underlining the fact that there are many poor households with children where nobody is unemployed and hence the importance of factors other than unemployment in holding children in poverty. Higher education has a clear pay-off: very few persistently poor households have a university graduate head while the share among the never poor is twelve times higher. The share of urban households is higher among the households never found poor, pointing again to greater market opportunities in towns and cities. The impact of household size is confirmed, with persistently poor households having more dependent children than those found poor only once or never at all. The difference between persistently and never poor households is even larger when one looks at young children (aged 0–6). The average number of elderly people, on the other hand, is lowest among the persistently poor households. There are very substantial regional variations in chronic poverty. None of the households poor at all three interviews are in Moscow or St Petersburg while one in four households is in the Urals and one in five in the Central region.

These results are also suggestive of a failure of existing social protection programmes to reach the persistently poor. The share of households with children that had not received any child benefits at each of the three interviews was actually higher in the persistently poor group than among transitory and never poor households. Though this difference is not statistically significant, it is nonetheless surprising that public transfers are not reaching the chronically poor.[19] This finding underlines just how grave is the problem of errors of exclusion described earlier in the chapter.

11.7 Conclusions

This chapter is the first study of mobility and poverty dynamics among children in Russia. The longitudinal data collected in the RLMS have proved

[19] Since child benefit is very small even for those receiving it, this result (if confirmed in future samples) is best interpreted as a failure of benefit targeting (not reaching the most disadvantaged) rather than as evidence that child benefits are lifting children out of poverty.

very useful in highlighting the challenges facing the country. They have allowed us to identify the high rates of persistent poverty among children, and especially very young children. The findings that emerged in many ways confirmed our a priori expectations, but they also confirmed the seriousness of the poverty prospects facing many of Russia's children.

First, there is a very high level of expenditure mobility among children. The extent of mobility is, however, limited and varies substantially across children. In particular, children in rural households and in lone-parent families were less likely to move up the expenditure distribution during the period under review and, where they had been relatively well off, children in these groups were more likely to experience a movement down the distribution.

Second, we examined the flows into and out of absolute poverty among different groups of children. During the period of tremendous economic change that has characterised the transition in Russia, there has been substantial turnover in the population of children who are poor. The exit as well as the entry rate was high over 1994–5 (these rates averaging 48 and 17 per cent respectively) despite a sharp rise in the overall child poverty rate. Reflecting the results on expenditure mobility, the risk of entering poverty was found to be higher for rural children than urban children. The risk was also higher among the youngest age groups and among lone-parent children.

The third set of results relates to the vulnerability of children in terms of persistent poverty. Repeated poverty is present despite the substantial turnover and 5 per cent of children were found poor at each of three successive annual interviews. Of major concern is our finding that long-term poverty rates are higher among children than among working-age adults and pensioners. Hence the individuals who are perhaps at their most vulnerable time in the life cycle appear to be most at risk of being persistently poor. This could in turn be expected to have adverse repercussions for child development along the dimensions of health and schooling, and therefore also longer-term prospects for productivity and well-being.

What then are the policy implications? Levels of public spending on social assistance are low, and seriously undermine the effectiveness of the system of social protection. Even for the limited amounts of money being spent, targeting of children in poor and chronically poor households could be improved. There is clearly a need to tackle the non-receipt of child benefits which was extensive among poor children in our sample.

Our study has also pointed to serious challenges facing policymakers in terms of regional development. Children in rural areas are significantly disadvantaged at present. This highlights the need for adequate social welfare support systems and adequate financing and provision of basic social services. Such measures could help overcome disadvantage at the household level in the short term and, just as important perhaps, work to avert the perpetuation of existing disadvantage over time. This implies the need for a re-focus on ways to redistribute fiscal resources across regions to help ensure equitable access to social services.

Clearly a major part of the challenge will be a general renewal of economic and employment growth. However, further consideration needs to be given to problems of regional development and to ways to expand economic opportunities in rural areas. This may have implications for policies in the areas of infrastructure and transport, for example. Another challenge, which was highlighted in this chapter in the context of single parents, is how to overcome pervasive gender disadvantage in the labour market, both in terms of rates of pay and alternative career possibilities (see UNICEF 1999).

There are important differences between Russia and the other industrial countries that are the subject of study in this volume. Most obviously, child poverty rates were on a steep upward trend through much of the 1990s and are now at high levels. Hence the extent of the child poverty problem is much greater. We noted early in the chapter that average incomes in Russia are relatively low, and the institutional capacity of the state is quite limited. Indeed the resources of government – both fiscal and institutional – limit the available policy options to a much greater extent than in the OECD countries studied in this volume.

References

Atkinson, A. B. and Micklewright J., 1992, *Economic Transformation in Eastern Europe and the Distribution of Income*, Cambridge University Press, Cambridge.

Braithwaite, J., 1997, 'The old and new poor in Russia', in Klugman (1997).

Commander, S., Tolstopiatenko, A. and Yemtsov, R., 1999, 'Channels of redistribution: inequality and poverty in the Russian transition', *Economics of Transition*, 7: 411–47.

Desai, P., 1997, *Going Global: Transition from Plan to Market in the World Economy*, MIT Press, Cambridge MA.

Doyle, C., 1996, 'The distributional consequences during the early stages of Russia's transition', *Review of Income and Wealth*, 42: 493–505.

Flemming, J. and Micklewright, J., 2000, 'Income distribution, economic systems and transition', in Atkinson, A. B. and Bourguignon, F. (eds.), *Handbook of Income Distribution*, North-Holland, Amsterdam.

Foley, M., 1997, 'Static and dynamic analyses of poverty in Russia', in Klugman (1997).

Foley, M. and Klugman, J., 1997, 'The impact of social support: errors of leakage and exclusion', in Klugman (1997).

Goskomstat, 1998, *Statistical Yearbook of the Russian Federation*, Moscow.

Jarvis, S. and Jenkins, S., 1999, 'Marital splits and income changes: evidence from the British Household Panel Survey', *Population Studies*, 53: 237–54.

Klugman, J. (ed.), 1997, *Poverty in Russia. Public Policy and Private Responses*, Economic Development Institute, World Bank, Washington DC.

Klugman, J. and Braithwaite, J., 1998, 'Poverty in Russia: an overview', *World Bank Research Observer*, 13: 37–58.

Klugman, J. and Kolev, A., 1999, 'The role of the safety net and the labour market on falling cash consumption in Russia 1994–96: a quintile-based decomposition analysis', EUI Working Paper ECO 99/41, European University Institute, Florence.

Klugman, J. and Kolev, A., 2000, 'The welfare repercussions of single parenthood in Russia in transition', in Klugman, J. and Motivans, A. (eds.), *Single Parents and Child Welfare in the New Russia*, Macmillan, London.

Klugman, J. and Marnie, S., forthcoming, 'Poverty and inequality', in Granville, B. and Oppenheimer, P. (eds.), *The Russian Economy in the 1990s*, Oxford University Press, Oxford.

Klugman, J. and McAuley, A., 2000, 'Social policies for single-parent families: Russia in transition', in Klugman, J. and Motivans, A. (eds.), *Single Parents and Child Welfare in the New Russia*, Macmillan, London.

Koen, V., 1996, 'Russian macroeconomic data: existence, access, interpretation', *Communist Economies and Economic Transformation*, 8: 321–33.

Kolev, A., 1996, 'Poverty in Russia: what can we learn from round VI of the RLMS?', unpublished paper, European University Institute, Florence.

Lehmann, H., Wadsworth, J. and Acquisti, A., 1999, 'Crime and punishment: job insecurity and wage arrears in the Russian Federation', *Journal of Comparative Economics*, 27: 595–617.

Micklewright, J., 1999, 'Education, inequality and transition', *Economics of Transition*, 7: 343–76.

Milanovic, B., 1998, *Income, Inequality and Poverty during the Transition from Planned to Market Economy*, World Bank, Washington DC.

Mozhina, M. and Prokofieva, L., 1997, 'Living standard of families in Russia', unpublished paper, Institute for Socio-Economic Studies of the Population, Russian Academy of Sciences, Moscow.

OECD, 1998, *Reviews of National Policies for Education: Russian Federation*, OECD, Paris.

Popkin, B. M., Zahoori, N. and Baturin, A., 1995, 'Elderly nutrition in Russia: is there a problem?', unpublished paper, University of North Carolina, Chapel Hill NC.

Popov, V., 1996, 'A Russian puzzle: what makes the Russian transformation a special case?', *Research for Action 29*, United Nations University/World Institute for Development Economics Research, Helsinki.

Standing, G., 1997, *Russian Unemployment and Enterprise Restructuring*, Macmillan, London.

Stewart, K., 2000, *Fiscal Federalism in Russia: Intergovernmental Transfers and the Financing of Education*, Edward Elgar, Cheltenham.

UNDP, 1996, *Human Development Report*, Oxford University Press, New York.

UNICEF, 1998, 'Education for all?', *Regional Monitoring Report No. 5*, UNICEF International Child Development Centre, Florence.

UNICEF, 1999, 'Women in transition', *Regional Monitoring Report No. 6*, UNICEF International Child Development Centre, Florence.

World Bank, 1994, 'Russia: social protection during transition and beyond', Report No. 11748–RU, Washington DC.

World Bank, 1995, 'Poverty in Russia: an assessment', Report 14110–RU, Washington DC.

World Bank, 1999, 'Russian social protection malaise: key reform policies as a response to the crisis', Social Protection Discussion Paper 9909, Washington DC.

Yeltsin, B., 1997, Radio address to the Russian population, Radio Free Europe, October 1997.

Summary and policy conclusions

12   Thinking about children in time

J. LAWRENCE ABER AND DAVID T. ELLWOOD

12.1 What have we learned from this book?

The papers collected in this book demonstrate the power, the promise and some of the current limits of examining the dynamics of child poverty. They reveal both striking consistencies and sharp differences across countries in the depth and persistence of economic distress among families rearing children. They illustrate which families seem to struggle the most. They help us understand when high poverty is offset by high mobility and the situations where it is not. And they point to the causes of more serious, longer-term poverty. In doing so these papers also help to chart a course for the future of research on policy, offering the reader both challenges and opportunities.

In this concluding chapter we seek first to summarise what was learned about child poverty; second, to identify limits to the current research and suggest elements of a future research agenda; and, third, to draw on the research in order to reflect on policy directions stimulated by research on dynamics. Throughout, we endeavour to illustrate how thinking about child poverty in time may help us to identify solutions to child poverty in time.

Dynamic analysis steps beyond the static world of counting how many are poor in a host of exciting and important ways. Until recently, discussions of poverty focused primarily on the question of who is poor at any one time. The answer was derived typically by comparing annual income to a poverty standard. Families with incomes below the line were poor; those above it, not poor. And knowing who was poor, the policymaker was left with only one real policy question: how much should we give the poor to try and reduce or eliminate their poverty? The dynamic analyses here dig deeper and point to a richer set of policy options.

Chapter 2 offers a wonderfully comprehensive discussion of the models and methods involved in the examination of child poverty dynamics. Such work requires longitudinal data with repeated observations of individuals over time. With such data one can first ask not just who is poor, but who is poor for how long. The authors note that deprivation takes on a very different meaning if it is fleeting rather than if it lasts for years and years. A family may be able to smooth out the financial and emotional distress caused by temporary unemployment or illness by dipping into savings, turning to family or friends, selling assets or delaying major purchases. But as the duration of poverty increases, the financial options narrow and the emotional cost may grow. The impact of short versus long poverty spells may be particularly important in childhood, as both child psychologists and specialists on brain development emphasise the critical time of early childhood.

Dynamic analysis also helps in understanding mobility. Who moves up or down? How far do they move? A society with more ladders out of poverty would seem to offer more hope and opportunity than one with fewer. There might even be trade-offs between the level of poverty and the extent of mobility. Indeed, one might be more comfortable with a slightly higher level of poverty if mobility was much greater.

Finally, a number of these chapters illustrate that longitudinal data offer a glimpse at the *why* of poverty not just the who. If one finds a lone-parent family in poverty, one can make some inferences about what led the family there. But if one finds the woman was middle class until she and her husband split up or, instead, that she was earning a decent salary until being laid off from her job, or even that she was poor all her life and then had a child outside of marriage, one gets rather different pictures of the origins of the poverty and its likely longevity.

12.2 Important lessons

The country chapters in this book are important for their variety of economic settings, data sources, methods and topical foci. Appropriately each confronts a somewhat different question that is likely to be of particular interest to the domestic audience as well as the international community. Still, a number of powerful generalisations emerge from the chapters taken together.

Variation in the persistence of child poverty

Researchers have known for some time that poverty rates vary widely across countries, and that point was well illustrated in chapter 3. Moreover, the way in which poverty is measured – as an absolute standard common across countries or as a percentage of country median income – also affects poverty levels and rankings. Using the 'percentage of country median income' poverty rate favoured by the authors of the seven-country chapters, child poverty in the early 1990s ranged from roughly 12 per cent in Hungary and Germany to 27 per cent in the USA and Russia (table 3.2). Using an absolute standard equivalent to the US poverty line, the rates for the seven countries ranged from 12 per cent in Germany to 20–30 per cent in the USA and UK to roughly 50 per cent in Spain and Ireland to 90 per cent or more in Hungary and Russia (table 3.2). The book demonstrates that there is also enormous variability in the persistence of child poverty. In Britain and the USA, over 15 per cent of children were poor for two consecutive years, and nearly 10 per cent or more were poor for five years out of five. Yet in Hungary and Germany only about 4 per cent were poor even two consecutive years and just 2 per cent of children were poor for five straight years (table 4.7).

Children have higher rates of persistent poverty than other groups

One might anticipate that children would have much shorter spells of poverty than others. After all they are typically living in a home at the early stages of their parents' work life when incomes are likely to be rising faster. Yet for the countries where the issue was addressed, persistent poverty seems to be at least as high and often higher than for the general population. Schluter reports that, for Germany, the fractions who were poor throughout the observation period were essentially identical for children as for all persons (table 6.2). Hill and Jenkins estimate that, for Britain, chronic poverty (defined to be having a six-year average income below the poverty line) accounted for 60 per cent of the total poverty among children while it was 'only' 55 per cent of poverty for those over 18 (table 7.2).

Poverty rates are highest for the youngest children

In every country where children were broken down by age groups, younger children were at higher risk of poverty, often much higher. For example, in West Germany children aged 0–6 had a 9 per cent poverty rate versus 8 per cent for all children, in East Germany the corresponding rates were 20 per cent and 16 per cent (table 6.1). In Britain the poverty rate for younger children was much higher than for all children combined (chapter 7). In Russia, 45 per cent of children aged 0–6 were poor in at least one of the three survey years, while 38 per cent of older children experienced poverty (table 11.5). In Hungary the poverty rate was 25 per cent for young children in 1996 (defined here as being in the bottom fifth of the income distribution) versus 20 per cent for older ones (table 10.3).

Extending the argument made above concerning the higher risk of poverty for children relative to others in the population, it should not be surprising that poverty is greatest among young children. Biology and economic structures conspire to lead to most children being born when parents' wages are typically at their lowest. Moreover, the nurturing and care needs of the children themselves may limit the labour-market options of the parents (or parent, if only one is present). Still, the results could be a potentially serious policy concern, for both the child psychology literature and the recent work in brain development point to the first three years of life being a particularly crucial time for the child. That poverty rates for young children are often among the highest of any group in society raises important questions about its longer-term consequences.

Mobility and long-term poverty varies widely within countries

We have already noted that the youngest children often seem to have long poverty episodes. Other factors seem to play an even larger role. Gottschalk and Danziger show that the probability of remaining in the poorest fifth of the US income distribution varies widely among children from different family backgrounds. Whereas over half of all white children in the poorest fifth rose out of that group ten years later, less than a quarter of blacks did (table 5.2). Similarly, children in single-parent families or those receiving 'welfare' (means-tested benefits) were far less likely to escape poverty. Schluter reports that German children of guestworkers and single parents were far more likely to experience long-term poverty (table 6.2). According to Hill and Jenkins, only about a third of poverty in the early 1990s among British adults aged 30–59 was chronic, whereas among the elderly and young children the figure exceeded two thirds (table 7.2). Children from lone-parent families were far more likely to be persistently poor in Hungary (table 10.4) and to a lesser extent in Russia (tables 11.4, 11.5).

Higher poverty rates do not mean higher rates of economic mobility (except in Russia)

These chapters shed light on the critical question of whether there is a trade-off between poverty and mobility. Arguably, highly open and economically energetic societies create more temporary hardship, but also offer their people many more chances to reach a better life. The chapters in this book offer no support for this thesis. There is little variation across the seven countries in the proportions of children who change decile group over one year – about 60 per cent – with the notable exception of Russia where the proportion is over 80 per cent (table 4.3). And the chances of being stuck in the poorest fifth of the distribution are broadly similar, again with the exception of Russia (table 4.4). In the more limited group of countries for which five years of data are available, the USA, which has the *highest* poverty rate (measured using half median income as the poverty line), has the *lowest* proportion of children in a different group in year 5 compared to year 1 (table 4.3) and the highest fraction of children remaining stuck five years out of five in the poorest fifth or with an income below half the median (tables 4.4, 4.7). Gottschalk and Danziger offer a particularly poignant picture for the United States. It is well known that, during the 1980s and 1990s, wage inequality and family income inequality grew markedly in the USA. Yet the relative mobility of children aged 0–5 (as measured, for example, by the chances of rising out of the poorest fifth) appears not to have changed (table 5.1). Over this time period, at least, rising inequality and unchanged mobility seem to have been the pattern.

One should be cautious in interpreting these results or about jumping to conclusions about economic structures and any mobility and poverty trade-offs. If dynamic open economies grow faster, there may be greater gains in absolute income of the poor even if their relative status is unchanged or worsens. Indeed Gottschalk and Danziger do find a modest increase in the absolute mobility (i.e. more growth in incomes) for the poorest young children during the period of rising inequality, although the difference is not statistically significant (table 5.3). Moreover, in comparing poverty levels with measures of income mobility and drawing conclusions about economic structures, we should remember that family formation patterns and social policies also influence poverty levels and mobility. Nonetheless it is striking that there seems to be no connection between poverty and relative mobility, with the exception of Russia.

The transition countries exhibit a variety of patterns

One would expect transition economies to be turbulent and the chapters in this book provide interesting contrasts. According to Galasi and Nagy and Klugman and Kolev, Hungary and Russia have both experienced rising poverty rates especially among children. Russia also has the highest level of economic mobility of any of the countries studied. Over half of the children in the poorest fifth of the income distribution in one year had risen above it in the next (tables 11.2–11.4). The mobility may be evidence of the turmoil of the Russian economy. Although real incomes have been falling in Russia, measures of relative mobility reveal that 'upward mobility' among children can still occur provided other children in the society are losing ground even faster.

It is interesting to contrast the experiences of the transition countries. Hungary's economic transition has been less turbulent than Russia's. Its child poverty rate in 1994 put Hungary in the middle of the international league table while Russia was at the top (table 3.2). But, nonetheless, the position of children deteriorated, especially relative to elderly people (figures 3.2, 10.2). The former East Germany experienced a different pattern. In the years following re-unification child poverty rates in the East were higher than those in the West, and so too were a child's chances of being poor at least once over a five-year period (table 6.2). However, child poverty rates in the East fell and converged dramatically towards those of the West (figure 6.2).

Using annual income is inadequate

Several of the chapters in this book pay particular attention to the advantages of using annual or current income as the basis for determining deprivation and for targeting interventions. Economists have long argued that 'permanent' income is a more important measure of a family's real level of deprivation because families can use various means to smooth out the effects of economic shocks in their lives. Current and 'permanent' income can differ significantly. Hill and Jenkins find that roughly half of the children who were chronically poor if one averaged income over six years were not currently poor in any one year. Similarly, over half of those children poor in a single year were not chronically poor (table 7.3).

Nolan, Maître, and Watson offer another way to get at the 'real' level of economic deprivation. Chronic poverty can diminish access to items such as food and housing far more than short-term poverty that is the result of a temporary setback, since families will work to smooth their consumption. Nolan and his co-authors find that the link to annual income is not as tight as some might have imagined (table 8.5). Indeed families with the lowest measured income in one year often appear to be less poor according to their consumption than people with incomes just around the poverty line. Presumably the former group was only temporarily poor (or perhaps were not reporting some income).

These two chapters, indeed all the chapters in the book, raise the critical question of whether we can do better than to simply target resources on people who are poor at one point in time. Unfortunately we cannot determine six-year average income until six years have passed, even if we had the resources to measure income over such a long period of time, and consumption is extremely hard to measure even under the best of circumstances.

Two causes of poverty stand out: job loss and family change

One of the greatest advantages of longitudinal data is the capacity to begin to understand some causes of poverty. The chapters in this book only scratch the surface of this potentially powerful line of research. Looking for immediate causes of poverty requires comparing the timing of key events such as job loss, childbearing, divorce or separation, exit or entry of other family members, and wage changes with the timing of entry and exit into poverty. This methodology is exploited usefully in the work of Cantó and Mercader-Prats where they show that poverty entry can be greatly affected by the departure of a youth aged 18–29. Indeed they go further, to show that the presence of an employed youth reduces poverty while an unemployed one increases it. Thus the authors are able to show that youth unemployment is 'causally' linked to family poverty and worthy of policy attention. Similarly, Galasi and Nagy show that poverty episodes in Hungary are linked to the falls and rises in the employment of household adults, although they also stress the importance of other factors (table 10.6).

Other chapters in this book point to the critical role of job loss and family structure without comparing the timing of events. We have already noted the widespread finding that children living with a lone parent are more likely to be chronically poor. Several of the chapters (for example, those about Germany and Hungary) find a close association between job loss and poverty, as one might expect. But ultimately questions of which events lead to long-term versus short-term poverty are among the many that are left open for future research.

12.3 What more would we like to know?

We applaud the important advances made by these new studies of the dynamics of child poverty. They represent an important beginning to finding out answers to crucial research and policy questions. To learn some of those answers will require some advances in both methods and data.

Richer descriptions of patterns of income dynamics

The real promise in the study of dynamics is learning about the events and processes that lead into and out of deprivation. Analysis of dynamics requires tracing something that begins and ends. Unfortunately, in the need to find measurable events, one faces the real danger of creating false ones. And when researchers focus on particular defined events, policy will often follow. As was emphasised in chapter 2, if you choose a specific poverty line and measure movements into and out of poverty, you treat equally a person whose income had been well above the poverty line and then fell dramatically, and a person whose income was only $1 above the poverty line whose earnings fell by a few dollars. These are not comparable events. The person whose income changed so little probably did not experience anything that he or she would describe as significant. The goal, as noted in chapter 2, is to have transitions that 'mean something'. Yet often we may have created an arbitrary event.

The reason for our preoccupation with highly subjective event classification arises in part because of the promise we perceive for dynamic analysis. With longitudinal data we begin to pierce the veil of causality. In social science, there are elaborate models for causality tests using time series data. There are methods for deciding if event A caused event B or vice versa. In principle we can use the same methods to ask whether work leads to marriage, or marriage leads to work. But if a couple lived together for several years before marriage, is marriage the big event? Applying such methods to longitudinal data for individuals is very dangerous when false events can create incorrect inferences. Often one will miss the real causal forces because of misclassification. There are a number of responses to this concern.

First, one can seek to work around the limitations while still studying poverty dynamics. Certainly one can very sensibly ask whether someone is poor five years out of seven, and one can further ask by how much the person's income fell below the poverty line during those years. One can, as several of the chapters do here, average income or consumption over a longer time period. Then the data provide a picture about more permanent deprivation. One can also seek to classify transitions into and out of poverty into larger and smaller movements, and focus on the larger ones. The use of non-monetary indicators of deprivation to trace discrete changes in living standards, as in chapter 8's analysis of Ireland, could be another route forward. (More attention in this approach could be focused on indicators of child deprivation as opposed to the household in general, as noted by Nolan and his co-authors.)

A second approach is to shift the analysis to a focus on threshold events that really are meaningful. In many nations, public assistance and benefit programmes are limited to people with income and or assets below some threshold. People usually need to apply for such aid and they are readily aware of when they are or are not receiving assistance. In this case, there is still an arbitrary point at which aid is cut off, but because there are concrete administrative eligibility steps and well-defined benefits associated with the receipt of assistance, the notion that movements onto and off benefit receipt represent a genuine event seems far more credible. It was precisely for this reason that after their initial work on poverty dynamics, Bane and Ellwood shifted much of their focus to welfare dynamics (cf. Bane and Ellwood 1986, 1994). Similar reasons may explain why much of the work about income dynamics in Germany, for example, has been concerned with the dynamics of social assistance receipt and based on administrative record data (Leisering and Leibfried 1999), even though panel data suitable for analysing income dynamics have long been available.

The problem with focusing on the dynamics of benefit receipt and programme participation, though, is that they are governed in part by the particular rules and features of the programmes themselves. If one is trying to understand the underlying economic and demographic forces that influence economic well-being beyond the programme rules, these can be easily obscured by the unique and changing policy climate. As noted in chapter 2, some of the features of programme participation dynamics may not have great meaning in terms of real changes in standard of living. Recent 'welfare reforms' in the USA illustrate the issue: receipt of welfare benefits almost halved between 1996 and early 1999 – from five million recipient families to less than three million (US Department of Health and Human Services 1999). But poverty has declined far less: the official rate of child poverty fell only from 20.8 per cent in 1995, the year preceding the major welfare reforms, to 18.9 per cent in 1998.[1] Programme change may lead to the 'welfare' poor becoming the working poor. This may be important and interesting in and of itself, but it does not capture the same idea as movements into and out of poverty. Finally, comparisons across groups and countries become far more difficult if one is examining programme dynamics of very different policies for very different populations in very different economic and cultural environments.

A third strategy is to characterise the dynamics of the economic processes more fully. Some have championed use of so-called growth trajectories and growth curve modelling as a means to better understand the rates

---

[1] The experimental improved poverty measures calculated by the US Census Bureau show somewhat larger falls (Short *et al.* 1999).

and shape of change over time (see, for example, Bryk and Raudenbush 1992). In this case, one seeks to characterise the initial level of income, its rate of growth, even its variance over time. Thus families with similar numbers of poverty episodes in a fixed timeframe might actually look quite different. One family might have started poor but moved up rapidly. Another might have shown no real growth in income but experienced dramatic fluctuations over time. Still another family might have been on an upward trajectory until a spell of unemployment, which led to a temporary decline in income. (Different patterns of income growth are also discussed by Gardiner and Hills 1999.) Of course the hard question is how to summarise the heterogeneous income patterns over time in a parsimonious and yet informative manner. Looking both for events that affect income and the income trends for particular types of families could be more revealing than focusing exclusively on poverty dynamics.

More use of ethnographic research

The type of quantitative analysis showcased in this book may be incapable of generating, by itself, a truly powerful understanding on the dynamics of child poverty. So much of the dynamics depends on the personal meaning made of the events by the individual and institutional factors and of the complex interplay between persons and contexts. Moreover, personal meaning and complex person/context interactions are poorly studied using quantitative panel survey methodology.

For these and other reasons, we believe that qualitative ethnographic research is needed to complement quantitative longitudinal research on the dynamics of child poverty. Evaluation of the US anti-poverty programme called New Hope provides an example of the potential for this. Using both experimental and longitudinal designs, the researchers have found that a package of guaranteed work, wage supplements, health insurance and childcare not only reduced the experimental families' welfare benefit dependency and increased their income, but also had an indirect effect on the social competence and academic achievement of their sons, though not their daughters. The quantitative analysis was unable to answer the very important questions about the mediating and moderating processes that led to gender differences in the impact of the programme on children. Fortunately, the evaluators had also mounted an ethnography of a smaller number of families which was able to generate and test several hypotheses about the mechanisms of effects (Bos *et al.* 1999). Several other US examples of the successful integration of quantitative and qualitative approaches to the study of employment dynamics and developmental dynamics in low-income communities come to mind, including studies by Newman (1999) and Stack (1974) of low-income workers and their contexts, and by Sullivan (1989) and his colleagues of children and school violence. These examples suggest that including ethnographic components to studies of the dynamics of child poverty will assist researchers in identifying and testing hypotheses about the mechanisms of effects revealed by the panel data.

Exploiting policy variation in space and time

Perhaps the most important limitation to the use of the current studies to guide policy development is the lack of systematic attention to the variations among the countries in policies affecting child poverty. No single study or set of studies can or should be expected to accomplish all desirable goals, but the variations in child poverty rates and child poverty dynamics cry out for a comparative analysis across countries. What packages of policies are associated with which income levels and which patterns of growth?

Of course, to conduct such comparative analyses in a rigorous quantitative or qualitative fashion, many more countries (or perhaps large semi-autonomous regions within countries) would be particularly valuable. Fortunately, there are researchers who are tackling the imposing question of how to quantify or qualitatively classify across-jurisdiction variation in policies that could be associated with variations in critical child and family outcomes net of those social, demographic and economic factors known to predict the outcomes. For instance, Gornick *et al.* (1999) have developed an approach to quantify cross-national differences in policies that are designed to promote women's labour-force participation. Similar efforts are underway in the USA to create state-by-state typologies of 'welfare' policies that could be used to investigate how differences in child and family outcomes are associated with differences in policy (Bell 1999).

As these researchers continue to make progress in quantifying across-jurisdiction variation in policies, this research should be integrated with the types of panel studies of child poverty dynamics described in this book. We recognise that this vision for research is conceptually and technically very ambitious. But we believe that exploiting policy variation over space and time will yield deeper, more policy-relevant insights into the dynamics of child poverty.

The need for longer panels of longitudinal data

Two years of data do not a dynamic picture make. A real problem with several of the chapters in this book is that they are based on only a few years of data. The remarkable feature of longitudinal data is that their value rises exponentially as the timeframe expands. The most interesting questions, including the incidence of really long-term deprivation and the intergenerational aspects of poverty, require very long timeframes. Unfortunately the natural myopia of the political process, the pressure on academics to publish and the limited attention spans of even the most committed data gatherers all conspire to make panels shorter rather than longer. Arguably the real value of longitudinal data in the US context only appeared when panels had been running for ten years and more. And now that the Panel Study of Income Dynamics has been running for three decades it is providing new pay-offs, in the form of information about intergenerational factors, including the links between family income and other circumstances during childhood and outcomes during adulthood. Academics and policymakers alike need to seek to preserve and extend the lengths of time covered by panel and other longitudinal data.

12.4 Policy directions and questions

Static analysis with its focus on 'who is poor' generally leads to the question of 'who should get how much money?' Some of the debate in this domain centres around questions of universal versus means-tested benefits (those for which the amount received depends on income). Means-tested benefits offer the virtue that one can focus aid on those who need it most and thereby minimise total budget expenditures. Universal benefits are appealing for their smaller work disincentives, their avoidance of stigma, the collective and community values they seem to embody, and for their simplicity and lower administrative costs.

The analysis here helps inform this existing debate. All of the chapters in this book, and particularly those by Hill and Jenkins and by Nolan, Maître and Watson illustrate that providing benefits based on current income poverty may not be as well targeted to those truly in need as one might have thought. Many of the short-term poor are not the long-term poor. Hill and Jenkins implicitly argue that this may tilt us more in favour of more universal benefits. And one could interpret the results of Nolan *et al.* as suggesting an approach targeted more on specific consumption deficiencies (though the authors do not make this inference). Perhaps even more importantly, the finding that young children have the highest risks of persistent poverty in many countries suggests that a particular focus on them is essential. For example, there may be merit in introducing greater targeting by child's age in family and child benefits.

Longitudinal analysis at its best should presumably do more than simply indicate where the problems are greatest. It ought to provide us with alternative policy ideas as well. The USA provides a useful case study of a country where dynamic analysis has sharply influenced policy. The experience carries lessons about the benefits and dangers of thinking about policies from a dynamic perspective.

Dynamic perspectives and 'welfare' reforms

Over the past five to ten years and partly as a result of studies of dynamics, the USA began explicitly to look for ways to encourage movements into work and mobility out of poverty. Support to low-income working families expanded considerably, particularly using tax credits to raise the effective pay of working parents. The goal of these policies was to encourage people to enter work, and to ensure that working families were not poor. Policymakers did not want low pay to be a primary cause of poverty. Support to low-income working families grew dramatically. The USA spent just $5 billion on such families in 1986; by 1999 the figure exceeded $50 billion.

At the same time the structure of public assistance was also changed. The largest changes were to 'welfare', the term used to describe means-tested benefit programmes for the poor, in particular Aid to Families with Dependent Children (AFDC), most of whose recipients were lone mothers. It was a federal scheme, though the generosity of the benefits paid varied between states. It was replaced in 1996 by Temporary Assistance for Needy Families (TANF), which gives the states substantial discretion in the design and operation of their programmes. The goal of welfare programmes has changed from the assessment of eligibility and payment of benefits (a policy linked to a focus on poverty at a point in time) to one focused on ways to encourage – even require – people to work. Some states offer training. Others push immediate job placement. None are allowed to pay benefits indefinitely. After two years of receipt, most parents are expected to be working; after five years of receipt, benefits are usually terminated (US Department of Health and Human Services 1999).

The US case illustrates that targeting cash aid efficiently to the very long-term poor may not always be seen as a desirable policy outcome. A major impetus behind the US welfare reforms was the research finding that a sub-stantial fraction of those receiving means-tested public assistance had been poor for a long time. The public, and many policymakers, it seems, were comfortable offering short-term support while people 'got on their feet', but they were far more troubled about giving on-going unrestricted cash support to able-bodied parents who seemed mired in poverty. Those from the political centre and left were troubled that people were not really moving upwards and that they were not achieving a measure of control and independence in their lives. Those from the political right argued that government benefits themselves discouraged people from working and led to 'dependency'. Nearly everyone in the debate seemed to agree that a more appropriate goal than simply targeting money to the most needy was finding a way to enable people to overcome the barriers that left them poor in the first place.

The US example illustrates that dynamic analysis can lead to a policy focus on shortening the duration of poverty and finding strategies for increasing the opportunities for people to move up and out. It might be seen as a search for solutions to poverty not by treating the symptoms (lack of money), but rather by treating the causes (lack of work, low pay, etc.). Of course, there is a very real sense in which a lack of money *is* the cause of poverty. Still, if one could create mechanisms whereby poor families achieved a higher standard of living through some combination of their own efforts and government support, there could be advantages. 'Thinking in time' does at least open the question of whether downward mobility can be diminished while upward mobility increased.[2]

The time-limiting of eligibility is an important issue when moving from dynamic analysis to policy. When thinking longitudinally, policymakers end up asking how long a person's receipt of benefits should be allowed to continue. For example, should someone be able to collect aid for eighteen years? That question never arises in the question of 'who is currently poor and how much shall we give them?' But when you think about what event follows another, you must confront the 'and then what?' question. If the policy is to give people training and education when they enter the system, the next question is 'and then what?' If people will be offered a subsidised job if they cannot find an unsubsidised private job, people ask 'how long

---

[2] Of course some definitions of income mobility, including the relative one used in parts of this book, imply that for everyone who rises out of an income group, someone else must fall. For everyone who leaves the bottom fifth, someone else must join it or it will no longer contain 20 per cent of the population. This is not true for poverty dynamics. It is possible to increase mobility out of, and minimise movement into, poverty and thus lower its incidence.

do we provide that public job? One year? Eighteen years? And then what?' Eventually it seems almost everyone reaches a point where the answer to 'and then what?' becomes 'perhaps we have done enough'. In the US context, this led to the explicit consideration and adoption of time limits to the receipt of assistance.

It is worth noting, however, that the draft proposals for US welfare reform combined time limits with commitments to provision of training and education for the former welfare recipients. But these measures were very much diluted or lost altogether during the legislative process. The goal of 'ending welfare as we know it' was indeed achieved, but in quite a different way from what was originally envisaged. In the contemporary political climate, politicians found it easy to de-couple the carrots of training and education from the stick of time limits. Introduction of what would have been new active labour-market policies did not fit with the political mood of the majority.[3]

The US experience provides an important lesson to would-be welfare state reformers around the world. Without large majorities to push reforms through as originally proposed, key elements of a package may be lost in the process of political negotiation and compromise. The recent UK experience contrasts with the US one. The Labour government which came to power in 1997 had, and has, welfare state reform – along with the 'eradication of child poverty' – high on its list of priorities. It has introduced a substantial change in emphasis away from simply providing benefits to those currently eligible to getting benefit recipients into work – as in the USA. And, also as in the USA, substantial resources have been directed towards assisting low-income working families, thus increasing the incentive to enter employment. (The UK Working Family Tax Credit which replaced Family Credit in October 1999 was much influenced by the US Earned Income Tax Credit, and the UK, like the USA, now has a statutory minimum wage.) A series of so-called New Deal policies have been introduced recently for groups such as lone parents and young people explicitly aimed at helping get them into work. The in-coming government's very large majority undoubtedly helped in getting all the components of their reform programme introduced largely as planned. (Opposition to elements has also been muted by other policies which have explicitly redistributed resources to children – see chapter 7.)

Of course it is not only the size of political majorities that shapes the nature of feasible 'welfare' reforms in different countries. Differences in history and social values matter too. The UK welfare state remains more

---

[3] The US experience is discussed further by Ellwood (1998).

comprehensive in coverage then the US one, despite the changes described earlier. And in marked contrast to the USA, there has been no time-limiting of mean-tested benefits in the UK.[4] Leisering and Leibfried (1999: chapter 12) discuss the increased influence of dynamic perspectives on policy in Germany, but emphasise how the German state-orientated approach to provision severely constrains the possibility of US-type welfare reforms being implemented there.

Support for families with children in the UK, as in other parts of Europe, differs from that in the USA in several respects. One important difference is the UK's Child Benefit, a universal family allowance paid in respect of all children. This type of benefit also exists elsewhere in Europe: for example, the Netherlands and Hungary (see chapter 10's concluding remarks). Conventional static analysis of child poverty can lead one to conclude that a universal family allowance is badly targeted on the poor, the great bulk of expenditure going to families with incomes above the poverty line. This is the reason why calls for reform of such benefits are often made by some commentators. A dynamic perspective provides a counter-argument. Chapter 4's cross-country analysis shows that around 40 per cent of children were in the poorest fifth at least once over a period of five years in Germany, Hungary and Britain, and a third in the USA (table 4.4). Universal allowances go to many families that will be poor at some time, even if they are not poor at any given moment, providing an element of security as incomes fluctuate.

The limits of seeing individuals as the behavioural unit

The biggest danger with bringing a dynamic perspective to policy may be the tendency to treat the individual as the critical behavioural unit. When one starts doing dynamic analysis, one is essentially forced to look at the events facing individuals rather than families, households or other groups in the economy. How long were people poor? How long did they receive benefits or other assistance? What events led them onto or off benefit receipt? One is forced to answer such questions using individuals as the unit

---

[4] They have been suggested, however. For example, a leading opposition party politician in Britain recently suggested that lone parents who refused 'reasonable' job offers should lose benefit when their youngest child turned 11 ('Lone parents should look for work when children reach 11, say Tories', *Guardian*, 23 November 1999). One might also interpret the recent restriction of eligibility to non-means-tested unemployment insurance benefit from twelve months to six months as a step in the time-limits direction (assistance after six months is now means-tested).

of analysis rather than any other unit, because over time families, firms and communities undergo transformations as smaller units within leave or join the larger unit (see chapter 2). So methodological reasons lead us to follow an individual and measure the changes and events in his or her life. A focus on the individual is problematic for at least two reasons.

First, much information on dynamics has been gained from the dynamics of benefit receipt, as noted earlier, and the focus in this approach is on the person who claims these benefits, the child's carer and guardian, rather than the child itself. Moving the focus to the parents may take us away from our original concern with the well-being of children. How then can we be sure that money paid to parents for children reaches the intended targets? In the UK the universal Child Benefit is, and means-tested Family Credit was, paid directly to the mother rather than the father, reflecting the belief that payments into her purse were more effective in helping children than payments into his wallet. Under the new Working Family Tax Credit (which has replaced Family Credit), parents may choose which one of them the payments are made to, but nonetheless there has been debate about whether 'selfish' husbands will allow this choice to be exercised and thence retain money intended to help children. In the US debate on welfare reform, there has been concern that the focus on the numbers of parents who move off benefit and into work means that much less attention is paid to the key question of whether children benefit from the reforms, and whether their economic well-being, their schooling, their health and so on improve as a result (see Collins and Aber 1997).

A second potential problem with the individual focus of dynamic analysis is that it may lend itself more easily to questions like 'what is wrong with those people?' than to questions such as 'what is wrong with that society or economy?' Dynamic analysis highlights the heterogeneity of outcomes. Some people stopped receiving benefit, so why can't the others? Part of the answer may be that some of them had more education (for example), but the differences may also reflect differences in the availability of jobs or affordable childcare. And arguably governments and societies can, in principle, alter the socio-economic environment and larger forces that influence individuals. Thus larger structural relationships should be examined. If we have a policy tool that myopically homes in on the individual, these larger opportunities will be missed. And we may thereby inadvertently support those who would deny any significance to these forces.

One of the most important benefits of this book is its examination of dynamics across countries, not just across individuals. In this context, it is much harder to ignore the larger social and economic forces because they so clearly differ across countries. The reason for the high poverty and high mobility of children in the transition economies of Eastern Europe obviously has far more to do with the nature of the economic changes underway than the particulars of individuals. Similarly examining differences in dynamics across OECD countries forces researchers to look beyond individualist explanations to systemic ones.

12.5 The next steps in child poverty analysis

Thus dynamic analysis does not provide a magic guide to policy. It may provide a lens which helps us decide what needs to be focused upon. Considering what can be done about the fact that so much poverty seems to be concentrated among young children brings alternative strategies into sharp relief. We have already noted the unhappy coincidence that children tend to be born at a time when parental earning capacity is relatively low. One obvious solution is to provide or expand a universal child allowance. Such a plan can obviously reduce the poverty of children directly. Yet many of the benefits will go to families whose children are not at all poor, so such plans are expensive. An alternative is means-tested assistance. But there is clear evidence, in the USA at least, that means-tested benefits can reduce parents' work efforts. Given that young people are at the very start of their work careers, some policymakers will be particularly troubled by a strategy that might discourage work.

A dynamic view might instead lead one to consider what can be done to enable young families with children to earn more money. Then a number of other strategies can be considered. In a setting like the USA where jobs are relatively plentiful, but pay levels are often woefully low, particularly for the young, one might instead consider a set of policies such as wage subsidies or tax credits which will increase the effective earnings of low-wage workers with children. Expanded training and higher-quality and more accessible childcare might provide more opportunities for parents to work outside the home and help their young children. If job turnover is high among certain groups, policies designed to encourage both employees and employers to extend jobs could be considered. In places or times when unemployment is high among the young, the problem is more difficult. But some form of job creation programme or subsidised job strategy might be considered as a way to keep families moving upwards. Jobs programmes might be more effective in the long run than cash aid that compensates for a lack of work.

There is no universal policy message that emerges from the book. Indeed, the very diversity, not only of the findings but even of the questions asked, suggests that different countries at different times will see different causes for poverty dynamics and look for different types of policy solutions. What longitudinal analysis can and does point towards is the consideration of a set of strategies with two explicit features. First, they may be designed to influence the factors that create the poverty dynamics in the first place. Thus such policies are far more likely to be designed to change the behaviour of individuals, the workings of the market place or both. Second, they include a temporal dimension of policy, so that one policy follows the success or failure of another in helping to eliminate the poverty of particular families. Thus open-ended policies might be replaced by ones which include a sequence of steps.

Of course, adding a time dimension as an element of our thinking about policy design does not really solve the hard problems that poverty creates – it only opens some other perspectives. Basic philosophical differences will remain. Some people will argue that social policy itself is a cause of 'dependency' and that removing support is actually a way of encouraging greater economic independence and success in the long run. Others will see very large social, societal or structural causes that are not easily overcome by policy. But adding a time dimension does tend to move the focus to attempts to reduce the perceived causes of poverty. Still, the chapters in this book do point to a clear message. In many countries, long-term poverty among children is a serious problem and it is often getting worse. The causes are many: low pay, unemployment, single parenthood, limited social benefits. The challenge for researchers is to learn still more about the incidence of long-term poverty and especially its causes and consequences, and to push for high-quality long-timeframe longitudinal data. The challenge for policymakers is to find ways to help children and their families move up and out of poverty or avoid it in the first place. The challenge for everyone is to find appropriate solutions in time.

Dynamic analysis has thus revealed a series of important insights into the nature of deprivation, particularly long-term deprivation in these countries. Some obvious policy conclusions follow directly from the findings above. In many respects the finding that long-term poverty is particularly high among the youngest children in most countries raises serious doubts about the current structure of policies. If the earliest childhood years really are as important as some current research suggests, countries may want to think about adding or redirecting resources towards families with young children.

References
Bane, M. J. and Ellwood, D. T., 1986, 'Slipping into and out of poverty: the dynamics of spells', *Journal of Human Resources*, 21: 1–23.
Bane, M. J. and Ellwood, D. T., 1994, *Welfare Realities. From Rhetoric to Reform*, Harvard University Press, Cambridge MA.

Bell, S., 1999, 'New federalism and research: rearranging old methods to study new social policies in the States', Assessing the New Federalism Project Discussion Paper 99–08, Urban Institute, Washington DC.

Bos, H., Huston, A., Granger, R., Duncan, G., Brock, T. and McLoyd, V., 1999, 'New hope for people with low incomes: two-year results of a program to reduce poverty and reform welfare', unpublished paper, Joint Center for Policy Research, Northwestern University, Evanston IL.

Bryk, A. S. and Raudenbush, S. W., 1992, *Hierarchical Linear Models: Applications and Data Analysis Methods*, Sage, Newbury Park CA.

Collins, A. and Aber, J. L., 1997, 'How welfare reform can help or hurt children', Children and Welfare Reform Issue Brief 1, National Center for Children in Poverty, New York.

Ellwood, D., 1998, 'Dynamic policy making: an insider's account of reforming US welfare', in Leisering, L. and Walker, R. (eds.), *The Dynamics of Modern Society: Policy, Poverty and Welfare*, The Policy Press, Bristol.

Gardiner, K. and Hills, J., 1999, 'Policy implications of new data on income mobility', *Economic Journal*, 109: F91–F111.

Gornick, J., Meyers, M. and Ross, K., 1999, 'Supporting the employment of mothers: policy variation across fourteen welfare states', *Journal of European Social Policy*, 7: 45–70.

Leisering, L. and Leibfried, S., 1999, *Time and Poverty in Western Welfare States*, Cambridge University Press, Cambridge.

Newman, K., 1999, *No Shame in my Game: The Working Poor in the Inner City*, Knopf, New York.

Short, K., Ireland, J. and Garner, T. I., 1999, 'Experimental poverty measures: 1998', unpublished paper, US Bureau of the Census, Washington DC. http://www.census.gov/hhes/poverty/povmeas/exppov/exppov.html

Stack, C. B., 1974, *All Our Kin: Strategies for Survival in a Black Community*, Harper and Row, New York.

Sullivan, M. L., 1989, *Getting Paid: Youth Crime and Work in the Inner City*, Cornell University Press, Ithaca NY.

US Department of Health and Human Services, 1999, *Temporary Assistance for Needy Families (TANF) Program*, Second Annual Report to Congress, US Department of Health and Human Services, Administration for Children and Families, Washington DC.

Index of authors

Index by subject

304

cross-national differences in
dynamics 92–134
cross-national differences in rates
63–91
definitions 28, 69–72, 137, 155, 198,
224–5
entry to *see* poverty, movements into
and out of
exit from *see* poverty, movements
into and out of
'Fab Five' longitudinal indicators of
poverty 45
and household structure 223–8,
230–2
see also households, changes in
structure
importance of money *see* money,
importance of
income versus consumption *see*
consumption versus income
line *see* poverty line
measures of dynamics 44–52, 112–3
movements into and out of 1–2, 4–5,
8–10, 12–3, 19, 27, 28, 30, 32, 35,
37, 42–5, 49–50, 52–8, 92, 93–4,
102, 113, 114–9, 122, 126, 130–1,
159, 163, 196, 231, 246, 263, 265,
267–9, 274, 288, 293–4
near poverty 112–6, 163–4
patterns over time *see* poverty, rates
persistence 12, 106–10, 119–22,
166–9, 171, 244–6, 270–3, 282–4
see also poverty, chronic
rates 63–91, 73–77, 115–6, 135–6,
152, 155, 159–63, 169–70, 181–3,
197, 226, 240–1, 257–8, 297
reduction programmes 188
repeated spells 34, 37–8, 176, 184–8
taxes and transfers, combined effect
on 82–4
transitory 52, 135, 155, 166, 175,
177, 184–93
trends *see* poverty, rates
see also deprivation; income
mobility; inequality; poverty,
persistence

poverty dynamics *see* poverty cross-
national differences in dynamics;
poverty, measures of dynamics;
poverty, movements into and out
of; poverty, persistence
poverty line
absolute and relative 42–4, 65–6
definitions 101, 158, 180, 224–5,
240–1, 262–3
moves across 49–50, 122–6
US official 66, 70–1, 136, 140
poverty rates *see* poverty, cross-
national differences in rates;
poverty, rates

racial differences in poverty flows *see*
United States, racial differences in
flows
residence-based panels *see* panel
surveys, residence-based panels
Russia 7–8, 13, 67–88, 254–75, 283,
284
economy 255–6
expenditure mobility 102–11, 263–7
divorce 57
Longitudinal Monitoring Survey
(RLMS) 257, 259, 260–1, 267,
270, 273
poverty dynamics 19–20, 92–131,
255–75
poverty line 262–3
rising poverty 254, 257, 259
transition 285–6
wage arrears 262, 266

single parent families, see lone-parent
families
Slovakia 67–88
social expenditure 11, 32, 80–2, 236–7,
255
see also benefits; social protection;
targeting; welfare state
social protection 1, 215, 219, 233,
258–9, 273
see also benefits; social expenditure;
targeting; welfare state